50
Country Quilting Projects

DIALOGUE

By Dee Danley Brown. *See page 83*

50
Country Quilting
Projects

Edited by MARGIT ECHOLS

RODALE PRESS

Emmaus, Pennsylvania

Produced for Rodale Press by
TENTH AVENUE EDITIONS, INC.
625 Broadway, Suite 903
New York, New York 10012
Editor-in-Chief: Clive Giboire
Managing Editor: Rose Hass
Technical Writer: Cheri Raymond
Graphic Artist: Pat O'Brien
Editorial Assistant: Peter Wagner
Project Coordinator: Mark Muday
Production: Romeo Enriquez

RODALE PRESS
Editor-in-Chief: William Gottlieb
Senior Managing Editor: Margaret Lydic Balitas
Crafts Editor: Suzanne Nelson
Cover Photographer: Mitch Mandel
Cover Stylist: Kay Lichthardt
Cover Designer: Darlene Schneck

About the cover: The Iris Medallion quilt was designed by Mary Gomez and was sewn and quilted by members of the Wandering Foot Quilt Guild, Duarte, California. It is owned by Rick Eakins. The white-on-white Roses Galore quilt used in the background was quilted by Gayle Shelhamer. Special assistance was provided by Julie Brenner, owner of The Sewing Basket, Emmaus, Pennsylvania.

The designs and instructions for the projects in this book are under copyright. Readers are encouraged to reproduce these projects for their personal use or for gifts. However, reproduction for sale or profit is forbidden by law.

The editors who compiled this book have tried to make all the contents as accurate and as correct as possible. Illustrations, photographs, and text have all been carefully checked and cross-checked. All instructions and diagrams should be carefully studied and clearly understood before beginning any project.

Printed in the United States of America on acid-free paper ∞

If you have any questions or comments concerning this book, please write:
Rodale Press, Book Reader Service, 33 East Minor Street, Emmaus, PA 18049

Library of Congress Cataloging-in-Publication Data
50 country quilting projects.
p.   cm.
ISBN 0-87857-886-2
1. Quilting-Patterns. 2. Patchwork—Patterns. I. Title: Fifty
country quilting projects.
TT835.A15 1990
746.46—dc20   89-37580
                                                          CIP

Distributed in the book trade by St. Martin's Press

2 4 6 8 10 9 7 5 3 1 hardcover

DEDICATED TO EUGENIA MITCHELL
AND ALL THOSE WHO
HAVE BEEN QUILTING A LIFETIME

ACKNOWLEDGMENTS

We thank all the artists listed below for graciously allowing us to include their work in *50 COUNTRY QUILTING PROJECTS.* We also thank V.I.P. Fabrics, Stearns Technical Textiles Company, and the publishers of *Quilt World*, *Quilt World Omnibook*, *Stitch'n Sew*, *Country Needlecraft*, *Quilter's Newsletter Magazine*, *Lady's Circle Patchwork Quilts*, and *Designs by Doris* for their valuable assistance.

AMERICAN EAGLE QUILT by Eugenia Mitchell, Golden, Colorado; adapted from a quilt in the Smithsonian Institution collection, Washington, D. C.

ANNIVERSARY by Karen Felicity Berkenfeld, New York City

AN EXTRA BATCH OF BISCUIT PROJECTS (Puff Quilt, Pillow, and Cushion) by Doris Carmack, author, teacher of quilting and machine arts. Other projects found in *Easy Biscuit Quilting* available from the author, Fountain Valley, California

APPLIQUÉD COASTERS & NAPKIN RINGS, by Sheri Kawahara Fisher, Victoria, British Columbia, Canada

BIRDS ON THE TRACKS Owner: Sandra L. Hatch; courtesy of *Quilt World*, Berne, Indiana

CALICO CUPBOARD TULIP WALL QUILT by Janet Page-Kessler; courtesy Calico Cupboard Collection, V.I.P. Fabrics, New York City

CAROLINA BASKETS by Karen Felicity Berkenfeld, New York City; owner: Carolina Restaurant, New York City

COUNTRY LANES Courtesy of Mountain Mist Collection, Stearns Technical Textiles Company, Cincinnati, Ohio

COUNTRY PLACEMATS by Barbara Clayton; courtesy of *Country Needlecraft*, Berne, Indiana

COUNTRY VILLAGE WALL HANGING by Cheri Tamm Raymond, Rockland, Maine

COTTAGE TEA COZY by Barbara Macaulay of Treadle Crafts, Victoria, British Columbia, Canada; owner: Sheri Kawahara Fisher, Victoria, British Columbia, Canada

CRAZY CAT by Dee Danley-Brown, New York City

DIALOGUE by Dee Danley-Brown, New York City

EASTER BUNNY WALL HANGING by Diane Rode Schneck, Copyright © 1989. New York City

GEESE & TULIPS PILLOW by Barbara Clayton; courtesy of *Country Neddlecraft*, Berne, Indiana

IRIS MEDALLION by Mary Gomez, co-founder of the Schoolhouse Quilters Guild of Rosemead, California and owner of A.M. Creations; sewn and quilted by the Wandering Foot Quilt Guild of Duarte, California; owner: Rick Eakins

IRISH CHAIN VARIATION Owner: Stillwater Historical Society Collection, Stillwater, Minnesota; courtesy *Lady's Circle Patchwork Quilts*, New York City; photograph by Myron Miller, New York City

KITCHEN BISCUITS (Bulletin Board, Potholders, and Country Basket Lining) by Doris Carmack, author, teacher of quilting and machine arts. Other projects found in *Easy Biscuit Quilting* available from the author, Fountain Valley, California

LIGHT AND DARK SQUARES QUILT by Diane Rode Schneck, based upon a design by Kathleen McCrady appearing in *Quilter's Newsletter Magazine*, used with permission of the designer

MINIATURE MAY BASKETS by Vivian Ritter; courtesy of *Quilter's Newletter Magazine*, Wheatridge, Colorado

MINI MARINER'S COMPASS by Barbara Zygiel, Alexandria, Virginia; courtesy *Quilter's Newsletter Magazine*, Wheatridge, Colorado

MINI PATCHWORK ORNAMENTS (Monkey Wrench, Bowtie, Amish Square) by Margit Echols, New York City

PATCHWORK BOXES by Cheri Tamm Raymond, Rockland, Maine

PATCHWORK & LACE CHRISTMAS TREE SKIRT by Doris Carmack, Fountain Valley, California

PINE TREE MEDALLION by Jane Noble; courtesy of *Quilt World*, Berne, Indiana

QUILTED BEDSIDE POCKET by Anna Mae Schack; courtesy of *Quilt World*, Berne, Indiana

ROSE FEVER Inspired by April Wreath in *Scrap Quilts* by Judy Martin; courtesy of Rose Fever Collection, V.I.P. Fabrics, New York City

SHADOW QUILTED COIN PURSE by Sheri Kawahara Fisher, Victoria, British Columbia, Canada

SHAMROCK PILLOW by Diane Rode Schneck, Copyright © 1989. New York City

SPICED TEA MAT by Sheri Kawahara Fisher, Victoria, British Columbia, Canada

STAR QUILT by Loret Race; courtesy of *Quilt World*, Berne, Indiana

THANKSGIVING BANNER by Diane Rode Schneck, Copyright © 1989. New York City

TOUCHING STARS (late 19th century) Owner: Lincoln Home Collection, Springfield, Illinois; courtesy *Lady's Circle Patchwork Quilts* New York City; photograph by Myron Miller, New York City

TRICK OR TREAT BAG by Diane Rode Schneck, Copyright © 1989. New York City

VALENTINE QUILT by Diane Rode Schneck, Copyright © 1989. New York City

WAITING FOR THE MAIL by Marilyn Lawhon; courtesy of *Quilt World Omnibook*, Berne, Indiana

WINDBLOWN TULIP (1983) by Kathy Patrick, Nicholasville, Kentucky; courtesy Mountain Mist Collection, Stearns Technical Textiles Company, Cincinnati, Ohio

YOUNG MAN'S FANCY (1940) by Sarah Barnett; owner: Sarah Jones Rogers; courtesy of *Quilter's Newsletter Magazine*, Wheatridge, Colorado

 CONTENTS

COZY KITCHEN COMPANIONS

DOWN THE GARDEN PATH

FARMER'S MARKET

All of these projects are ranked by skill level and size.
At the start of each project you will find the following symbols:

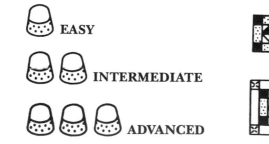 **EASY**

INTERMEDIATE

ADVANCED

 **SMALL TO MEDIUM-SIZE PROJECT**

 **LARGE PROJECT**

# PREFACE

WELCOME to our selection of country quilting projects. Many were created especially for this book by accomplished quilt makers and designers, while others come from their own or private collections. Some projects you may recognize as having appeared in national quilt magazines, which we're sure you'll be glad to see here as part of a more permanent collection. The advantage of gathering everything together into a book is that there is space for full-size patterns, detailed instructions, and lots of diagrams. More attention can be paid to every aspect of making each quilt.

Ever since I started writing how-to books on quiltmaking, I've been dedicated to providing easy-to-follow instructions and accurate, full-size patterns that include seam allowance. When I was working on my first book, there was a tense moment when the art director told me that if all the patterns were full size it would look like a coloring book. "Then it will look like a coloring book," I said, determined to spare the reader the chore of enlarging patterns. I was prepared to drop the project if he insisted. Fortunately he agreed to my request, or my career in quilting books might never have gotten off the ground! I've been working this way ever since.

The process of creating this book started three years ago, when Rose Hass began the search for fifty of the best country-style quilting projects she could find. As the projects came in, I drew each design to size and redrafted the patterns in pencil, which I checked against the originals. I also made sketches for lots of diagrams to accompany the written instructions for quick visual reference.

Then everything was sent to our writer, a very fine quilt maker, Cheri Tamm Raymond, who wrote the instructions, checked the numbers and dimensions, and figured out the yardages. Our work was then meticulously gone over by our editor, Suzanne Nelson, who has an impressive background in needlework and a keen eye for detail. Even the artist, Pat O'Brien, who did all the final drawings for the patterns and diagrams, made sure that the numbers added up and all the pieces fit together, just for his own satisfaction. Clive Giboire, who designed the book, made sure that all the diagrams were placed right next to corresponding text in the final layout, so you won't have to hunt around for them. Working with such a good and thorough team makes me confident that what we pass on to you here is not only accurate and easy to use, but probably one of the finest quilting books around.

Every book I've worked on includes a section on quiltmaking techniques. It grows longer with each writing as I refine it and add new information. I expect that soon it will grow long enough to become a book of its own. In the meantime, I offer you my latest version with useful tips on basic and special techniques, which will tell you all you need to know to complete each project. Also included is a basic section on making pillows to help with the pillow projects in the book.

In the table of contents and on the first page of each project, you will see symbols for skill level and size. One thimble means the project is easy to make; two thimbles mean it requires intermediate skills; and three thimbles mean the project is challenging. The size of the quilt block symbol will tell you whether the project is large or small-to-medium in size.

Even though the colors in all the quilts are quite beautiful, we believe that you'll probably want to select colors of your own. For this reason we've omitted color references in most of the cutting instructions and materials lists, except for those projects where the instructions might be confusing without them.

Included in our selection of fifty projects is a variety of country styles and quilting techniques. Recreate a classic quilt design from the lovely assortment in the section called Bright and Beautiful. Choose from a garden full of florals to piece and appliqué in Down the Garden Path, and from a trunk full of traditional patchwork designs in Geometrics Great and Small. Bring quilting into your kitchen with tea cozies, pot holders, and matching placemats and napkins from Cozy Kitchen Companions. Find gifts for family and friends or projects to offer at fairs and bazaars from Farmer's Market. Decorate the house year-round in festive style with projects from Celebrating the Holidays. No matter what you're looking for, there's bound to be plenty of projects here that will strike your fancy.

HAPPY QUILTING!

Margit Echols

QUILTING BASICS

To assure that every project you make from this book is a success, this chapter covers many of the basic techniques that are essential to completing a quilt. It will take you from the initial steps of preparing patterns and choosing fabric to the last step of handstitching the binding to the back. On the way you will find pointers on how to mark and cut the fabric; how to piece and appliqué; how to assemble the layers that make up a quilt and attach them to a frame; and how to do the actual quilting. If you are new to quiltmaking, this section will serve as a good introduction to basic techniques. If you are experienced, you'll enjoy reading the tips and special pointers, and perhaps you'll discover new ways of doing things.

USING THE PATTERNS

The full-size patterns in this book are drawn with ¼-inch seam allowances. All of the projects use this as a standard seam allowance, unless otherwise specified in the directions.

The pattern pieces have several features that are intended to make cutting and sewing easier. First of all, cutting and sewing lines are clearly marked (**Diagram 1**). The arrows on some pattern pieces indicate which side or sides should line up with the horizontal or vertical grain of the fabric. Patterns with straight edges that do not have arrows, such as squares or rectangles, should be positioned along the horizontal and vertical grains of the fabric.

Some pattern pieces have notches; these should be clipped into the fabric where indicated, up to but not through the stitching line. Use the notches to match edges when sewing pieces together.

You will notice that corners on triangular-, diamond-, and odd-shaped pieces have been squared off. This was done to eliminate excess bulk at the intersections and to make it easier to match the sides when sewing the pieces together.

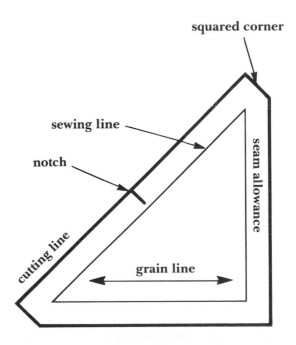

Diagram 1. Sample pattern piece showing features that will be helpful in cutting and sewing

Before beginning a project, the patterns will need to be photocopied or traced. Photocopying is easiest, but be aware that some copiers may alter the size of the originals slightly. Check the accuracy of your copy by placing it on top of the original and holding them both up to the light. If there has been any change in size, adjust the copier, if possible, and try again.

Trace the patterns by hand using a pencil, tracing paper, and a straightedge. Work carefully; inaccurate patterns can create problems. Write the name of the design, the identification letter, and any other important markings, such as notches and arrows, on each piece.

Once you copy the pattern pieces, you can cut them out and use them as is by pinning them directly onto the fabric. If you plan to use the patterns often or share them with friends, it is helpful to make sturdier templates. You can mount the paper pattern pieces on cardboard with rubber cement or spray glue. First apply the glue to a piece of cardboard the same size as or slightly larger than the sheet of paper on which the patterns have been copied. Place the paper on top of the cardboard and smooth it down with your hand. When the glue has dried, cut out the pieces with scissors or use an X-Acto knife and a steel straightedge. **Tip:** *Work in a well-ventilated area when using spray glue, and avoid inhaling.*

You can also make stronger templates out of nonslip sheets of plastic. Instead of making photocopies, trace the patterns directly out of the book onto the plastic with a pencil (the surface has a slight texture and will accept the markings easily). Be sure to transfer all features like arrows and notches. Cut out the templates with scissors or an X-Acto knife and steel straightedge. Some template plastic comes marked with a ¼-inch grid, which is handy for tracing most square or rectangular pattern pieces. **Tip:** *The tools and materials referred to throughout this section are available in most sewing and quilt supply stores and from many mail-order catalogs that specialize in quilting.*

ENLARGING PATTERNS

A few projects have patterns that are so large they had to be reduced to fit on a page in the book, so you will need to enlarge them. If you've never done this before, don't be intimidated, because it is a very simple procedure. Dimensions are given for oversize squares and rectangles that you can draw on graph paper, on ruled template plastic, or directly onto the fabric. (When drawing on fabric, be sure to keep the sides square.)

Other patterns, such as curvilinear designs for appliqué, are drawn on a grid that breaks up the design into manageable parts that can be transferred onto a larger, usually one-inch grid for a full-size, ready-to-use pattern. Use a large piece of graph paper as is or trace a one-inch grid (or whatever size the pattern calls for) onto another sheet of plain paper. Transfer the design by drawing the lines as you see them in each box of the grid in the book onto the corresponding box of the larger grid.

CHOOSING FABRICS

The best fabric for quilts is 100 percent cotton, but if that isn't available, cotton blends can be used as well. To preshrink and test colorfastness, machine wash and dry all cottons or cotton blends at least once before cutting. Some fabrics may need more than one washing to remove residual dye.

Each project has a materials list and cutting chart. The materials list gives you the amount of yardage needed in each color to complete the project. The cutting chart tells you how many of each pattern piece to cut from each color fabric. In some cases, when a project calls for only small quantities of different fabrics, there is no yardage amount provided. Instead you'll find the phrase "scraps of assorted fabrics." This gives you a good opportunity to use up bits of leftover fabric. **Tip:** *Experienced quilters know that it doesn't hurt to purchase a little more than called for to allow for mistakes in cutting.*

MARKING THE FABRIC

When using cardboard or plastic templates, you'll need some sort of marker to trace the pattern onto the fabric. You can use any pencil with a sharp point. Yellow and white pencils are good on dark fabrics. Chalk markers, which contain refillable powdered chalk, are easy to use and quite accurate. They dispense a thin line when drawn across the fabric that can be easily brushed off. These markers come in more than one shape and the chalk is available in an assortment of colors.

As you're tracing around templates with a pencil or marker, hold the point firmly against the edge of the template. Any extra seam allowance that results from marking cutting lines even slightly larger than the pattern will cause a piece to "grow." This can create a real headache when the time comes to join all the various sections of the quilt together.

CUTTING TECHNIQUES

With a pair of good, sharp scissors you can work more quickly by cutting through four layers of fabric at a time instead of two. For cutting out many pieces with straight sides, such as strips for strip piecing, use a rotary cutter and cutting mat. Hold the circular blade against a steel or thick plastic straightedge, apply pressure, and roll the blade along the side of the straightedge. Thick straightedges are safer than thin ones, and those made with ridges on the underside will grip the fabric and stay in place as you cut. **Tip:** *Handle a rotary cutter with care! Always push it away from you as you cut. Make sure the blade stays against the straightedge and doesn't jump over the edge and cut your hand.*

All woven fabric has threads that run in either a vertical or horizontal direction called the grain. The 45-degree angle across the grain is called the bias. The sides of square or rectangular patterns should be aligned with the grain. Other patterns, such as triangles, may have arrows which should also be aligned with the grain. In most sewing, using the lengthwise direction of the grain is recommended for best results. But in quiltmaking, it usually doesn't matter unless the fabric is printed with a one-way design. For the best and most strategic use of stripes, for example, the overall design of the quilt should be taken into consideration.

Pin paper patterns directly onto the fabric and cut. **Tip:** *Be very careful when cutting with paper pattern pieces. If you accidentally trim away some of the pattern as you cut, the difference in size, however slight, can compound itself and make it difficult to assemble the project later on.* If you are using cardboard or plastic templates, carefully cut along the outlines you have traced. Be sure not to lose or add seam allowance when cutting. Precise marking and cutting will ensure ease of assembly and prevent the pulling and puckering that inevitably result from inaccurate work.

PIECING

Quilting enthusiasts are divided over whether piecing is best done by hand or machine. Some feel a pieced quilt must be entirely hand sewn, just as it was done in the old days. But other quilters see no reason not to take advantage of the speed and ease of sewing that technology has provided. The decision to hand- or machine-stitch your quilt should be based purely on your preference and whatever is the most comfortable for you.

Accurate sewing is just as important as accurate marking and cutting. Beginners may need to mark stitching lines (always on the wrong side of the fabric) until sewing accurate $1/4$-inch seams becomes automatic. **Tip:** *Using a quilter's quarter, a $1/4$-inch-wide metal or plastic sewing aid, is a handy way to mark seam allowances. Align the edge of the quilter's quarter with the edge of the fabric and mark with a pencil or chalk marker along the inside edge.*

You can skip this step of marking the seam allowance if your sewing machine has a seam allowance gauge. If your machine doesn't have one, place a piece of masking tape so that the edge of the tape is $1/4$-inch away from the needle and parallel to the side of the zipper foot. By keeping the edge of your fabric even with the edge of the tape, you will maintain a ¼-inch seam allowance.

PRESSING SEAMS

Your work will look its best if you take the time to press the seams after each step. Most quilters press seams to one side, which is thought to add strength. This is certainly true of hand piecing, but not as critical for machine piecing. Pressing seams open has some advantages. The seams will lie flatter and they will be easier to join at intersections. Overall the finished work will have a neater, flatter look. Whichever method you use, be sure not to pull any of the pieces out of shape as you press.

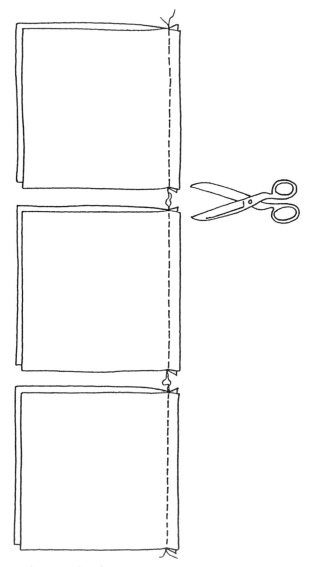

Diagram 2. Time-saving assembly piecing

QUICK PIECING

Many of the projects in this book call for sewing together multiple sets of pieces of the same size and shape. You can save a substantial amount of time by sewing them together, one after the other, without raising the presser foot. You'll be able to zip through a sizable stack of pieces in no time at all.

To start, sew the first set of pieces together. Without raising the presser foot, sew about ½ inch beyond the end of the seam and feed the next set of pieces through. Continue in this manner until all the sets you need are sewn together (**Diagram 2**). You will end up with a long chain of pieces connected by thread. A few quick snips with the scissors will separate the sets. **Tip:** *The threads on the end will stay twisted and keep the seams secure enough to hold the pieces together when pressing and sewing them to other pieces in subsequent steps.*

STRIP PIECING

Strip piecing is a time-saving technique that has many creative possibilities. The basic principle is easy. You cut long strips of fabric into any width and sew them together in a band. This band is then cut into more strips at right angles (or any other angle you desire). These strips are rearranged into checkerboard or other patterns and sewn together into another band. For a wonderful example of how effective this technique can be, turn to Touching Stars on page 68.

Throughout the projects in the book, you will find recommendations to use strip piecing whenever it is appropriate. Refer to the step-by-step directions given here to complete the strip-piecing portion of the project. The cutting instructions for the projects will indicate the number and width of the strips required.

1. Cut fabric into strips of designated width. For quick cutting, fold a length of fabric in half to make two layers. If more than one color is required, fold another length in half and place it on top of the first so all the sides are even.

Mark off strips the width you need (preferably along the lengthwise grain of the fabric to minimize stretch) with a straightedge and pencil (**Diagram 3**). Cut out the strips. **Tip:** *For the quickest cutting, use a thick plastic or metal straightedge, a rotary cutter, and cutting mat.*

2. Sew strips together into a band. Be sure to assemble the strips with accurately sewn ¼-inch seams. Sewing all the seams together before pressing can minimize any stretching that may result. However, you may prefer to sew strips together into pairs, press the seams open, then sew the pairs together until the band is complete.

3. Place the straightedge across the band at the angle designated in the directions and mark off strips in desired widths (**Diagram 4**). Cut the strips, rearrange them into the final design, and sew them together.

APPLIQUÉ

Appliqué involves placing fabric shapes on top of a fabric background and stitching them down. There is great freedom in this technique because you can place the shapes anywhere you like; you are not restricted by the precise fitting together of geometric shapes that piecing requires.

In its simplest form, traditional appliqué is done by hand. You place a shape on top of the background fabric, turn the edges under, and hand stitch the edges to the fabric underneath. For the best results, blind stitch with the same color thread as the appliqué. All corners should be sharp and the curves smooth.

Easier and quicker ways to appliqué include using freezer paper, machine appliqué, and fusible webbing. These are explained in the step-by-step directions that follow. Projects throughout the book will refer to one of these techniques. Turn back to this section to assist you in completing the appliqué portion of the project.

Freezer-Paper Appliqué

Supermarket freezer paper can make hand appliqué much easier, allowing you to appliqué shapes with perfect edges and nice, sharp points and corners.

1. Trace a shape, without seam allowance, on the dull side of the freezer paper. Cut out the shape and lay it, shiny side down, on the wrong side of the fabric, leaving enough fabric around the edges for seam allowance. Press in place with a hot, dry iron. The paper will stick to the fabric.

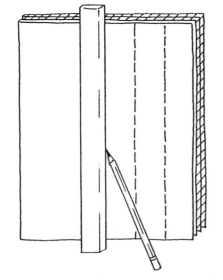

Diagram 3. Mark off the strips in parallel lines

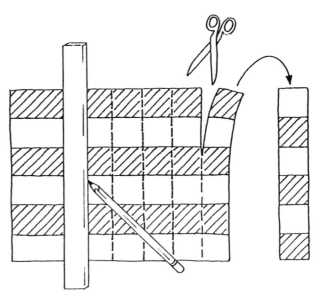

Diagram 4. Mark parallel lines across the band

2. By eye, cut the fabric with a ¼-inch seam allowance around the outside edge of the freezer paper. Clip concave curves up to the edge of the paper just a hair's breadth short of the edge.

3. Place the shape, paper side down, on top of the background fabric and pin or baste in place. Turn the edges under and blind stitch in place. Because the freezer paper adds stability to the shape, it's easier to turn the seam allowance under and sew it accurately with very little effort. **Tip:** *Some quilters turn over the seam allowance and baste it to the freezer paper before applying the shape to the background.*

4. For points and corners, blind stitch all the way up to the point and take an extra stitch. Turn the seam allowance under with the tip of the needle (**Diagram 5**) and continue blind stitching along the next side. You can clip away some of the excess fabric at the corner, but be careful—it's better to have too much fabric than too little.

5. To remove the freezer paper from the appliquéd shape after it is sewn in place, turn the work over to the wrong side, cut away the background fabric to within ¼-inch of the stitching inside the stitch line, and remove the freezer paper. Or, remove the paper through

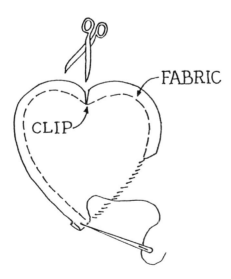

Diagram 5. Turn the seam allowance under and continue stitching

a small slit in the background. If you want the background fabric to remain intact, remove the freezer paper just before you finish sewing up to your starting point. The paper can be wiggled and crunched up to loosen it. If the edges were basted before appliquéing, remove the basting before removing the freezer paper.

Machine Appliqué

Unless machine appliqué is done with clear nylon thread, it will be visible and should therefore be considered ornamental. Each piece will be outlined with a row of zigzag stitching wider than straight stitching in thread of the same or contrasting color.

1. Cut out a shape without seam allowance and place it, right side up, on top of the background fabric.

2. Using a tight zigzag stitch, sew around the shape, concealing the raw edges under the stitching.

Appliqué With Fusible Webbing

When shapes are fused to the background they stay flat and anchored in place, making it easier to machine stitch around the edges. The most practical type of fusible webbing has a paper backing on one side, such as Pellon's Wonder Under.

1. Trace a shape without seam allowance on the paper side of the fusible webbing. Cut around the shape approximately ¼-inch from the pencil line.

2. Place the webbing, rough side down, on the wrong side of the fabric and fuse it in place with a hot, dry iron. Cut out the shape following the pencil line. Peel the paper away, place the shape, webbing side down, on the background, and fuse. **Tip:** *If you find it difficult to remove the paper without fraying the edges (especially if the pieces are small), consider fusing a larger piece of webbing to the fabric. Peel the paper away, then trace and cut out the design and fuse it to the background. Be careful not to iron the wrong side of the web—it will stick to the iron. Protect*

the ironing board from residual stickiness with a piece of discarded fabric or a portion of an old sheet.

3. Once the shape is fused in place on the background, zigzag around the edges.

MITERING BORDERS

Once the quilt top is finished, it is time to think about borders. Some of the projects in this book call for mitered borders, which are sewn together at the corners at a 45-degree angle. Mitered corners on borders are nice-looking, but the measurements are not always easy to calculate correctly. To avoid cutting them the wrong length or at the wrong angle, cut them longer than necessary and miter them after they are sewn to the sides of the project. Measurements for mitered borders are listed for various projects in this book. You may wish to cut them slightly longer and trim to fit in case the size of your project changes during assembly.

1. Sew the borders to the sides of the project, stopping ¼ inch from the corners. Press seams open or to one side.

2. Fold over both ends of each border at the corner to make a 45-degree diagonal line from the inner edge to the outer edge. Press these folds to make a crease. Trim the fabric to within ¼-inch of the fold line (**Diagram 6**).

3. Sew the diagonal ends together at each corner. Press seams open.

CHOOSING THE BEST BATTING

There are a number of different types of quilt batting available. The batting material, weight, and size you choose will depend on your project and what you feel most comfortable working with. Today's commercial battings hold their shape over the years through many washings, so the extensive quilting that was required in the past to prevent the batting from moving between the layers is unnecessary unless desired.

Most brands of quilt batting on the market are made of 100 percent polyester. This material is lightweight and easy to handle. One drawback is that the fibers tend to migrate between the layers of fabric during use and washing. Polyester is considered to be the easiest batting to hand quilt. Although cotton batting is harder to "needle," or hand quilt, some people prefer to work with it because it gives an old-fashioned look to the quilt. Cotton batting is available in an updated version, blended with a small amount of polyester, which makes the hand stitching easier.

Batting comes in several different weights. The thinner the batting, such as light, low loft, or extra low loft, the easier it is to produce smaller hand stitches. Thin batting is also a good choice for quilted craft projects like placemats, since it doesn't add bulk. High loft or extra-loft batting is thicker and suitable for puffy quilts that will be tied instead of hand quilted.

Most weights are available in several sizes: craft-size for small projects, 36 x 45 inches; crib size, 45 x 60; twin size, 72 x 90; full size, 81 x 96; queen size, 90 x 108; and king size, 120 x 120. The size of batting needed for each quilt project is given in the materials list.

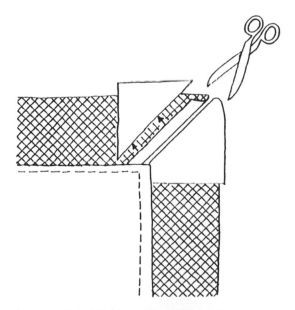

Diagram 6. Fold the ends of the border at a 45-degree angle and trim within ¼ inch of the crease

BACKING THE QUILT

The color you choose for the back of the quilt is really a matter of personal preference. The usual choice is white or a light color. However, you could also use fabric in one of the colors in the top or a contrasting color. The only combination that may not work is a dark fabric back for a light colored quilt top (especially when the batting is thin). The back is likely to show through and darken the light colors.

The most common width for cotton and cotton-blend fabrics is 45 to 48 inches, although you may find some that are 36 inches wide. If the project you are making is larger than the width of the fabric, you may need to piece together two or more lengths for the back. For example, if a quilt measures 90 x 90 inches, two 2 1/2-yard lengths of 48-inch fabric, or a total of 5 yards will be needed for the back. When you join several lengths of fabric together, trim the selvages from the sides. They are more tightly woven than the rest of the fabric and will prevent the seams from lying flat.

ASSEMBLY

Once the quilt top is finished, it is ready to be combined with the batting and back.

1. Spread the back, wrong side up, on the floor. **Tip:** *The nap on a low-pile carpet will keep the fabric from moving, making the assembly process a lot easier. On a bare floor, secure the edges of the fabric to the floor with masking tape. This keeps the back from slipping underneath the batting and quilt top.*

2. Place the batting on top of the back. Smooth it out, stretching it slightly to ease out any slack.

3. Place the quilt top right side up on top of the batting. Smooth it until it is square, flat, and free of puckers.

4. Pin all three layers together, working from the center of the quilt toward the edges. Pin in a square grid pattern throughout the quilt with the pins no more than 1 foot apart. Turn over the quilt, and straighten it out facedown on the floor. Make sure that the back hasn't moved

during pinning and is free from pulls and puckers. If necessary, turn over the quilt and repin until all layers are smooth and straight.

5. Starting from the center and working toward the sides in a sunburst pattern or square grid, baste all three layers together by hand. Your quilt is now ready to mark and attach to a frame.

MARKING THE QUILT

For most of the projects in the book, the last step of the directions will be to quilt as desired. Choose a quilting design that complements the quilt top.

The simplest and most frequently used design is to outline each shape with stitching 1/4-inch outside the seamline. As a guide, use a quilter's quarter, a transparent ruler marked in 1/4-inch increments, or special 1/4-inch-wide masking tape sold in quilting supply stores. If you plan to use a frame, marking for outline quilting can be done one section at a time after the quilt is in the frame.

Quilting in the ditch is another familiar method, in which you quilt directly into the seam line. No marking is needed for this type of quilting.

Distinct overall patterns like square or diamond grids are commonly marked 1 inch apart throughout the quilt top or in the plain areas outside any piecing or appliqué. Overall patterns should be marked on the top before it is in the frame. To mark a grid, start by drawing just two guidelines (diagonally from corner to corner in an X, for example) while the quilt is spread out on the floor. From these lines other parallel lines can be drawn later, after the quilt is in the frame.

For elaborate designs like feathers, hearts, flowers, or scallops you can use homemade or commercial templates. To make your own, draw the design on lightweight cardboard and cut it out with an X-Acto knife. Stencil-cutting kits containing electric hot pens and a roll of plastic are available through some mail-order quilt and craft suppliers.

Because you will be marking these quilting designs on the right side of the fabric, they should be as light as possible. Pencil lines, as long as they're made lightly, will all but disappear with the handling that goes on during quilting. Any that remain will come out during laundering.

Chalk markers are useful for marking and quilting one line at a time. If you mark more than one, the other lines will be rubbed off almost instantly as you touch them while working. It is not a good idea to mark elaborate patterns with chalk markers since the lines will disappear as you quilt.

Water-soluble marking pens are handy because the ink can be removed with a damp cloth. But before you start marking a project, be sure the ink will really come off your fabric by testing a sample piece. Don't hold the pen point in one place too long; the ink will continue to flow and become difficult to remove. Use a light touch and mark quickly for best results.

QUILTING WITH A FRAME

While it is true that quilting can be done without one, a frame helps to create a finished piece with an especially smooth and flat appearance. Because the quilt surface is taut and resists flexing as the needle is pushed at an angle up and down through the layers, it may take a little time to feel comfortable quilting this way. But with practice you will soon become used to stitching in a frame.

If you're a serious quiltmaker, treat yourself to a good frame, one that will make long working hours a pleasure instead of a chore. Norwood Looms makes a wonderful maple quilt frame with crossbars that are so heavy and stable they won't bow toward the center no matter how tightly the quilt is stretched.

Q-Snap frames, made of PVC pipe, come in several sizes for lap quilting and in a floor model that is lightweight, easy to assemble and take apart, and convenient to pack up and take anywhere. Snap-on caps hold the quilt to the frame so no pinning or basting is necessary. Turning the caps outward tightens the tension.

Whichever frame you select, it should come with instructions on how to attach the quilt. In case you're borrowing a frame or have misplaced the instructions, here is the general procedure for pinning or basting a quilt into a standard floor frame.

1. Pin or baste the top and bottom of the quilt to the cloth tape attached to each crossbar. Stretch the edge of the quilt slightly as you pin or baste. To assure that there is no diagonal pulling when you roll up the quilt, keep the top and bottom edges aligned.

2. Roll up the quilt tightly away from the center at both ends. Continue rolling until the center of the quilt is tightly stretched between the crossbars.

3. Lash the sides of the quilt to the sides of the frame with a needle and thread, or use a length of cloth tape pinned to the sides. The quilt will retain the shape it has acquired during this step, so stretch the quilt firmly and evenly (**Diagram 7**).

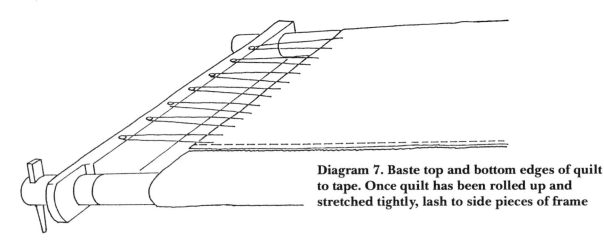

Diagram 7. Baste top and bottom edges of quilt to tape. Once quilt has been rolled up and stretched tightly, lash to side pieces of frame

Quilting hoops are a good choice for people who don't have room for a floor frame. These hoops, which include lap or standing models, are portable and allow you to work on a project from any angle. Some quilters feel that hoops don't stretch the quilt with an even tension, resulting in finished work that doesn't lie as flat. But the convenience and portability may be worth the difference. **Tip:** *Hoops and small Q-Snap frames are great for smaller projects like wall quilts and pillow tops. To get into the corners and up to the edges while you quilt you may need to add fabric panels to extend the sides. These extensions will allow you to center the work in the frame.*

Inserting a quilt into a hoop is much less time-consuming than attaching it to a frame.

1. Spread the quilt over the top of the inner ring with the section you wish to work directly over the ring.

2. Place the outer ring on top of the quilt and press it down over the inner ring.

3. Tighten the screw on the outer ring to hold the quilt in place.

QUILTING BY HAND

Quilting is a two-handed procedure. The hand above the quilt holds the needle over the surface and pushes it down through the layers. The hand beneath the quilt feels the needle as it comes through the fabric and directs it back up

to the top. Use a thimble to protect the finger on the upper hand that pushes the needle through (and even one on the finger of the hand underneath if it becomes tender). A short, thin needle is best to work with. If you have difficulty threading the small eye on a quilting needle, mechanical needle threaders are available for those of us whose eyesight isn't what it was. **Tip:** *Before you begin to quilt, pull the thread through a piece of beeswax. This will help keep it from twisting and knotting as you stitch.*

Knots shouldn't be visible on the front or back of your quilt. There are two simple techniques to secure the thread invisibly when starting and ending the stitching. Before you start, knot one end of the thread. Insert the needle through the quilt top *only*—not through the back—about an inch away from where the quilting stitch is to begin. Push the needle through the fabric until it comes out at this starting point. Pull the thread right up to the knot. Tug gently until the knot pops through the top layer and is hidden between the quilt top and back (**Diagram 8**).

To finish a line of quilting, use a similar technique to conceal the knot. When the needle comes through the top at the place where the stitching is to end, hold the needle down on the surface of the quilt. Wind the thread around the needle one or two times and pull the needle

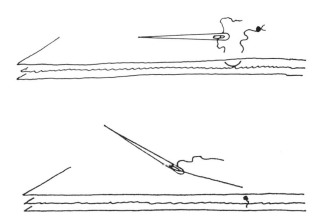

Diagram 8. To hide the knot at the start of stitching, insert needle through top layer and pull until knot pops through to the inside

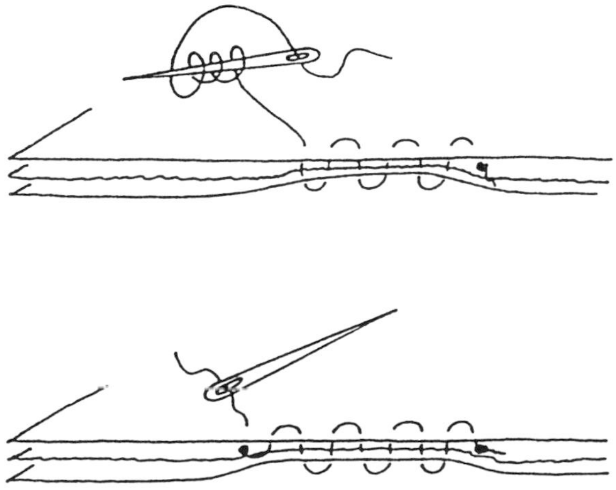

Diagram 9. To end line of quilting, wind thread around needle several times to make a knot. Insert needle through top of fabric and pull to pop knot through to the inside. Clip thread

through to make a knot. Insert the needle just one stitch length beyond this point between the top and back. Bring it up about an inch away and tug on the thread to pop the knot through the quilt top (**Diagram 9**). Pull the thread slightly and clip it off right where it exits the fabric. This end will slide back under the quilt top.

The quilting stitch technique you use between making those starting and ending knots is a matter of preference. Most experienced quilters make a series of running stitches at least two to four at a time, before pulling the thread through the fabric. Until they become comfortable with the running stitch, many beginners take one stitch at a time. Running stitches usually produce a straighter line than single stitches.

As you quilt, try to keep the stitches as even and small as possible. Some quilters believe that 10 to 13 stitches per inch is the sign of fine quilting. A quilt in which the stitches are even, but not nearly that small, is just as lovely.

Tip: *If you are using quilting thread in a color that contrasts markedly with the top or the back, it is especially important to keep the stitches regular in size. Uneven stitches will be much more obvious on a contrasting color.*

BINDING THE QUILT

Once all the quilting is completed and you have removed the quilt from the frame, it is time to add binding to finish the edges. Depending on your color choice, the binding can be a subtle or eye-catching addition to the overall design. The binding can match the quilt or it can be a contrasting color.

Binding can be made with strips cut on the straight or bias. Straight-grain binding is easy to cut. Bias binding takes a little more time but it is the binding of preference, especially for quilts with curves like scalloped edges. It gives slightly as it is sewn to the quilt and wraps nicely around the thickness of the quilt's edge. **Tip:** *Be careful not to create wrinkles in the binding while turning and sewing it to the back of the quilt.* The following

directions make ¹/₂-inch straight or bias binding for a low-loft quilt.

Straight Binding

1. Cut enough 2-inch-wide strips along the vertical or horizontal grain of the fabric to equal the desired total length of binding plus seam allowances. **Tip:** *To estimate yardage for binding, there are handy charts available in quilting supply stores and mail-order catalogs.*

2. Stitch the ends together to make one continuous strip. Press seams open.

Bias Binding (Small Quantity)

1. Fold a square of fabric in half on the diagonal and press a crease. Cut along the crease to make two triangles (**Diagram 10**). Sew the two triangles together along their short sides to make a parallelogram (**Diagram 11**).

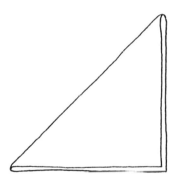

Diagram 10. Fold fabric diagonally in half and cut into two triangles

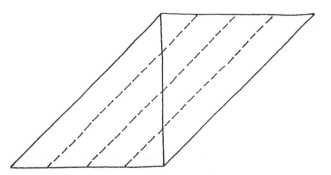

Diagram 11. Sew the triangles together along short sides. Mark and cut 2-inch-wide strips

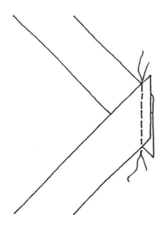

Diagram 12. Stitch ends of strips together to make one continuous strip

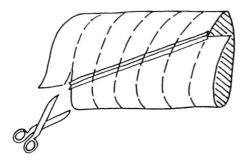

Diagram 13. Pin edges of fabric together, right sides facing. Stagger strips by moving them over one place

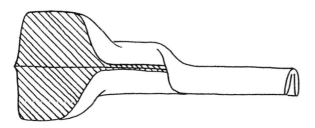

Diagram 14. Preshape bias binding by pressing in half, then folding sides toward the middle and pressing in half again

2. Mark off 2-inch-wide strips along the diagonal side, and cut as many bias strips as needed to go around the perimeter of the quilt. Stitch the ends together to make one continuous strip (**Diagram 12**). Press seams open.

Bias Binding (Large Quantity)

1. Begin with a square of fabric and make it into a parallelogram as described in Step 1 for Bias Binding (Small Quantity) above. Mark diagonal cutting lines 2 inches apart on the parallelogram.

2. With right sides facing, pin the edges of the fabric together, staggering the strips so that the bottom ends move over one place (**Diagram 13**). Machine stitch the edges together in this position to make a tube.

3. Starting at one end of the tube, cut out one continuous bias strip, following the marked lines.

Attaching The Binding

Before attaching the completed binding strip to the quilt, you can preshape it (optional) by folding and pressing it in half and then folding the sides in toward the middle and pressing in half again (**Diagram 14**). **Tip:** *A tape-pressing aid makes this step go quickly and easily.* The directions that follow are for both straight and bias binding.

1. Start the binding in the middle of one side of the quilt, not at a corner. Fold under the end of the binding and, using a ¹/₂ -inch seam allowance, sew the binding along one edge on the top of the quilt, matching the edge of the binding to the edge of the quilt (**Diagram 15**).

2. Stitch to within ¹/₂ inch of the corner and then backstitch. Lift the presser foot and move the work a short distance away from the presser foot.

3. Fold the binding up at a 45-degree angle, crease the fold, and pin (**Diagram 16**).

4. Fold the binding down to form a ¹/₂-inch tuck. Insert the needle directly where first line

of stitches ends, lower the presser foot, and continue to sew (**Diagram 17**). Sew for a few inches then stop to make sure the corner will miter neatly with just the right amount of binding. If any corrections are needed, make them before you go on to the other corners.

5. Continue sewing about 1 inch beyond the starting point and trim.

6. To finish, turn the binding over to the back of the quilt, fold the edge under ½ inch and slipstitch the binding to the quilt by hand. Also slipstitch the fold at the beginning of the binding (which is now on top) to the end of the binding underneath (**Diagram 18**). Fold the corners into neat miters.

FINISHING TOUCHES

Since you invest so much of your time and talent in your work, it is a nice idea to add your name and the date. Some quilters like to add other information as well, like the name of their town and whom the quilt was made for if it is a gift. You can embroider additional personal information on the front or back of the quilt in matching or contrasting thread depending on how visible you want it to be. If you plan to exhibit your work, consider adding a copyright symbol (c inside a circle) next to your name and the date to protect it.

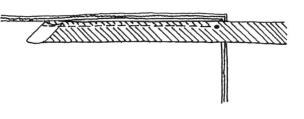

Diagram 15. Fold over end of binding and stitch to quilt, using 1/2-inch seam allowance

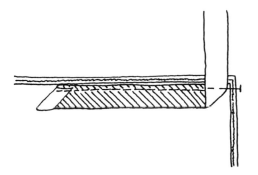

Diagram 16. Fold binding up at 45-degree angle, crease, and pin

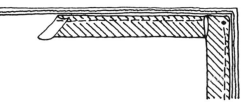

Diagram 17. After folding binding down at corner, insert needle at same spot where first line of stitching ends

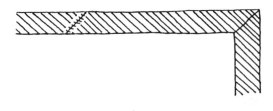

Diagram 18. Slip stitch folded end of binding closed

⬛ PILLOW PRIMER ⬛

The directions that follow will take you step-by-step through preparing the pillow top, finishing the edges, and assembling the pillow. Check the basic materials list before you start to make sure you have everything you need on hand.

Basic Materials List for Pillow

- Finished pillow top
- Fabric to line pillow top (preferably white)
- Batting (optional)*
- Fabric for pillow back (matching or contrasting)
- Edging (fabric for ruffle, lace, bias binding, or piping)
- Piping or cotton cord for self-piping (optional)
- Zipper (optional)
- Pillow form the same size or an inch larger (for extra firmness) than the finished size of the top

*The layer of batting adds a soft, plump appearance to the pillow top and gives dimension to your hand quilting. It is not essential, however, and can be omitted if you don't plan to quilt the pillow top.

PREPARING THE PILLOW TOP

1. Spread out the lining and lay batting (if used) on top. Smooth out any wrinkles. Lay pillow top right side up on batting (or on top of lining if batting is not used).

2. Pin all layers together and machine baste ⅛ inch along outside edge. Trim lining and batting to the same size as the pillow top.

3. Quilt, by machine or hand, as desired. For best results, use a small quilting hoop or frame to hold the layers taut as you quilt. **Tip**: *To quilt close to the edges and in the corners, baste a strip of fabric to each side of the pillow top to serve as an extension. Make the strips wide enough for the frame or hoop to grip* (**Diagram 1**).

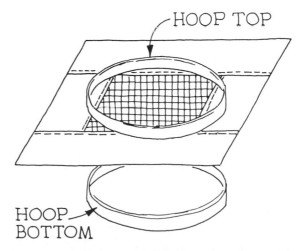

Diagram 1. To quilt easily along the edges and in the corners, baste extension strips onto all sides of the pillow top

FINISHING THE EDGES

Folded Ruffle

This ruffle is made with a strip of fabric folded in half lengthwise before gathering, which provides a finished edge without hemming and allows the right side of the fabric to show on both sides. The directions are for a 2-inch-wide finished ruffle. One-third yard of 44-inch-wide fabric is adequate to make a generous folded ruffle for a 10-, 12-, or 14-inch-square pillow.

1. Measure one side of the finished pillow top. Multiply that length by $1\frac{1}{2}$ or 2, depending on how tightly gathered you want the

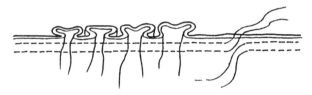

Diagram 2. Pull threads to gather ruffle

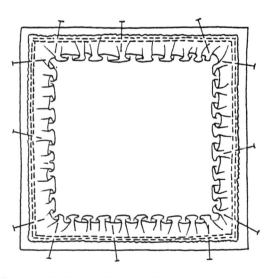

Diagram 3. Pin ruffle to pillow top, with folded edge toward the center

finished ruffle to be. Cut four 5-inch-wide strips to the required length. For example, for a 10-inch-square pillow, cut four 5 x 15- or four 5 x 20-inch fabric strips. Or, simply cut and piece a 5-inch-wide strip that measures $1\frac{1}{2}$ to 2 times the perimeter of the pillow top.

2. Sew the four strips or single strip together end to end to make one continuous loop. Press the seams open. Fold the ruffle in half lengthwise, right side out, and press the fold into the ruffle. **Tip**: *On a ruffle made of one strip, fold it in quarters, clip a notch at each fold, and use the notches as placement guides. On a ruffle made of four equal pieces, the seamlines can be matched with the corners or with the center on each side of the pillow top.* With the largest stitch on your machine, stitch through both thicknesses $\frac{1}{8}$ inch from the raw edges along the entire length of the ruffle. Add a second row of stitching $\frac{1}{8}$ inch away from the first, starting and stopping at the same place.

3. Pull the threads at one end of both rows of stitching at the same time to gather the ruffle, then pull the threads at the other end of both rows until the gathers meet in the middle (**Diagram 2**).

4. Pin the ruffle to the outside edge of the pillow top with the folded edge of the ruffle toward the center (**Diagram 3**).

5. Distribute the gathers with more fullness at the corners. Sew the ruffle to the pillow top just inside the stitch lines. To finish the pillow, follow the instructions for assembling on page xxx.

Single Ruffle

A single ruffle, as the name implies, is made from a single thickness of fabric. You use basically the same technique as for the folded ruffle, except that you must finish the outer edge with a hem or some trim. The directions given here are for a 2-inch-wide single ruffle (not including any decorative trim). One-quarter yard of 44-inch-wide fabric will provide enough for the ruffle plus a little extra.

1. Measure one side of the finished pillow top. Multiply that length by $1\frac{1}{2}$ or 2, depending

on how full you want the gathered ruffle to be. Cut four 3-inch-wide strips to the required lengths.

2. Sew the strips into one continuous loop. Press the seams open.

3. To make a hem, fold one of the sides over twice and stitch a $1/4$-inch hem along the entire edge. Add two rows of machine basting along the other edge for gathering and attach to the pillow top as described for the folded ruffle.

4. Add any decorative trim, if desired. Some trims, such as laces, are finished on both edges and can be attached to the ruffle with one row of stitching (**Diagram 4**). Others will have one raw edge that will have to be sewn into the edge of the ruffle as it is hemmed. To finish the pillow, follow the instructions for assembling on page xxx.

Piped Edge

Piping gives a pillow a handsome finished edge. Commercial piping is widely available, but for a perfect match you may wish to make your own with one of the fabrics in your pillow top. These directions make enough piping to edge a 10- or 12-inch-square pillow.

1. From a 9-inch square cut into 1-inch bias strips, cut and assemble approximately $1^{1/2}$ yards of bias binding according to instructions for binding the quilt on page xxiii.

2. On your sewing machine, replace the presser foot with a zipper foot. With the right side out, fold the bias strip over a $1^{1/2}$-yard length of cotton cord and stitch close to the cord.

3. Pin and stitch the raw edges of the piping to the outside edge of the right side of the pillow top. Before turning the corners, clip the seam allowance of the piping at the corners. Cut up to but not through the stitch line.

4. As you approach the point where the two ends of the piping will meet, trim the piping 1 inch past the starting point and fold under the end of the bias binding $1/2$ inch. Clip the ends of the cord so they meet without overlapping. Wrap the binding over the ends of the cord and stitch the sides down as for the rest of the binding (**Diagram 5**). To finish the pillow, follow the instructions for assembling on page xxx.

Bound Edge

For a simple yet attractive edging on a pillow, finish it in the same way you do your quilts, with a strip of binding that contrasts or coordinates with the fabrics in the pillow top. These directions are for binding a 10- or 12-inch-square pillow.

1. Prepare $1^{1/2}$ yards of 2-inch bias binding according to instructions for binding the quilt on page xxiii.

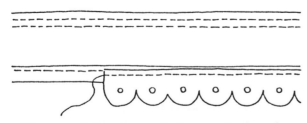

Diagram 4. Sew lace onto hemmed edge of single ruffle

Diagram 5. Wrap binding around cord where the ends meet

2. Place the right side of the binding against the right side of the pillow top, match the edges, and fold over the starting end of the binding ¹/₂ inch (**Diagram 6**).

3. Sew the binding around the pillow top ¹/₂ inch from the edge, mitering the corners (for details on mitering see page xix). Trim the binding ¹/₂ inch beyond the starting point.

4. Sew the pillow top to the pillow back, *wrong sides facing*, leaving one side open. Insert the pillow form and close the opening by hand or machine. Fold the binding over to the back of the pillow, tuck the raw edge under ¹/₂ inch, and slip stitch the binding to the pillow by hand. **Tip**: *To wash the pillow top, you will have to clip the stitching on one side and remove the pillow form, or you can use an overlapped back as an opening.*

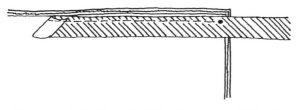

Diagram 6. Fold end of binding over 1/2 inch

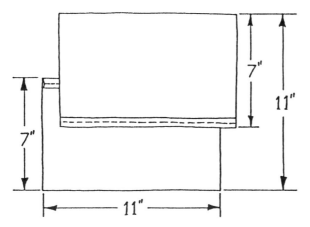

Diagram 7. Overlap hemmed edges of two back pieces

ASSEMBLING THE PILLOW

How you assemble your pillow will depend on the type of closing you choose. Three of the most common methods are described here: hand-stitched closing, overlapped back closing, and lapped zipper closing.

Hand-Stitched Closing

This is a very simple technique that hardly takes any time at all.

1. Pin the pillow back to the pillow top with right sides facing. If there is a ruffle, tuck it inside toward the center.

2. Choose one side as your starting point. Begin machine stitching 1 inch before the corner on this side. Continue sewing the top to the back around three sides. On the last side, end about 1 inch past the corner.

3. Clip the corners and turn the pillow right side out. Insert the pillow form, turn the edges of the opening inside ¹/₂ inch, and whipstitch closed by hand. **Tip**: *Before laundering the pillow, carefully snip open the hand stitching and remove the pillow form. If the fabric is loosely woven, baste the edges together to prevent fraying during laundering.*

Overlapped Back

This simple but effective method uses two pieces of overlapping fabric on the back of the pillow. You insert the pillow into the opening between the overlapped pieces.

1. Cut two pieces of backing fabric the same width as the top, but 2 inches longer than half the length. An 11-inch top, for example, requires two 11 x 7¹/₂-inch pieces. Fold one long side over twice on both pieces and stitch a ¹/₄-inch hem.

2. Lay one piece over the other so that together they measure 11 x 11 inches. The hemmed edges should overlap in the center (**Diagram 7**). Machine baste the pieces together at the sides where the edges overlap.

3. Lay the back on the pillow top with right sides facing and pin together. If there is a ruffle, tuck it out of the way toward the center of the pillow. Stitch around all four sides.

4. Clip the corners and turn right side out. Insert the pillow form through the opening where the two back pieces overlap.

Lapped Zipper

If you foresee the need to launder your pillow frequently, the little extra time it takes to install a zipper will be worthwhile. A zipper closing makes it easy to take the pillow form in and out.

1. Choose a zipper 2 inches shorter than the size of the finished pillow. For example, a 12-inch finished pillow needs a 10-inch zipper.

2. Arrange the pillow front and back pieces with the right sides facing. On one side, stitch them together 1 inch from each end, backstitching for strength (**Diagram 8**). Press open the seam along the entire side.

3. Place the wrong side of the back facing up and fold out the seam allowance of the pillow top. Lay the open zipper face down so the teeth match the center seamline. **Tip**: *Adjust the zipper so the tab and stop fall exactly where the stitching ends*. Using a zipper foot, stitch down the length of one side of the zipper, ¼ inch from the teeth, sewing through the pillow front seam allowance (**Diagram 9**).

4. Close the zipper, turn it face up, and smooth the seam allowance away from the zipper. Topstitch along the length of the zipper through the seam allowance, about ⅛ inch from the seam near the zipper teeth (**Diagram 10**).

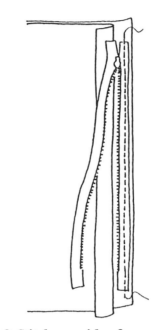

Diagram 9. Stitch one side of opened zipper to seam allowance on pillow front

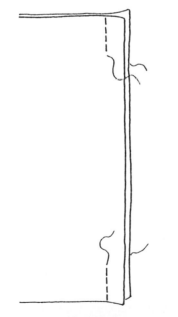

Diagram 8. Stitch 1 inch in from each end on one side

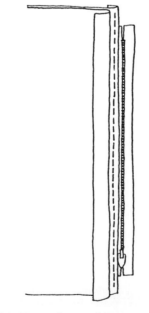

Diagram 10. Turn zipper face up and topstitch seam allowance to zipper tape

5. Spread open the front and back of the pillow and turn the closed zipper face down on the seam. Begin stitching at the top of the zipper, go across the seam from pillow front to pillow back, turn the corner and stitch the zipper tape to the pillow back down the length of the zipper. Turn the corner at the other end and stitch across from back to front (**Diagram 11**).

6. With right sides facing, pin pillow front and back together around three remaining sides. **Tip:** *Open the zipper a few inches after pinning the sides. This keeps you from inadvertently sewing the pillow shut with the zipper closed.* Sew around the three sides, starting and stopping above the tab and below the foot of the zipper (**Diagram 12**).

7. Clip corners and trim seams before turning the pillow right side out. Insert pillow form and zip closed.

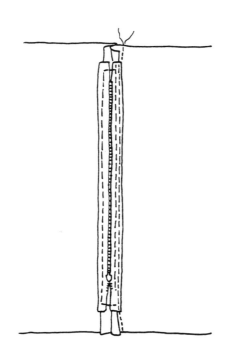

Diagram 11. Close zipper and stitch in place along other side

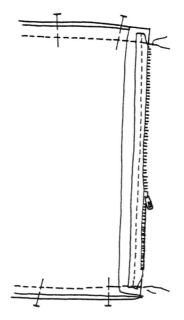

Diagram 12. Finish by stitching around other three sides of pillow

BRIGHT & BEAUTIFUL

COUNTRY LANES

Mountain Mist Collection

Country Lanes, inspired by the classic Irish Chain and Nine Patch quilts,
is easy to assemble, which makes it a good quilt for beginners.

SIZE

Block is 10 inches square
Finished quilt is 82 x 98 inches

MATERIALS

- 4½ yards white fabric
- ⅔ yard medium fabric
- ⅔ yard dark fabric
- 1¾ yards light fabric
- 6 yards fabric for quilt back
- 1 yard fabric for bias binding
- Template 10½ inches square (includes seam allowance) for E
- Template 6½ x 10½ inches (includes seam allowance) for rectangle F
- Queen-size batt

CUTTING

Blocks A, B, and C

Pattern Piece	Number of Pieces
A	110 white 116 medium 98 dark
B	82 white
C	28 white
D	20 medium 20 dark
E	17 light
F	14 white

Borders

Two strips 10½ x 98½ inches, white
Two strips 8½ x 82½ inches, white

PIECING DIAGRAMS

Block A

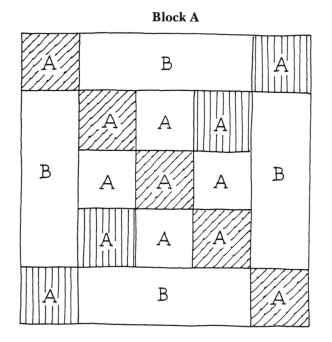

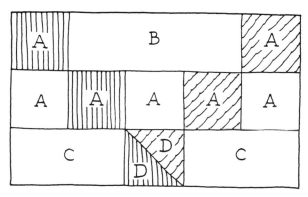

Block B

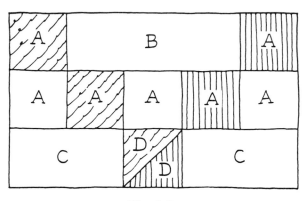

DARK

MEDIUM

Piecing Diagram: Block C

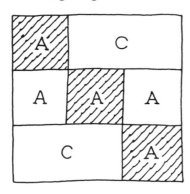

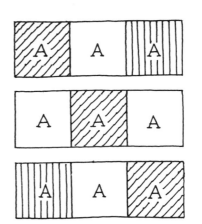

Diagram 1. Sew A pieces together in order shown, making central nine-patch square

PIECING

Block A

1. Sew a row of three A pieces. Repeat for three rows, alternating light, medium, and dark colors as shown in **Diagram 1**. Press seams open.

2. Matching seams at intersections, sew the three rows together to form a central nine-patch square. Repeat for a total of eighteen A units. Press seams open.

3. Sew one dark A and one medium A piece to opposite ends of one B (**Diagram 2**). Repeat for a total of thirty-six A-B-A units. Press seams open.

4. Sew two B pieces to opposite sides of each central nine-patch square (**Diagram 3**). Repeat for a total of eighteen B-A-B units. Press seams open.

5. Matching seams at intersections, sew A-B-A units to top and bottom of center square, with the medium squares in the upper left and lower right corners forming a diagonal line of medium squares across block (**Diagram 3**). Repeat for a total of eighteen A blocks. Press seams open.

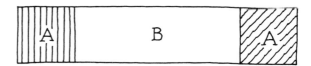

Diagram 2. Sew one dark and one medium A to opposite ends of one B

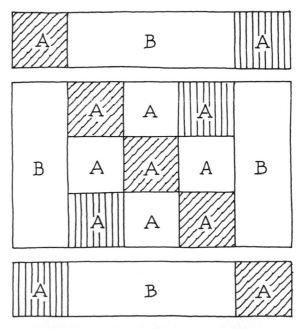

Diagram 3. Sew B pieces to opposite sides of A unit. Sew A-B-A units to top and bottom

Diagram 4. Sew one medium triangle (D) to one dark triangle to form a square

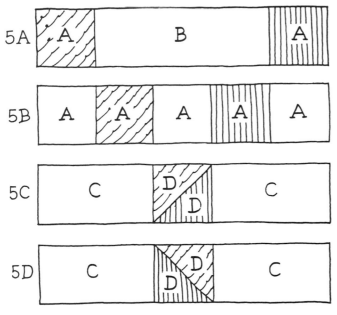

Diagram 5

Pieced Border, Block B

6. Sew together one medium and one dark D to form a square **(Diagram 4)**. Repeat for a total of ten D units. Press seams open.

7. Sew one medium A and one dark A to opposite ends of one B **(Diagram 5A)**. Repeat for a total of ten A-B-A units. Press seams open.

8. Sew together three white, one medium, and one dark A squares in order shown in **Diagram 5B**. Repeat for a total of ten A units. Press seams open.

9. Sew two white C pieces to opposite sides of one D unit with dark triangle on the bottom right **(Diagram 5C)**. Repeat for a total of six C-D-C units. Press seams open.

10. Sew two white C pieces to opposite sides of one D unit **(Diagram 5D)** with dark triangle on the bottom left. Repeat for a total of four C-D-C units. Press seams open.

11. Sew together A-B-A unit, A unit and C-D-C unit as shown in **Diagram 6**. Make six blocks with dark triangles on the bottom right and four blocks with dark triangles on the bottom left. Press seams open.

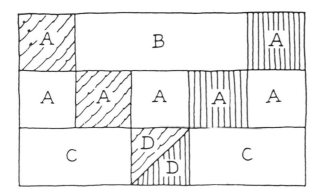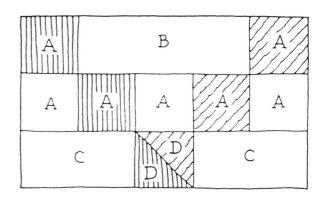

Diagram 6. Sew rows together to make B blocks

Block C

Note: There are four C blocks, two with dark A pieces and two with medium A pieces.

12. Sew one A to one end of one white C **(Diagram 7)**. Repeat for a total of eight A-C units, four with dark A pieces and four with medium A pieces. Press seams open.

13. Sew together three A pieces in a row. Repeat for a total of four A units, two with dark A center pieces and two with medium A center pieces **(Diagram 7)**.

14. Sew two A-C units to the top and bottom of one A unit to form block C, checking position of A pieces as in **Diagram 8**. Repeat for a total of four C blocks, two with dark A pieces and two with medium A pieces. Press seams open.

ASSEMBLY

15. To make top pieced border, sew together three F rectangles alternately with two B blocks as shown in Order of Assembly **(Diagram 9)**. Sew one dark/white C block to the left end of border strip, and one medium/white C block to the right end of border strip. Press seams open. Make bottom border in same manner, reversing the position of the dark and medium C blocks.

16. Sew together A blocks and plain E pieces in rows as shown in Order of Assembly **(Diagram 9)**. Press seams open. Sew one F piece to each end of the rows with A blocks on the ends. Sew one B block to each end of the rows with E pieces on the ends **(Diagram 9)**. Sew the rows together, matching seam intersections. Press seams open.

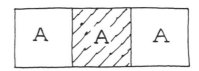

Diagram 7. Sew one A to the end of one C. Make four with dark A pieces and four with medium A pieces. Sew one white A to opposite sides of A. Make two with dark A centers and two with medium A centers.

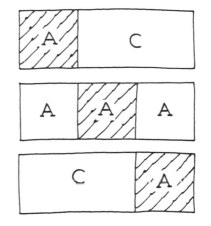

Diagram 8. Sew two A-C units to top and bottom of the A unit with A pieces in opposite corners

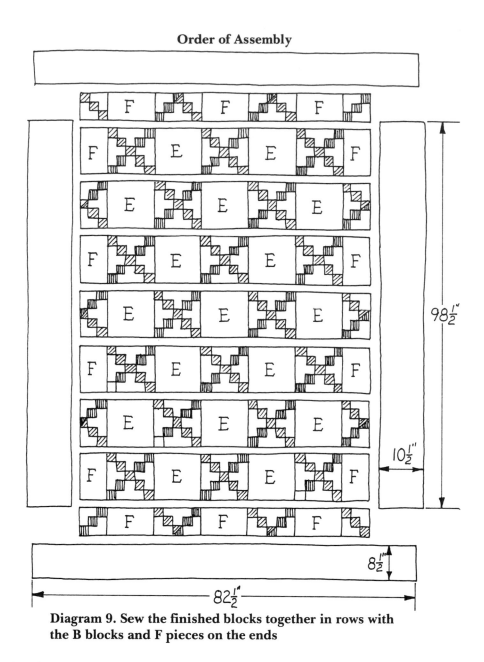

Diagram 9. Sew the finished blocks together in rows with the B blocks and F pieces on the ends

17. Sew the pieced borders (step 15) to top and bottom of quilt, matching seams at intersections. Press seams open.

18. Sew 10½ x 98½-inch white border strips to opposite sides of quilt top. Press seams open.

19. Sew 8½ x 82½-inch white border strips to top and bottom of quilt top. Press seams open.

FINISHING

20. Cut the 6-yard length of fabric for backing in half across the width. Trim selvages. Sew the two pieces together along one long side and press seam open.

21. Follow directions for assembling quilt top, batting, and back on page xx.

QUILTING

The original Country Lanes was quilted in a simple diagonal tile pattern, but this quilt offers many possibilities for creative quilting, such as small feathered wreaths in E pieces.

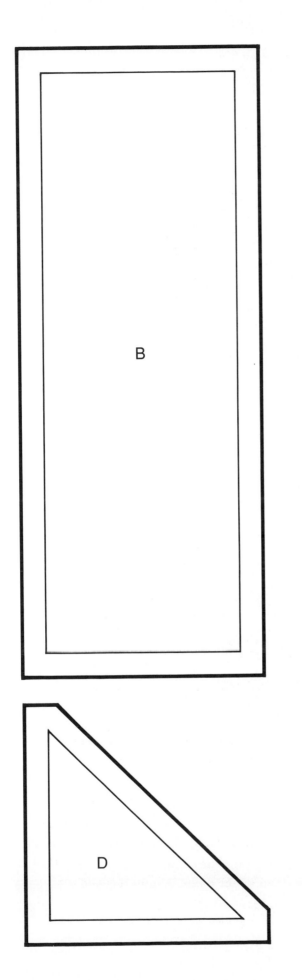

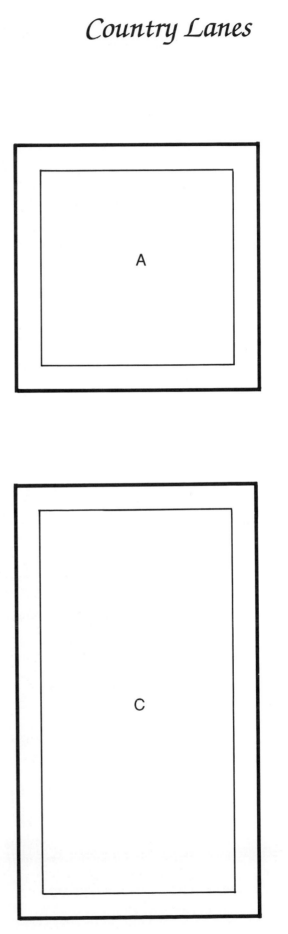

A

B

C

D

MINIATURE MAY BASKETS

By Vivian Ritter

A familiar quilt pattern in miniature is a delight to the eye. It's no wonder doll-size quilts and wall hangings are sweeping the country; besides their charm, they take less time to make than larger quilts. A quilt this size is perfect to make as a gift.

SIZE

Block is 2½ inches square
Finished quilt is 17 x 21¼ inches

MATERIALS

There are eighteen basket blocks, three each of six colors in dark, medium, and light shades. Each shade requires no more than ¼ yard fabric.

- ¼ yard fabric for outer triangles
- ¼ yard fabric for sashes and inner borders
- ⅛ yard fabric for outer borders
- ⅛ yard binding fabric
- ⅝ yard fabric for the quilt back
- 18 x 22-inch piece of batting

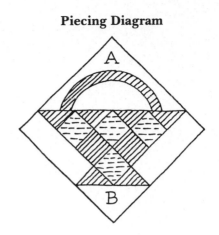

Piecing Diagram

2½-inch block

CUTTING

With the exception of pieces A and B, the baskets in this quilt are strip-pieced. See instructions on page xvi.

Use cutting instructions for each of six color combinations.

Three Basket Blocks for One Color Family

Strip Size	Number of Strips
1 x 3 inches	6 dark
1 x 6 inches	1 dark
1 x 3 inches	4 medium
2 x 6 inches	1 light
1 x 4-inch bias (basket handle)	3 dark

Pattern Piece	Number of Pieces
A	3 light
B	3 light

Edge Triangles

Pattern Piece	Number of Pieces
C	4 light
D	10 light

Sashes

Twenty-four strips 1 x 3 inches
Two strips 1 x 4 inches
Two strips 1 x 10 inches
Two strips 1 x 16 inches
One strip 1 x 19 inches

Borders

Two strips 1 x 19¼ inches
Two strips 1 x 15 inches
Two strips 1¾ x 21¾ inches
Two strips 1¾ x 17½ inches

PIECING

Blocks

The following instructions for strip piecing will make three basket blocks. Repeat for a total of eighteen basket blocks, three each of six color families.

1. Sew 1 x 3-inch dark and medium strips together as shown to make bands 1, 2, and 3 **(Diagram 1)**. One 1 x 3-inch dark strip will be left over. Sew 1 x 6-inch dark strip to light 2 x 6-inch strip to make band 4. Press seams open.

2. Cut all bands into 1-inch segments **(Diagram 2)**. Cut remaining 1 x 3-inch dark strip into three 1 x 1-inch squares.

For Three Baskets

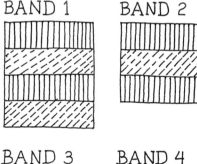

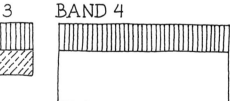

Diagram 1. Sew strips together into bands

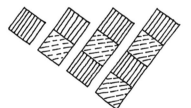

Diagram 3. Sew together segments from bands 1, 2, and 3 with one square on the left corner as shown

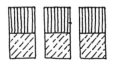

Diagram 2. Cut all bands into 1-inch segments

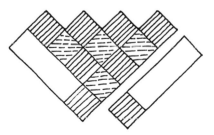

Diagram 4. Sew strips from band 4 to sides of basket

3. Matching seams at intersections, sew together one section cut from bands 1, 2, and 3 (**Diagram 3**). Sew one 1 x 1-inch dark square to the left corner. Press seams open.

4. Matching seam intersections, sew segments cut from Band 4 to sides of basket section made in step 3 (**Diagram 4**). Press seams open.

5. In order to attach pieces A and B, the basket must be trimmed across the top and bottom (**Diagram 5**). Note that the sewing line runs across the corners of the squares and that the cutting line is marked ¼ inch away from sewing line.

6. To make basket handle, fold 1 x 4-inch bias strip in half lengthwise, wrong sides together. Stitch ³⁄₁₆ inch from folded edge. Press the seam open down the center of the strip. Trim seam allowance if necessary.

7. With the seam on the underside, appliqué bias strip in a curve on piece A (**Diagram 6**). Trim ends of bias strip and press.

8. Sew A to top of basket and B to bottom of basket (**Diagram 6**). Press seams open.

9. Repeat steps 1 through 8 for each color family for a total of eighteen basket blocks.

ASSEMBLY

Refer to **Diagram 7** (next page) for visual aid with steps 10 through 13.

10. Sew 1 x 3-inch sashes between blocks to create six rows. Press seams toward sashes. Sew 1 x 4-inch sashes to third side of both corner blocks. Press seams toward sashes.

11. Sew long sashes of corresponding length between rows. Press seams toward sashes.

12. Sew D and C pieces to the ends of the rows. Press seams toward sashes.

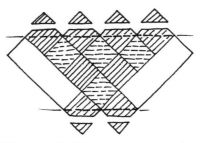

Diagram 5. Cut across top and bottom of basket so sewing line intersects corners of squares

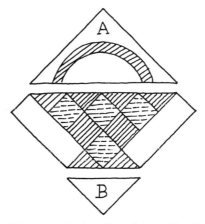

Diagram 6. Appliqué 1 x 4-inch bias strip to A to make handle. Sew A to top and B to bottom of basket

13. Sew 19¼-inch borders to opposite sides of quilt top, stopping ¼ inch from end. Press seams open. Sew 15-inch borders to top and bottom of quilt in the same manner. Press seams open.

14. Miter corners of borders following directions on page xix. Press seams open.

15. Sew 21¾-inch-wide borders to sides and 17½-inch borders to top and bottom of quilt as in step 13. Press seams open and miter corners of borders.

16. Proceed following instructions for assembling the quilt top, batting, and back on page xx.

QUILTING

Simple outline quilting following the shapes in the baskets would be appropriate on this quilt.

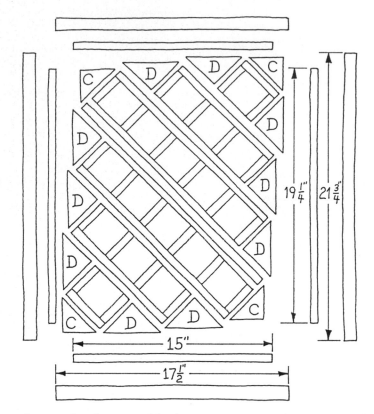

Diagram 7. Sew short sashes between blocks to create rows. Sew corner pieces D and C to the ends of the rows. Sew long sashes and rows together as shown

Miniature May Baskets

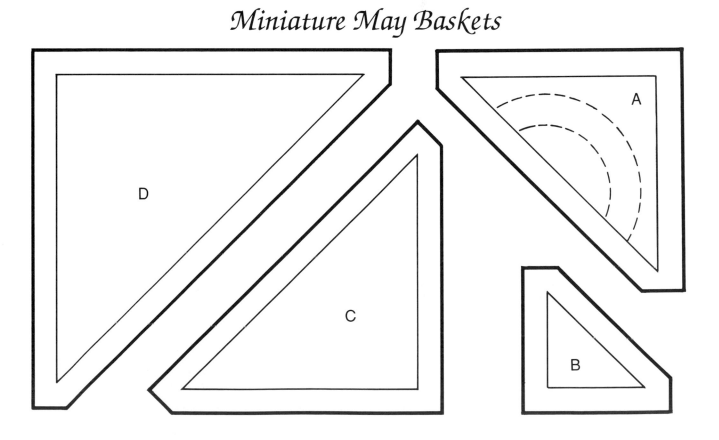

WAITING FOR THE MAIL

By Marilyn Lawhon

Appliqué and patchwork join to create a fetching wall hanging that captures the gentle ways of the Amish.

SIZE
The finished quilt is 40 inches square

MATERIALS
- 1⅛ yards black
- ½ yard lavender
- ¼ yard burgundy
- ¼ yard aqua
- Scraps of sky blue, brown, gray, muslin, and several shades of green for piecing background
- Assorted scraps for center appliqué
- Freezer paper or fusible webbing
- 1½ yards fabric for back
- Embroidery floss in black, lavender, yellow, blue, and red for details
- Crib-size batt
- Dressmaker's carbon

Appliqué Diagram

CUTTING

Pattern pieces for central appliquéd scene are given without seam allowance. Trace pattern for barn, trees, mailbox, and carriage group onto freezer-paper (see page xvii) or fusible webbing (see page xviii). If preferred, ¼-inch seam allowance can be added and turned under by hand, as in photo.

Piecing Diagram
1 square=2 inches

Using a 2-inch grid, enlarge drawing of center square foundation pieces (**Piecing Diagram**) to measure 24 inches square (see page xiv). Draw pattern pieces A through F and add ¼-inch seam allowances.

Pattern Piece	Number of Pieces
A	1 sky blue
B	1 brown
C	1 gray
D	1 medium green
E	1 muslin
F	1 light green
G	28 aqua 28 lavender 28 burgundy
H	4 lavender

Four 2½ x 26-inch strips black for inner borders
Four 2½ x 42-inch strips black for outer borders
Assorted appliqué pieces according to patterns

PIECING & APPLIQUÉ

Center Scene

1. Sew together A and B, then sew C to bottom of A-B unit **(Diagram 1)**. Press seams open after each step.

2. Sew together D, E, and F in a row **(Diagram 2)**, press seams open, and sew to bottom of A-B-C unit to complete center square foundation. Press seam open.

3. Iron freezer-paper or fusible webbing to wrong side of fabric scraps for barn, trees, mailbox, and carriage group. Referring to **Piecing Diagram** and **Appliqué Diagram**, cut out all appliqué pieces and appliqué or fuse to foundation square at this time. Place dressmaker's carbon under pattern pieces with embroidery details and trace directly onto fabric. Add embroidered details to appliqué design.

4. Sew 2½ x 26-inch black inner borders to all four sides of center and miter corners (see page xix). Press seams open.

5. Sew together three G's, one each of burgundy, aqua, and lavender, to make Rail Fence block **(Diagram 3)**. Press seams open. Repeat for a total of twenty-eight Rail Fence blocks.

6. Referring to **Appliqué Diagram**, sew together seven Rail Fence blocks, alternating stripes horizontally and vertically, with the colors in the position shown in the photo. Press seams open. Repeat for a total of four border strips of seven blocks each.

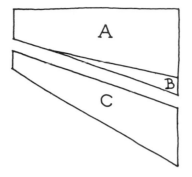

Diagram 1. Sew together A and B, then sew C to bottom of A-B unit

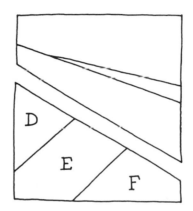

Diagram 2. Sew together D, E, and F pieces in a row

G

Diagram 3. Sew together three G's to make Rail Fence block. Make 28

7. Sew a Rail Fence border strip to opposite sides of the quilt top (**Diagram 4**). Press seams open.

8. Sew one H to each end of the remaining Rail Fence borders. Press seams open. Matching seams at intersections, sew these borders to the top and bottom of the quilt top (**Diagram 4**). Press seams open.

9. Sew $2^{1}/_{2}$ x 42-inch black outer borders to each side of quilt top. Trim excess at ends of strips if necessary and miter corners. Press seams open.

ASSEMBLY

10. Proceed following instructions for assembling the quilt on page xx. Quilt is bound with $1^{1}/_{2}$-inch straight strips of black fabric.

QUILTING

11. Waiting for the Mail was quilted along all seam lines, as well as along the contours of the land and roadway.

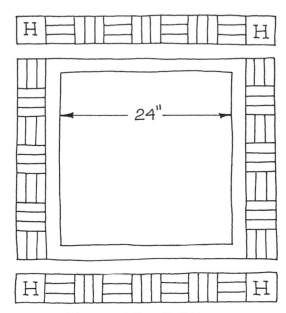

Diagram 4. Sew Rail Fence border to opposite sides of quilt center. Sew remaining borders to top and bottom of quilt center

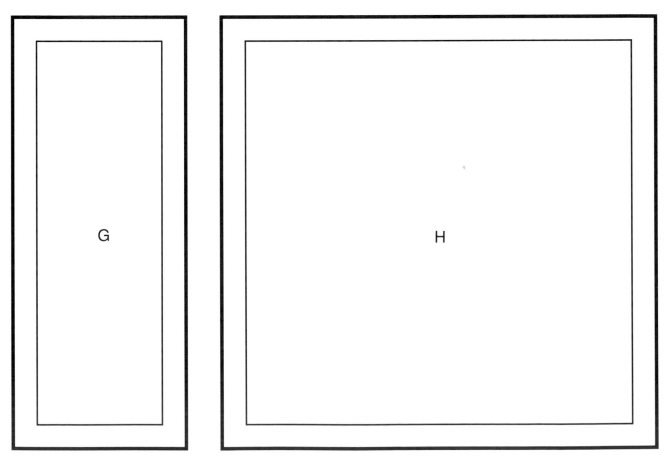

Waiting for the Mail

19

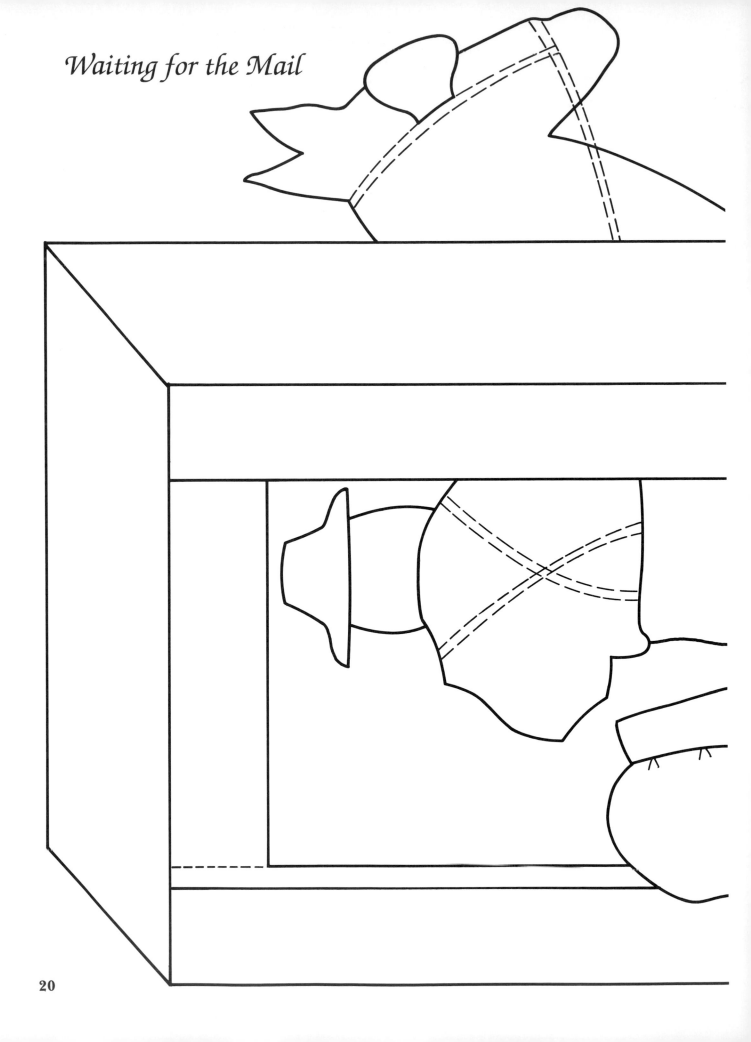

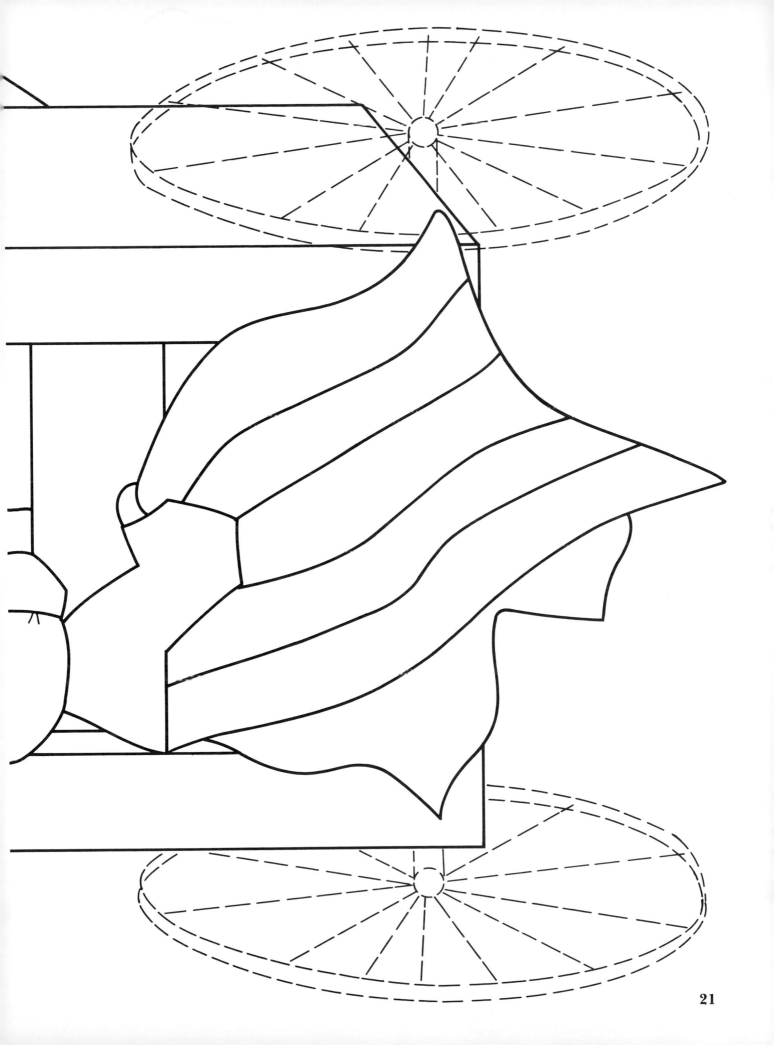

21

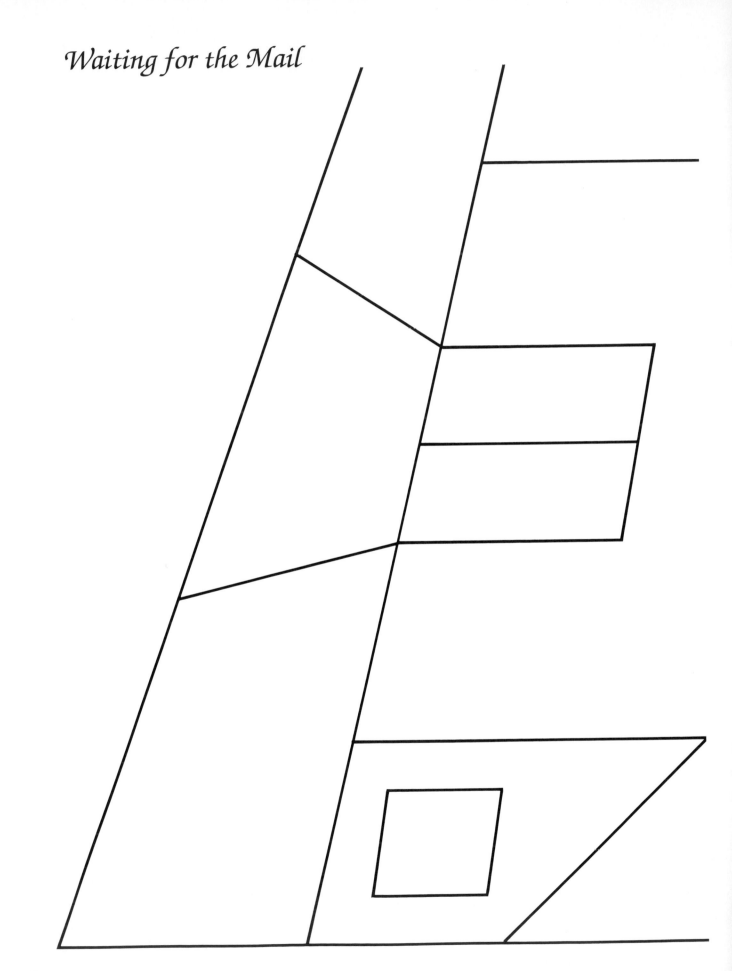

GEESE AND TULIPS PILLOW

By Barbara Clayton

Appliquéd geese in a tulip bed decorate a perky calico pillow. Make a number of these squares and you can have a matching quilt.

SIZE

Finished pillow is 16 inches square, including ruffles

MATERIALS

- 1 yard medium print fabric for corners, ruffle, and pillow back
- ¼ yard dark print fabric for ruffle
- One 9-inch square muslin
- Scraps of dark, medium, and light prints for appliqué
- Fusible webbing
- 13-inch square of light fabric for pillow top lining
- 13-inch square batting
- One 12-inch pillow form or stuffing
- Tracing paper
- Template for pattern piece A (draw 7-inch square and cut in half diagonally; includes seam allowance)

CUTTING

Corners

Pattern Piece	Number of Pieces
A	4 medium print

One 9-inch square muslin

Appliqué pieces from scraps

Two strips 4½ x 45-inch dark print for outer ruffle

Two strips 5 x 45-inch medium print for inner ruffle

PIECING, APPLIQUÉ, & ASSEMBLY

1. Trace geese appliqué design onto 9-inch muslin square, referring to photo of finished pillow for placement.

2. Sew the diagonal side of each A piece to each of the four sides of the 9-inch muslin square, making the pillow top. Press seams open.

3. To make appliqué pieces, trace appliqué designs onto tracing paper with dark pen. Turn tracing over, and trace motifs onto paper side of fusible webbing. Fuse to wrong side of appropriate fabric and cut out shapes without seam allowance. When ready to appliqué, remove paper before fusing pieces to background fabric.

4. Arrange appliqué pieces on pillow top tracing and fuse to pillow top.

5. Machine appliqué around each appliqué piece using a wide satin stitch.

6. Layer 13-inch light fabric square, batting, and pillow top, right side up, on top. Baste or pin layers together.

7. Hand quilt on both sides of diagonal seams and around appliqué design.

8. This pillow has two ruffles. The outer ruffle (navy pin-dot) is handled the same way as for Folded Ruffle, page xxviii. For the inner ruffle (light blue), sew the two 5 x 45-inch strips together end to end to make one long strip. Press seam open.

9. With right sides together, fold strip in half lengthwise and sew the sides together to make one long tube. Turn right side out through one end and press with the seamline approximately ½ inch from the fold on one side. With this seam on the wrong side, sew the ends together to make a loop. Press seam open.

10. Using the longest stitch on your machine, sew a row of stitching along the entire length of the ruffle ⅝ inch from the edge on the side without the seam. Pull one thread at each end to gather. Distribute the gathers evenly, with extra fullness at each corner, and sew the ruffle to the pillow top ¼ inch in from the outer ruffle.

11. To assemble the pillow, see page xxx.

Geese & Tulips Pillow

Geese Appliqué Pattern

ANNIVERSARY

By Karen Felicity Berkenfeld

Lovely stars emerge from the assembly of simple squares and rectangles, which have been subdivided to create triangles in each of their corners. This quilt was made as a gift to the quilt maker's parents on their golden anniversary.

PIECING DIAGRAMS

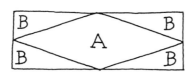

A-B Unit

C-D Unit

D-F-G Unit

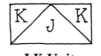

J-K Unit

SIZE

Finished quilt is 80 x 96 inches

MATERIALS

- 5 yards white fabric
- 2 yards fabric for inner and outer borders
- 11½ yards fabric in assorted prints and solids
- 6 yards fabric for quilt back
- Full-size batt
- Templates for:
    E: 9-inch square (includes seam allowance)
    H: 9 x 9 x 12¾-inch right triangle (includes seam allowance)

CUTTING

Cut B from fabric folded with right sides facing so the diagonal side in half the pieces slants in one direction, half in the other (B reversed).

Pattern Piece	Number of Pieces
A	80 white
B	160 assorted
B reversed	160 assorted
C	31 white
D	142 assorted
E	32 white
F	18 white
G	36 assorted
H	14 white
I	4 white

Flying Geese Borders

J	152 assorted
K	304 ivory
L	4 solid

Borders

Inner Border:

Two strips 2½ x 64½ inches
Two strips 2½ x 84½ inches

Outer Border:

Two strips 2½ x 76½ inches
Two strips 2½ x 96½ inches

PIECING

Note that the color of the B pieces on one side of A is different from those on the other, thereby creating stars of different colors when the pieces are assembled into the quilt top.

1. Sew one B to upper left and lower right sides of each A piece (**Diagram 1**). Press seams open. Sew one reversed B to upper right and lower left of each A. B pieces on the same side should be the same color. Repeat for a total of eighty A-B units. Press seams open.

2. Sew one D to upper left and lower right of C (**Diagram 2**). Press seams open. Sew one D to upper right and lower left of C. All four D pieces should be the same color. Repeat for a total of thirty-two C-D units. Press seams open.

3. Sew one G to right and left sides of F (**Diagram 3**). Press seams open. Sew one D to bottom of F piece. Repeat for a total of eighteen D-F-G units. Press seams open.

4. Sew one K to one short side of each J (**Diagram 4**). Press seams open. Sew one K to the other short side of each J. Press seams open. Repeat for a total of 152 J-K units.

5. To make corner units, sew one D-F-G unit to each end of one A-B unit (**Diagram 5**). Press seams open. Sew one I to the top. Press seam open. Repeat for a total of two corner units.

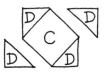

Diagram 2. Sew one D to the upper left and lower right sides of each C. Sew one D to upper right and lower left sides of each C

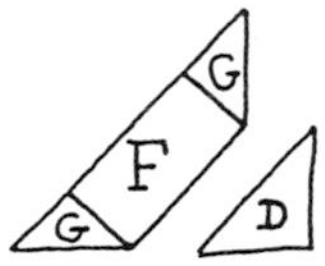

Diagram 3. Sew one G to right and left sides of each F. Sew one D to bottom of F

Border Unit

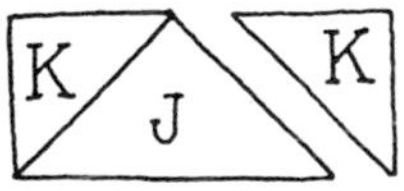

Diagram 4. Sew one K to each short side of J

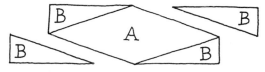

Diagram 1. Sew one B to upper left and lower right sides of each A. Sew one reversed B to upper right and lower left of each A

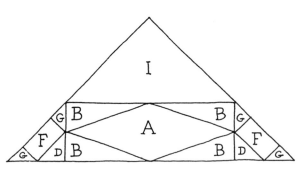

Corner Unit
Diagram 5. Constructing the corner unit

ASSEMBLY

The quilt top consists of two types of rows: one combining A-B units with C-D units; the other combining A-B units with the E pieces.

6. Matching seams at intersections, sew together the appropriate number of A-B and C-D units for each row as indicated in the **Order of Assembly Diagram**. Sew one D-F-G unit to ends of each row with the diagonal side facing outward. Press seams open.

7. Sew together alternating A-B units and E pieces for each row as shown in the **Order of Assembly Diagram**. With the exception of the two rows that require I pieces at the end, sew one H to each end of each row with the diagonal side facing outward. Press seams toward E.

8. Matching seams at intersections, sew the rows together in a diagonal formation, following the **Order of Assembly Diagram**. Sew corner units to upper left and lower right corners of the quilt top. Press seams open.

9. Sew 64½-inch inner border strips to top and bottom of quilt. Press seams toward border.

10. Sew 84½-inch inner border strips to sides of quilt. Press seams toward border.

11. To assemble top Flying Geese border, sew together thirty-four J-K units in a row **(Diagram 6)**, reversing direction of "geese" at center of row. Sew one L to each end. Repeat for bottom border. Press seams open.

12. To assemble side Flying Geese border, sew together forty-two J-K units **(Diagram 6)**, reversing direction of "geese" at center of row as done for top and bottom borders. Repeat for a total of two side borders. Press seams open.

13. Sew forty-two-unit borders to opposite sides of quilt. Press seams away from Flying Geese border.

14. Matching corner seams at intersections, sew thirty-four-unit borders to top and bottom of quilt. Press seams away from Flying Geese border.

15. Sew 76½-inch outer border strips to top and bottom of quilt. Press seams open.

16. Sew 96½-inch outer border strips to sides of quilt. Press seams open.

17. To piece quilt back, cut a full width of backing fabric 100 inches long. Cut two more pieces 20 x 100 inches. Trim selvages. Sew narrow pieces to each side of wide piece. Press seams open.

18. Proceed following instructions for assembling the quilt top, batting and back, on page xx. Quilt is bound by folding backing fabric to front of quilt, mitering corners, and blind stitching.

QUILTING

19. The Anniversary quilt was quilted with hearts and leaf designs in the A's, a woven ribbon in the E's, and simple outline quilting in the star designs.

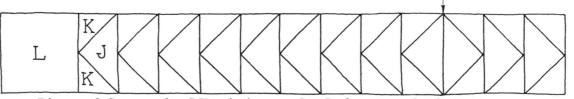

Diagram 6. Sew together J-K units in rows. Sew L pieces to ends of 34-unit rows

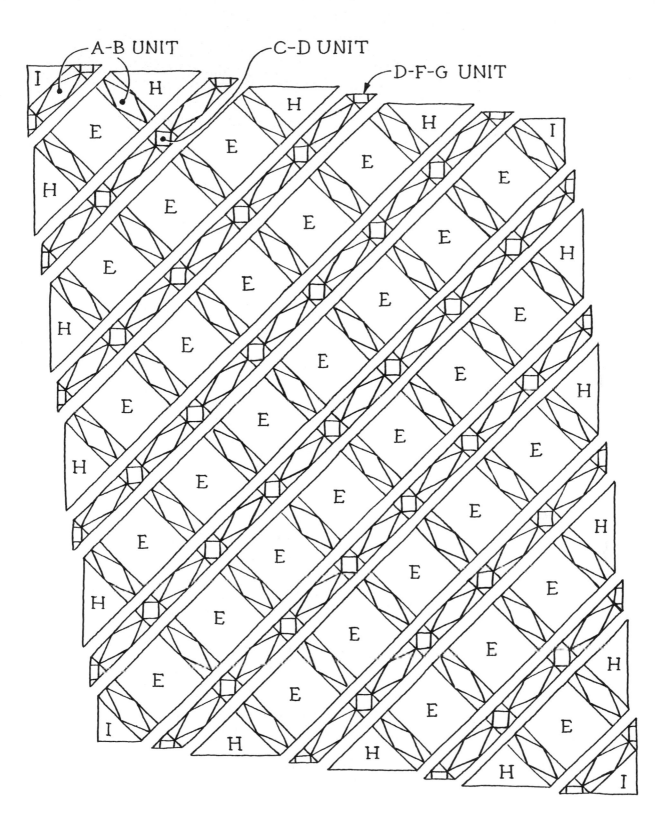

Order of Assembly

Anniversary

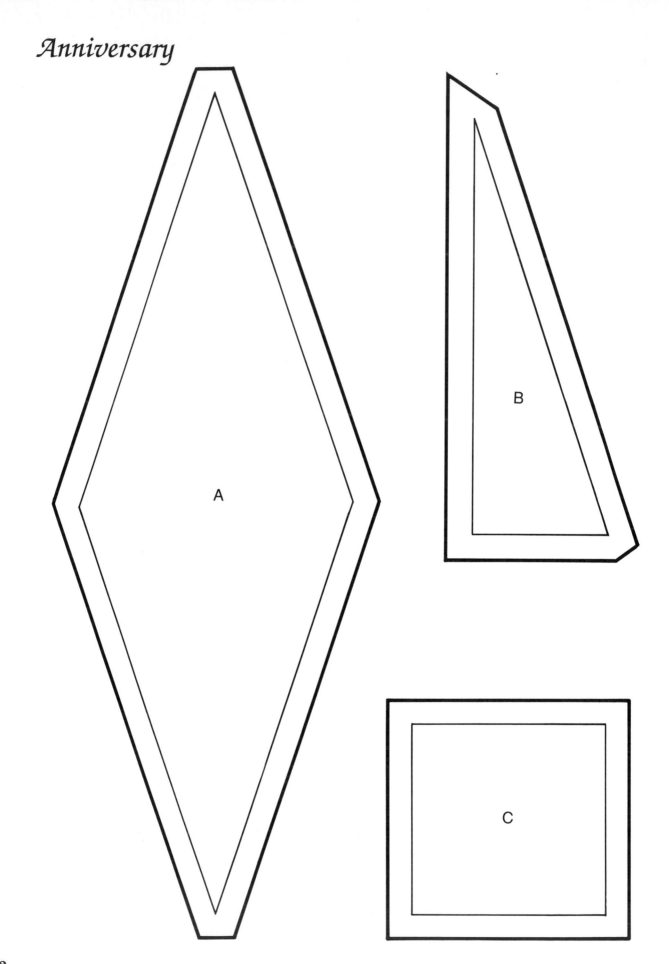

A

B

C

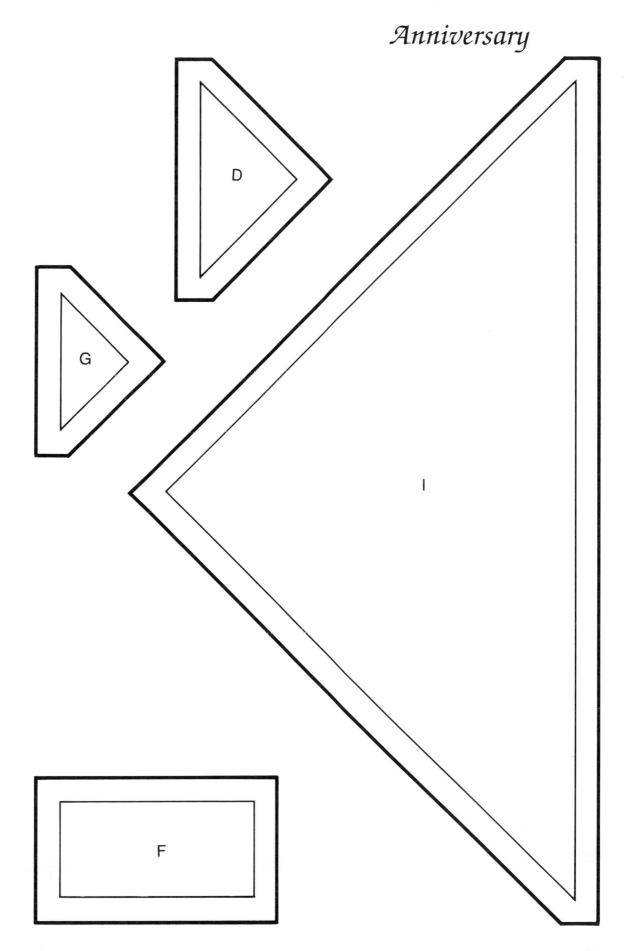

D

G

I

F

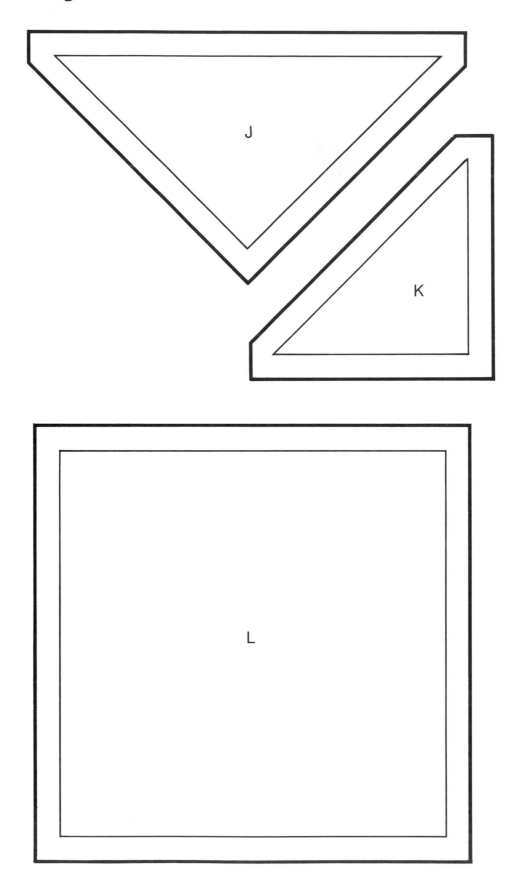

IRISH CHAIN
VARIATION

Stillwater, Minnesota, Historical Society Collection

This quilt is a colorful 19th-century variation of the Double Irish Chain.

SIZE

Block is 8 ¾ inches square
Four-block unit is 17½ inches square
Finished quilt is 52½ x 70 inches

MATERIALS

- 3¼ yards white fabric
- 1 yard yellow fabric
- 1¼ yards green fabric
- 1 yard red fabric
- 4 yards fabric for quilt back
- Twin-size batt
- 7 yards of 2-inch-wide white bias binding

CUTTING

Before cutting B pieces, see Piecing, Block B, for reference to strip piecing as an alternate method.

Pattern Piece	Number of Pieces
A	288 yellow 192 green 288 white
B	216 red 96 green 96 white
C	24 white

RED
GREEN
YELLOW

PIECING DIAGRAMS

Block A

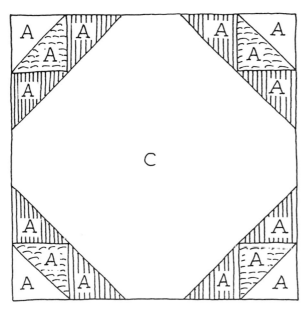

Block B

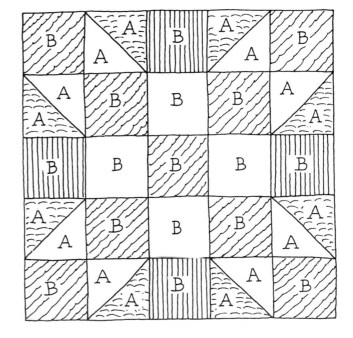

PIECING

Block A

1. Sew together one yellow A and one white A to form square (**Diagram 1**). Press seam open. Repeat for a total of 288 yellow/white squares, which will be used in both A and B blocks.

2. Sew one green A to one side of the yellow A of the square completed above. Press seam open. Sew another green A to adjacent side of the same yellow A, as shown in **Diagram 2**. Press seam open. Repeat for a total of ninety-six units.

3. Sew one A unit to each diagonal side of C (**Diagram 3**) to complete block A. Press seams open. Repeat for a total of twenty-four blocks.

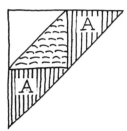

Diagram 1. Sew one yellow A to one white A to make A-A square

Diagram 2. Sew one green A to top of A-A square. Sew one green A to adjacent side of square to make A unit

**Piecing Diagram
Four-Block Unit**

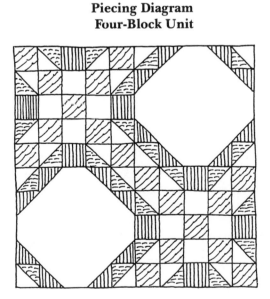

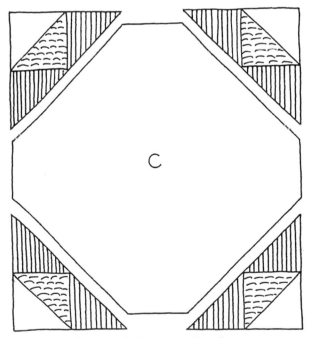

Diagram 3. Sew one A unit to each diagonal side of C

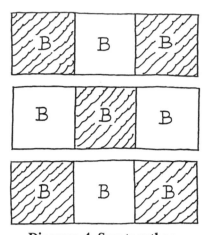

Diagram 4. Sew together white and red B pieces in three rows as shown

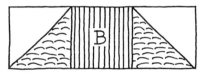

Diagram 5. Sew one A-A square to opposite sides of one B, making A-B unit

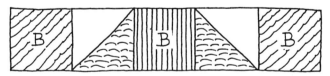

Diagram 6. Sew one red B piece to each end of A-B unit

Block B

To save time, strip-piecing methods (see page xvi) could be substituted for steps 4 and 5.

4. Sew together alternating red and white B pieces in three rows as shown in **Diagram 4**. Press seams open. Repeat for a total of forty-eight red/white/red rows (top and bottom) and twenty-four white/red/white rows (center).

5. Matching seams at intersections, sew three alternating rows together to form a nine-patch center square following order shown in **Diagram 4**. Press seams open. Repeat for a total of twenty-four nine-patch center squares.

6. Sew one A-A square (yellow/white square made in step 1) to opposite sides of one green B, with the yellow triangle next to the green square (**Diagram 5**). Press seams open. Repeat for a total of ninety-six A-B units.

7. Sew one red B to each end of one A-B unit (**Diagram 6**). Press seams open. Repeat for a total of forty-eight units.

8. Sew short A-B units (those without red B squares) to opposite sides of the nine-patch center square, matching seams at intersections (**Diagram 7**). Press seams open. Matching seams at intersections, sew long A-B units (those with red B squares) to top and bottom of block. Press seams open. Repeat for a total of twenty-four B blocks.

9. Referring to **Four-Block Unit Diagram**, sew together two A blocks and two B blocks in order shown. Press seams open. Repeat for a total of twelve four-block units.

ASSEMBLY

10. Matching seams at intersections, sew four-block units together into four rows of three four-block units each (**Assembly Diagram**). Press seams open.

11. Sew rows together. Press seams open.

12. Cut the 4-yard length of fabric for the quilt back in half across the width. Cut two 10 x 72-inch strips from one 2-yard panel. Trim selvages. Sew the 10 x 72-inch strips to opposite sides of full panel. Press seams open.

13. Proceed following instructions for assembling the quilt top, batting, and back on page xx.

14. Bind quilt with 2-inch white bias binding.

QUILTING

15. Quilt as desired. The original quilting was simple, echoing the geometric shapes of the piece.

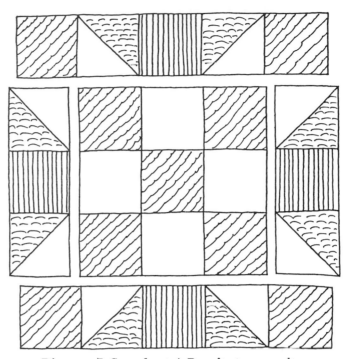

Diagram 7. Sew short A-B units to opposite sides of nine-patch center squares. Sew long A-B units to top and bottom of block

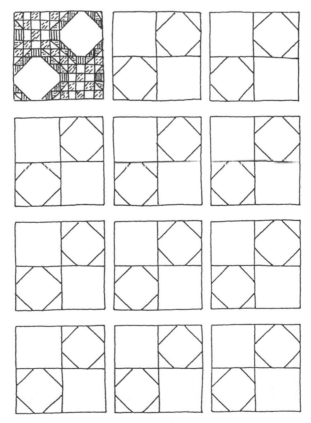

Assembly Diagram

Irish Chain Variation

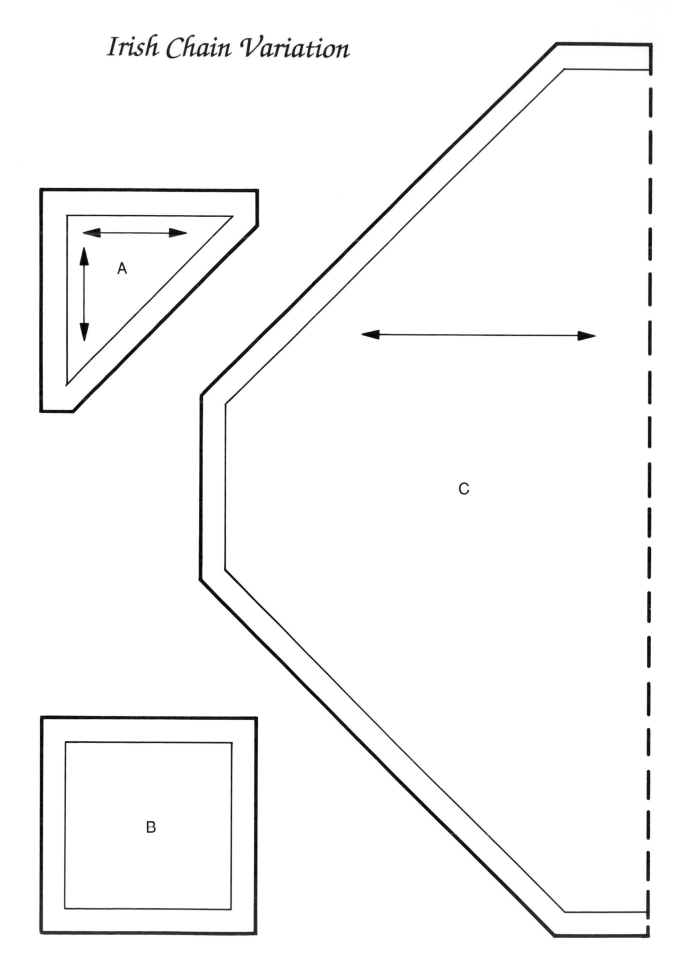

PINE TREE MEDALLION

By Jane Noble

What started out as a wall hanging grew, with the addition of borders, to a full-size quilt. The finished piece appears to be complex and highly detailed because of the borders, which are quite wonderful and fit together in a well-planned, logical manner. Even though this may seem to be a demanding, even daunting, project, don't be put off. All of the assembly details have been worked out for you so that even the borders are not difficult to construct.

The quiltmaker chose the Pine Tree block because she found the intricacy of the design appealing. If you like, you can replace the Pine Tree Medallion with any design, geometric or appliquéd, that's a 20-inch square (finished size). You can also use the medallion pattern or the substitute design to make a matching pillow top.

SIZE
Finished quilt measures 72 x 72 inches

MATERIALS
- 2¹/₂ yards dark blue*
- 1¹/₂ yards each of light blue, tan, brown, rust, and light rust.*
- One twin-size batt
- 4¹/₈ yards of 48-inch fabric for the back
- 8¹/₄ yards of 2-inch bias binding

* In case you wish to use your own color combination, the instructions refer to light, medium, and dark, rather than specific colors.

CUTTING

Medallion

Pattern Piece	Number of Pieces
A	78 (36 light, 42 dark)
B	3 light
C	3 light
D	1 dark
E	2 dark
F	2 light
G	2 dark
H*	4 medium

Border A
Four strips 2¹/₂ x 24¹/₂ inches, light

Border B

A	12 (2 dark, 2 light, 8 medium)
B	12 (6 light, 6 dark)
I*	96 (32 each of light, dark, medium)

Border C
Four strips 1¹/₂ x 32¹/₂ inches, light

Border D

J	36 dark
K	72 medium
A	144 light

Border E
Four strips 2¹/₂ x 44¹/₂ inches medium

Border F

L	92 (48 medium, 44 dark)
M	184 light
N*	8 light
O*	8 dark

Border G

A	368 (184 light, 184 dark)
B	60 (32 light, 28 dark)
E	8 medium
K	8 medium
P	52 (24 medium, 28 dark)
Q	8 dark

Border H
Four strips 2¹/₂ x 72¹/₂ inches dark

* Notes

H: Cut two squares measuring 10¹/₂ x 10¹/₂ inches and cut in half diagonally.
I, N, and O: Cut from fabric folded with right sides facing. In this way half of the pieces for each pattern will correctly face in the opposite direction.

PIECING

Medallion

To show how the Pine Tree Medallion is assembled, the major sections have been broken out in **Diagram 1**. Begin with the little triangles (A) and assemble the branch sections as follows:

1. Sew one light A to one dark A along the diagonal to form a square. Repeat for a total of thirty squares. Press seams open.

2. With the dark triangles pointing in one direction, sew five squares together in a row. Repeat for three rows. With the dark triangles facing in the opposite direction, sew five squares together in a row. Repeat for three rows. Press seams open.

3. Position the rows as indicated in **Diagram 2** and sew a light A to the top end of each row and a dark A to the bottom end of each row. Press seams open.

4. Matching seams at intersections, sew together three rows of A squares to form a set of branches for one side of the tree. Repeat for the other side **(Diagram 3)**. Press seams open.

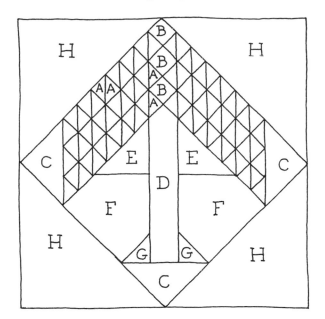

Diagram 1. Order of Assembly

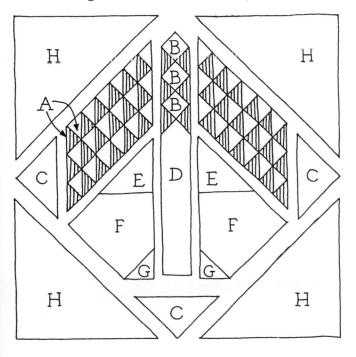

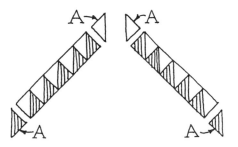

Diagram 2. Sew five A squares together into rows with light triangles on one end and dark triangles on the other end of each row

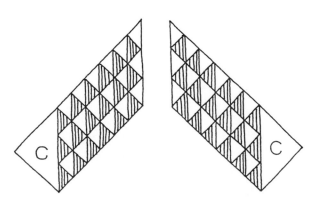

Diagram 3. Sew one C to the side of each branch section

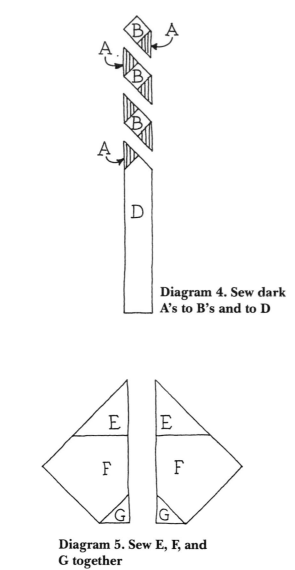

Diagram 4. Sew dark A's to B's and to D

5. Sew one C to the outer side of each set of branches (**Diagram 3**). Press seams open.

6. Sew one dark A to: the right side of one B; the opposite sides of two B pieces; and the left side of the top of D. Press seams open. Sew these units together as shown (**Diagram 4**), matching seams at intersections. Press seams open.

7. Sew E, F, and G together as shown (**Diagram 5**). Press seams open.

8. Sew the right branch section to the corresponding E-F-G unit (**Diagram 6**). Repeat for the left branch section. Press seams away from branches.

9. Sew the right side of the tree to the right side of the trunk (A-B-D), matching seams at intersections. Repeat for the left side (**Diagram 6**). Press seams open. Sew a C to the bottom of the tree. Press seam open.

10. To complete the center square for the Pine Tree Medallion, sew an H to opposite sides of the tree. Press seams toward H. Repeat for the remaining two opposite sides (**Diagram 6**).

Diagram 5. Sew E, F, and G together

Diagram 6. Sew branch sections to E-F-G units. Sew right and left sides of tree to the trunk (A-B-D). Sew one C to the bottom and one H to each side

Border A

11. Sew a 2½ x 24½-inch strip to each side of the medallion, mitering corners as described on page xix.

Border B

12. Note: *The position of the light and dark pieces in the center sections of the borders changes; it matches in opposite borders.*
Sew two B's together (one light and one dark) and one dark A and one light B together **(Diagram 7)**. Press seams open. Sew these two units together, matching seams at intersections. Repeat for two sets.

13. Make two more sets reversing the position of light and dark: sew together one dark B and one light B and one light A and one dark B. Press seams open. Sew these two units together, matching seams at intersections. Press seams open.

14. Note: *The position of dark and light I pieces changes in opposite borders.*
Starting with medium I pieces, sew one I to the top two sides of each center section. Press seams open. Add another I to each bottom side (dark I's on the two borders with dark A's, and light I's on the two borders with light A's as in **Diagram 8**). Continue to add I's in this manner, alternating light, medium, and dark, until each border has twenty-four I pieces. Sew one medium A to the bottom side at each end. Press seams open after each step, being careful not to stretch bias while pressing.

15. Sew one B border to each side of the quilt top, stopping ¼ inch from the corners. Press seams open. Sew the diagonal ends together at each corner, matching seams at intersections. Press seams open. Note: *The edges of the borders, which are on the bias, may stretch during handling. They can be eased back in to fit with a row of stay stitching. The bobbin thread can be pulled slightly for further easing. Careful pressing is essential.*

Border C

16. Sew a 1½ x 32½ -inch strip to each side of the quilt top and stop ¼ inch from the corners. Miter the corners following directions on page xix.

Border B

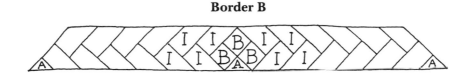

Diagram 7. Sew together two B's and one A and one B

Diagram 8. Sew I's to top and bottom sides of center section

Border D

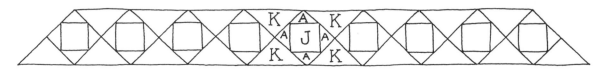

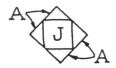

Diagram 9. Sew one A to
each side of J

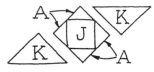

Diagram 10. Sew one K to each side
of A-J unit. Sew one K to lower left
side of remaining A-J units

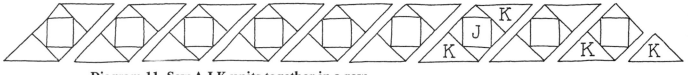

Diagram 11. Sew A-J-K units together in a row

Border D

17. Sew one A to each of two opposite sides of each J. Press seams open. Sew one A to the other two sides of each J for a total of thirty-two A-J units. Press seams open (**Diagram 9**).

18. Sew one K to the upper right and lower left sides of thirty-two A-J units. Sew one K to lower left side of each of the remaining four A-J units. Press seams open (**Diagram 10**).

19. Sew nine A-J-K units together in a row with the one that has only one K on the right end, matching seams at intersections (**Diagram 11**). Sew one of the remaining K pieces to the right end of the row. Repeat for four rows. Press seams open.

20. Sew the four borders to each side of the quilt top and stop ¼ inch from the corners. Press seams open. Sew the diagonal ends together at each corner, matching seams at intersections. Press seams open.

Border E

21. Sew one 2½ x 44½-inch strip to each side of the quilt top, mitering corners as described on page xix.

Border F

22. Sew one M to the upper right and lower left sides of each L (**Diagram 12**), matching notches, except for four medium L pieces; sew only one M to the lower left side of these four. Press seams open.

23. Starting with a medium L unit at the left end, sew twenty-three L-M units together in a row, alternating medium and dark L pieces and matching seams at intersections. Sew one of the medium L-M units with one M to the right end. Sew one of the remaining M pieces to the lower right side of the last L (**Diagram 12**). Repeat for four rows. Press seams open.

Border F

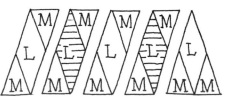

Diagram 12. Sew one M to each
of two opposite sides of L. Add
L-M unit at right end

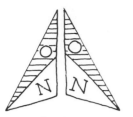

Diagram 13. Sew one N to each of the eight O pieces

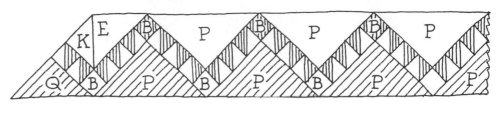

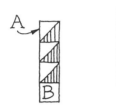

Diagram 14. Sew three squares together in rows

24. Matching notches, sew one N to each of the eight O pieces **(Diagram 13)**. Note that half of the N-O units will face in opposite directions. Press seams open. Sew one N-O unit to each end of each L-M border. Press seams open.

25. Sew the four borders to each side of the quilt top and stop ¼ inch from the corners. Press seams open. Sew the diagonal ends together at each corner, matching seams at intersections. Press seams open.

Border G

26. Sew one light A to one dark A along the diagonal to make a square. Continue in this manner until all the A pieces are used (You will have 184 pairs). Press seams open.

27. With the dark triangles pointing to the right, sew three squares together in a row. Repeat for twenty-eight rows. With the dark triangles pointing left, sew three squares together in a row. Repeat for twenty-eight rows **(Diagram 14)**. Press seams open. There will be sixteen squares left over for the ends of the borders.

28. Sew a light B to the bottom end of each of the twenty-eight rows of squares where the dark

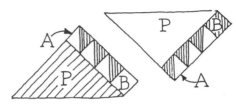

Diagram 15. Sew one row of squares to the right side of 28 dark P pieces. Sew one row of squares to the right side of 24 medium P pieces

triangles are pointing to the right **(Diagram 14)**. Sew a dark B to the top end of each of the twenty-eight rows of squares where the dark triangles are pointing to the left. Press seams open. There will be four light B pieces left over for the corners of the borders.

29. With the light B pieces on the lower right, sew a row of squares to the right side of the twenty-eight dark P pieces (check the position of the P pieces in **Diagram 15**). With the dark B on the upper right, sew a row of squares to the right side of the twenty-four medium P pieces. Four rows with dark B pieces will be left over for the left corners of the borders. Press seams open.

30. Sew a dark P-A-B unit to the left side of a medium one, matching seams at intersections **(Diagram 16)**. Press seams open. Sew a dark P-A-B unit to the right side of the section just completed. Press seams open. Proceed in this manner until you have a row with thirteen P-A-B units. Repeat for four rows.

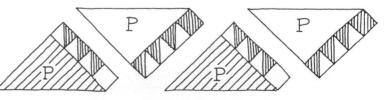

Diagram 16. Sew 13 P-A-B units together in a row

31. To finish the corners, sew one K to the left side of four E pieces. Sew one K to the right side of four E pieces (**Diagram 17**). Press seams open.

32. Sew the remaining squares (left over in step 27) of light and dark triangles (A) together in 8 rows of two squares: four rows with the dark triangles pointing to the right and four rows with the dark triangles pointing to the left (**Diagram 18**). Sew a light B to the bottom end of each of four rows of two squares where the dark triangles are pointing to the right. Press seams open.

33. Sew one row with a light B to the right sides of four Q pieces (check the position of the Q pieces in **Diagram 19**). With the dark B on the upper right, sew the four rows left over in step 29 to the diagonal side of E in the four E-K units with the K on the left. Sew the remaining four rows of two squares left over in step 32 to the lower right side of the remaining E-K units. Press seams open.

34. For the left corner, sew the Q section to the E-K unit. Press seam open. Sew this section to the left end of the border. For the right corner, sew the E-K unit to the last P unit. Press seams open. Sew the remaining Q to the lower right end of the border. Press seam open.

35. Sew the borders to each side of the quilt top, and stop ¼ inch from the corners. Press seams open. Sew the diagonal sides together at each corner, matching seams at intersections. Press seams open.

Border H

36. Sew a 2½ x 72½-inch strip to each side of the quilt top and stop ¼ inch from the corners. Miter the corners as described on page xix. Press seams open.

ASSEMBLY

37. Cut the 4⅛-yard length of fabric for the back in half across the width. Trim selvages. Sew the two pieces together along their long sides and press seams open.

38. Proceed following instructions for assembling the quilt top, batting, and back, on page xx.

QUILTING

39. To quilt the Pine Tree Medallion quilt, the quilt maker suggests "Simply let the geometric shapes dictate the quilting lines."

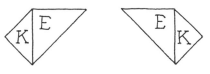

Diagram 17. Sew one K to the left side of four E pieces, and one K to the right side of four E pieces

Diagram 18. Sew leftover squares together in rows.

Left Corner   **Right Corner**

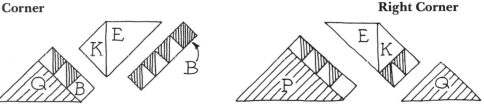

Diagram 19. For the left corner, sew a row of squares with a light B to a Q, and a row with a dark B to the E-K unit. Sew a row with a dark B to the E-K unit. For the right corner, sew a row of two squares to an E-K unit

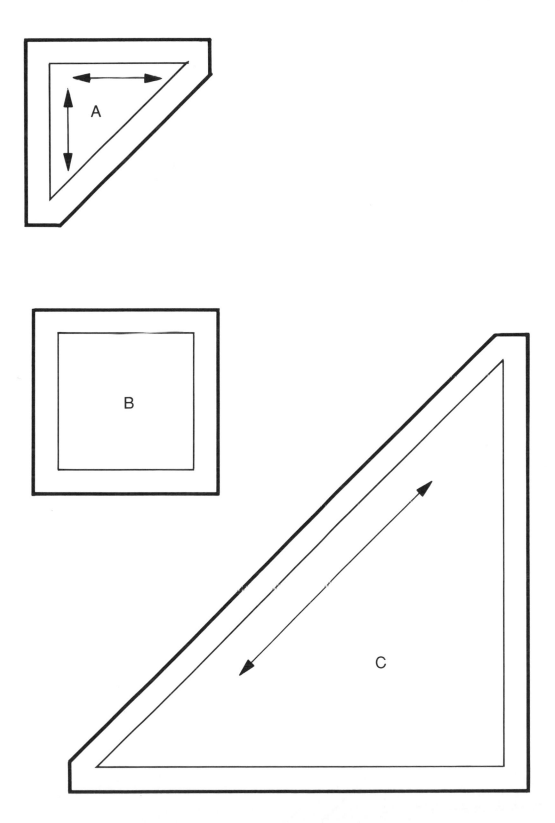

A

B

C

Pine Tree Medallion

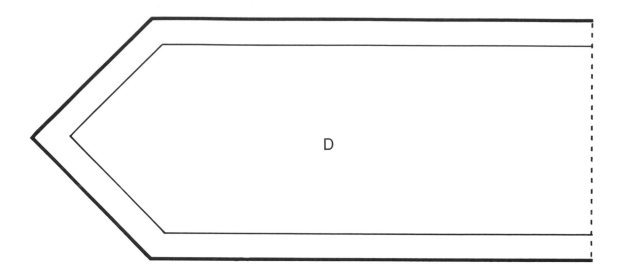

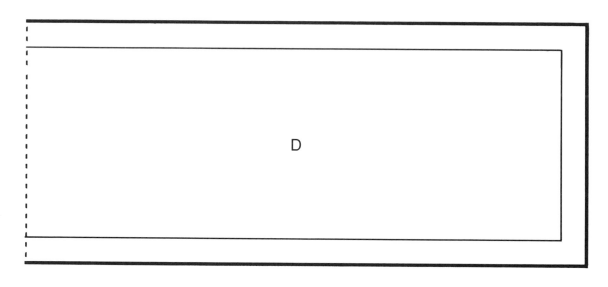

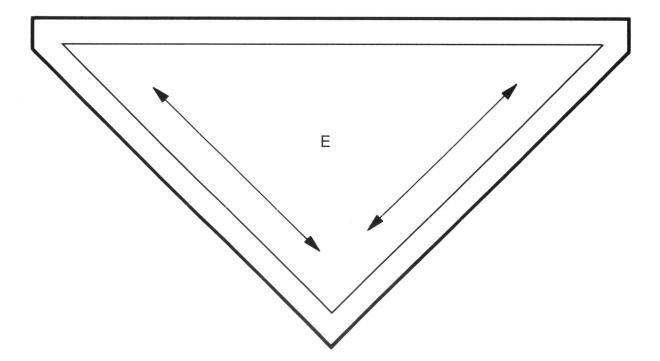

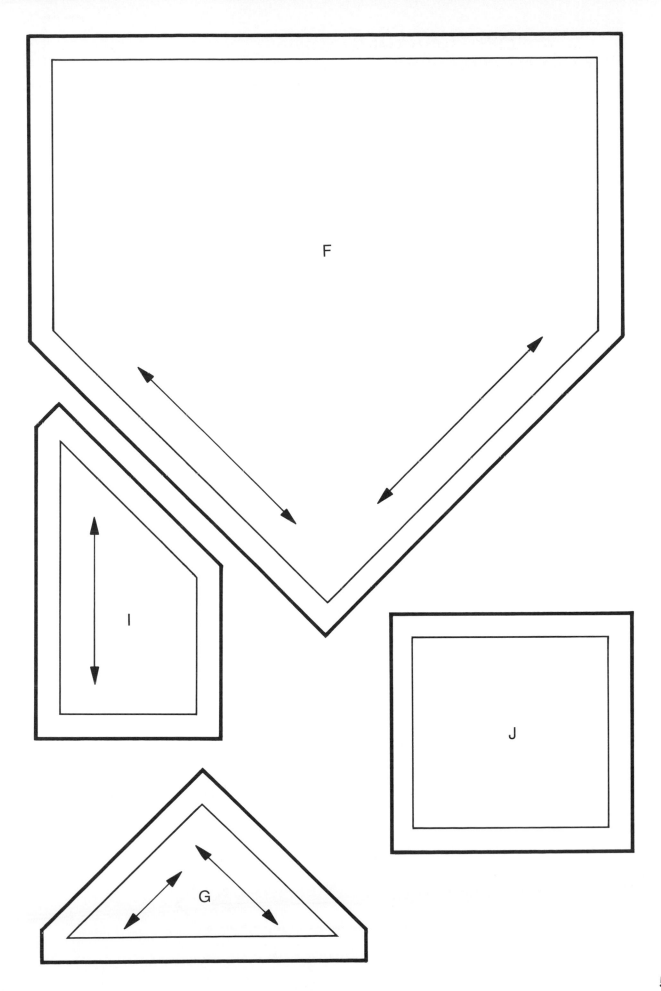

Pine Tree Medallion

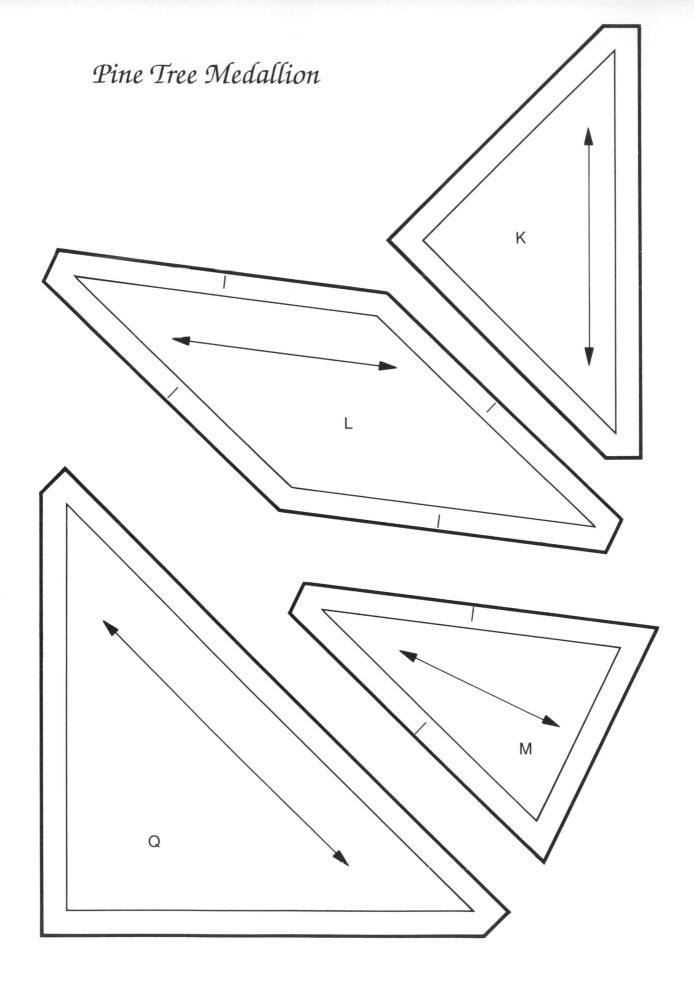

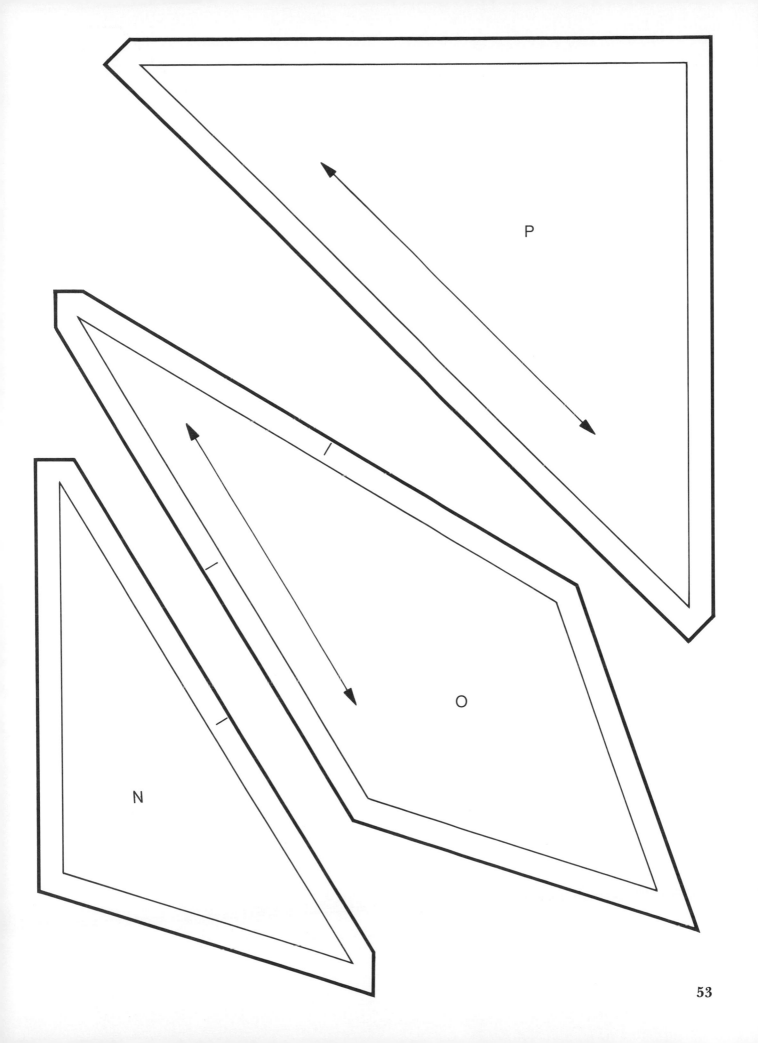

P

O

N

53

GEOMETRICS
GREAT & SMALL

BIRDS ON THE TRACKS

Sandra Hatch, owner

One of the delightful things about quilts is their names. After searching for this pattern, which she couldn't find listed in any of her quilt books, the owner named this antique quilt Birds on the Tracks because it seemed to be a combination of Railroad Crossing and Birds in the Air.

Piecing Diagram: 16-inch block

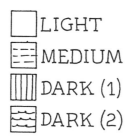

LIGHT
MEDIUM
DARK (1)
DARK (2)

Diagram 1. Sew one light and one dark triangle together

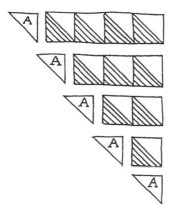

Diagram 2. Sew squares together in rows, adding A's as shown. Make four of each row

SIZE

Block is 16 inches square
Finished quilt is 76 x 79 inches

MATERIALS

- 3 yards light fabric
- 1½ yards medium fabric
- 2 yards dark fabric for blocks (small triangles)
- 2½ yards dark fabric for block centers, block corners, sashes, and borders
- 5⅛ yards dark fabric for quilt back and binding
- Full-size batt

CUTTING

Block cutting directions are for one block.
Repeat procedure for a total of sixteen blocks.

Block

Pattern Piece	Number of Pieces
A	100 (40 dark, 60 light)
B	1 dark
C	4 medium
D	4 dark

Sashes

Twelve strips 2¾ x 16½ inches, dark
Three strips 2¾ x 71¼ inches, dark

Borders

Two strips 4½ x 71¼ inches, dark
Two strips 2½ x 79¼ inches, dark

PIECING

Block

1. Sew one light A to one dark A along the diagonal to form a square (**Diagram 1**). Repeat for a total of forty squares. Press seams open.

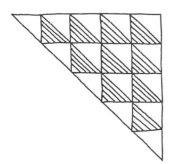

Diagram 3. Sew rows together to make one bird section

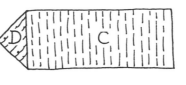
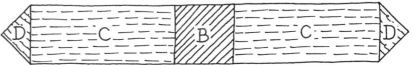

Diagram 4.
Top: Sew D to one end of each C
Bottom: Sew two C-D units to B

2. Arrange the squares in rows with light triangles on top as shown in **Diagram 2**. Sew squares into rows, with light triangles (A) at one end of each row as shown. Make three more of each row. Press seams open.

3. Sew rows together, matching seams at intersections, to complete one section of "birds" (**Diagram 3**). Repeat for a total of four bird sections. Press all seams open.

4. Sew one D to one end of each C (**Diagram 4**). Repeat for a total of four C-D units. Press seams open.

5. Sew two C-D units to opposite sides of B (**Diagram 4**). Press seams open.

6. Sew one bird section to each side of remaining C-D units. Press seams toward C-D unit. Sew these sections to each side of B-C-D section, carefully matching seams at intersections (**Diagram 5**). Press seams toward B-C-D unit.

7. Repeat steps 1 through 6 for a total of sixteen blocks.

Order of Assembly

Diagram 5. Sew bird sections to each side of two remaining C-D units.

Order of Assembly

Diagram 6. Sew short sashes between blocks. Sew long sashes between rows

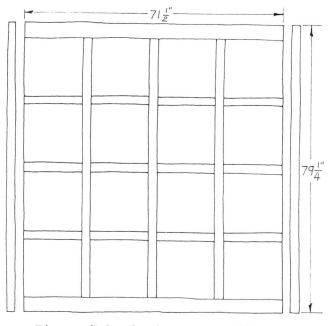

71½"

79¼"

Diagram 7. Sew borders to top and bottom and to each side

ASSEMBLY

Sashes and Borders

8. Sew the short sashes (2 ¾ x 16½-inch) between the blocks to make four rows of four blocks each (**Diagram 6**). Press seams toward sashes.

9. Sew long sashes (2 ¾ x 71¼-inch) between rows of blocks (**Diagram 6**). Press seams toward sashes.

10. Sew 4½ x 71¼-inch borders to top and bottom of quilt top (**Diagram 7**). Press seams toward border.

11. Sew 2½ x 79¼-inch borders to each side of quilt top (**Diagram 7**). Press seams toward border.

12. Cut the 5⅛-yard-length of fabric for the back in half across the width. Trim selvages. Sew the two pieces together along one long side and press seam open.

13. Proceed following instructions for assembling the quilt top, batting, and back on page xx. Also see page xxiii for instructions on binding.

QUILTING

This antique Birds on the Tracks quilt was quilted simply with diagonal lines, 1 inch apart, across the surface. However, pretty, decorative quilting could be done in the corners where the blocks join as well as in the central cross of each block. Complete with simple outline quilting. The original quilt was bound with the homespun fabric used to back the quilt.

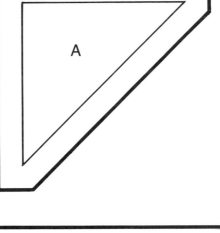

A

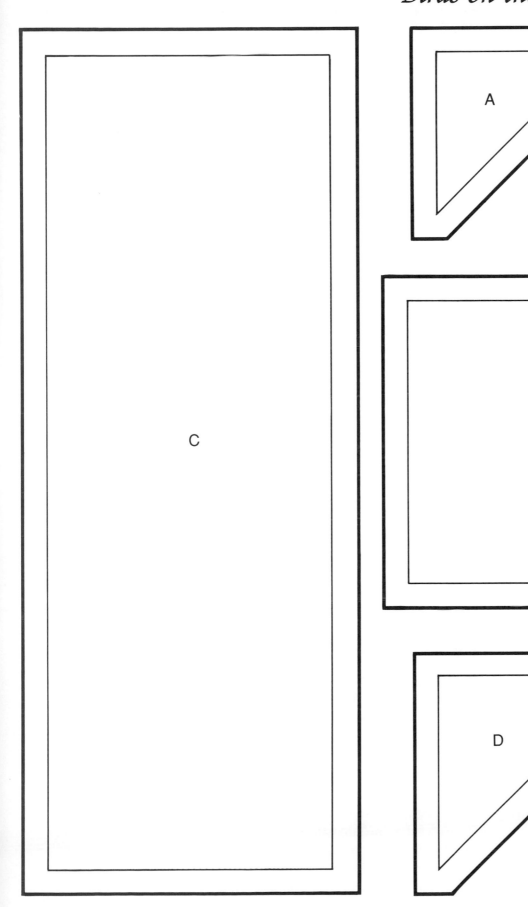

C

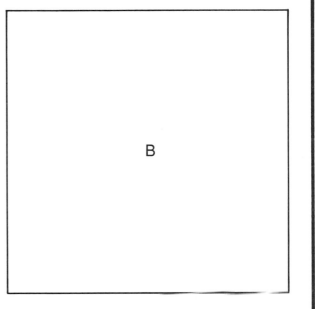

B

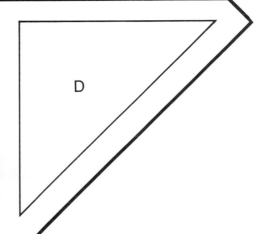

D

MINI MARINER'S COMPASS

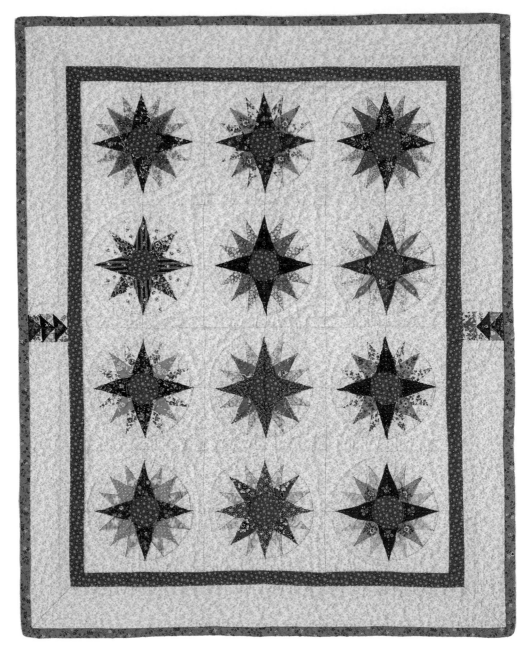

By Barbara Zygiel

A tiny version of an old favorite with blocks only four inches wide, this miniature quilt is constructed in the same way as its bigger brother, but a bit more care is needed to fit the smaller pieces together accurately.

SIZE

Block is 4¼ inches square
Finished quilt is 18½ x 23 inches

MATERIALS

- ⅝ yard fabric for background and outer borders
- ¼ yard fabric (compass centers and inner borders)
- ¼ yard total of dark, medium, and light scraps for compass points
- ¼ yard fabric for binding
- 22 x 26-inch piece of fabric for back
- 22 x 26-inch piece of polyester batting or cotton flannel

CUTTING

Compass Block

Pattern Piece	Number of Pieces
A	12
B	48 assorted dark
C	48 assorted medium
D	96 assorted light
E	192 background fabric
F	48 background fabric

Flying Geese Border Insert

Pattern Piece	Number of Pieces
G	6 assorted dark
H	12 assorted light

Borders

Inner Border (from inner border fabric):
    Two strips 1 x 19¾ inches
    Two strips 1 x 15¼ inches
Outer Border (from background fabric):
    Two strips 2 x 18¾ inches
    Four strips 2 x 11¼ inches

Binding

Cut 1½-inch-wide strips to make 2¼ yards of binding

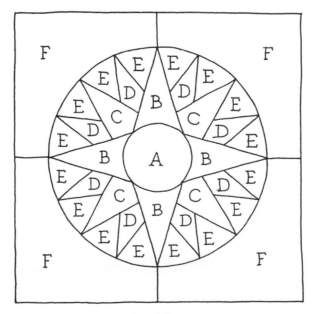

Piecing Diagram

Diagram 1. Sew one E piece to long sides of D

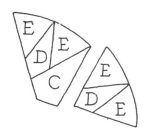

Diagram 2. Sew one D-E unit to long sides of C

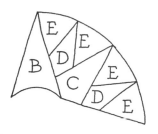

Diagram 3. Sew one C-D-E unit to right side of B

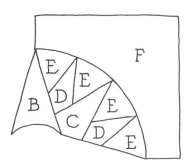

Diagram 4. Sew one F to B-C-D-E unit, matching notch on F to point of C

PIECING

The quilt maker recommends hand piecing the compass blocks and using ⅛-inch seam allowances. Press carefully to avoid stretching bias edges.

Compass Block

1. Sew one E to one long side of each D (**Diagram 1**). Press seams open. Sew one E to the other long side of each D. Press seams open.

2. Sew one D-E unit to one long side of each C (**Diagram 2**). Press seams open. Sew one D-E unit to the other long side of each C. Press seams open.

3. Sew one C-D-E unit to the right side of each B (**Diagram 3**). Press seams open.

4. Sew one F to outside curve of B-C-D-E unit, matching notch on F to point of C (**Diagram 4**). Repeat, sewing F pieces to the remaining three B-C-D-E units.

5. Assemble compass ring by sewing together the units made in step 4 (**Diagram 5**).

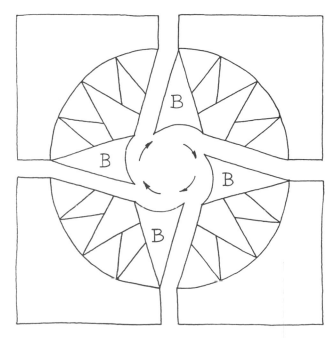

Diagram 5. Sew one B-C-D-E-F unit to right side of another, forming compass ring

6. To apply the compass center, use pattern A and cut a piece of heavy paper the size of the circle without the seam allowances. Run a gathering stitch around outer edge, in the seam allowance, of the fabric piece A. Center heavy paper circle on the fabric circle and pull up gathering stitch, fitting fabric snugly over paper circle and knot to hold stitching. Press the fabric circle and appliqué to center of compass block. Remove paper circle and gathering thread. Press entire block well.

7. Repeat steps 1 through 6, making a total of twelve Mariner's Compass blocks.

Flying Geese Border Insert

8. Sew one H to one short side of G (**Diagram 6**). Press seams open. Sew one H to the other short side of each G. Press seams open.

9. Sew together three G-H units in a row (**Flying Geese Border Insert Piecing Diagram**). Repeat for total of two Flying Geese border inserts. Press seams to one side.

10. Sew together a row of four Mariner's Compass blocks (**Diagram 7**). Press seams open. Repeat for a total of three rows of four blocks. Press seams open.

11. Matching seams at intersections, sew rows together. Press seams open.

Flying Geese Border Insert Piecing Diagram

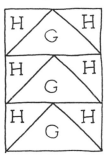

Diagram 6. Sew one H to both sides of G

Piecing Diagram

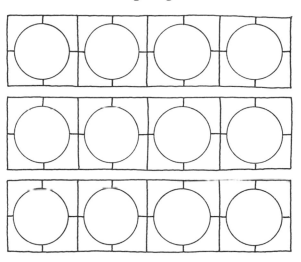

Diagram 7. Sew compass blocks together in rows as shown

Borders

Note: Border strips may be stitched by machine.

12. Beginning and ending ⅛ inch from corners, sew 1 x 15¼- inch inner borders to opposite sides of the quilt **(Diagram 8)**.

13. Beginning and ending ⅛ inch from corners, sew 1 x 19¾- inch inner borders to top and bottom of quilt **(Diagram 8)**.

14. Miter inner border corners by following directions on page xix. Press seams open.

15. Sew two 2 x 11¼-inch border strips to opposite sides of both Flying Geese inserts. Press seams open.

16. Beginning and ending ⅛ inch from corners, sew two 2 x 18¾-inch borders to opposite sides of quilt.

17. Beginning and ending ⅛ inch from corners, sew borders with Flying Geese inserts to top and bottom of quilt with "geese" pointing toward quilt center. Press seams open.

18. Miter outer border corners by following directions on page xix. Press seams open.

ASSEMBLY

19. Follow instructions for assembling quilt top, batting, and back, on page xx.

20. Quilt is bound with 1½-inch-wide straight-grain strips, but a bias binding can be used if desired. See instructions for binding on page xxiii.

QUILTING

21. The quilt shown was outline-quilted around compass centers and compass points, with a feathered wave quilting pattern in the borders.

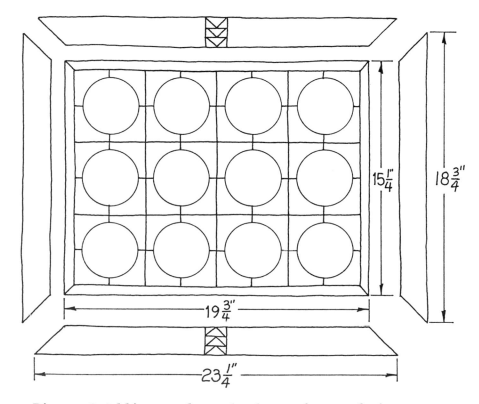

Diagram 8. Add inner and outer borders as shown and miter corners

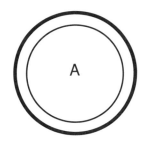

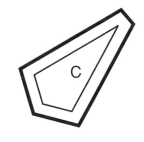

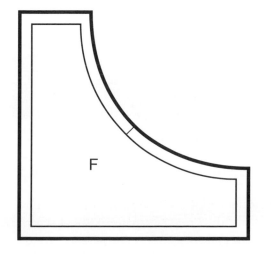

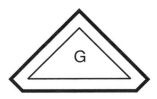

TOUCHING STARS

Lincoln Home Collection

An unusual star design covers this antique quilt from the Lincoln Home in Springfield, Illinois. Although similar to the Lone Star pattern, these stars have six points rather than the familiar eight.

SIZE

Pieced diamond is 10 ³⁄₈ x 10 ³⁄₈ inches
(18 inches point to point)
Finished quilt is 95 x 98 ³⁄₈ inches

MATERIALS

- 1 yard red fabric
- 2 yards green fabric
- 4 yards yellow fabric
- 4 yards white fabric, plus 1 yard for 10¹⁄₂ yards
  of 2-inch wide bias binding (optional)
- 5¹⁄₂ yards fabric for quilt back
- 1 queen-size batt, pieced to fit

CUTTING

To make the best use of the fabrics, cut strips
2 ³⁄₄ inches wide across the width of the fabric
(44 to 45 inches).

Stars

Color	Number of Strips
Red	8
Green	24
Yellow	20
White	12

Pattern Piece	Number of Pieces
B*	32 white
Half B*	2 white

* Note: Pattern piece B is too large for us to
provide as a full-size pattern, but it is simple
to make your own. First, trace B as shown on
page 74. Then, fold a large piece of paper in
half lengthwise, fold again across the width, and
align folds with fold lines on tracing and cut
out. To make half B template, fold large sheet of
paper in half widthwise and place fold on short
fold line of pattern. Trace, adding ¹⁄₄-inch seam
allowance on the remaining fold line, and cut
out.

**Piecing Diagram for One Diamond
(six per star)**

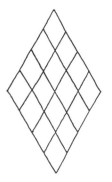

Borders

Two strips 2 ³⁄₄ x 93 ³⁄₄ inches, yellow
Two strips 2 ³⁄₄ x 95 inches, yellow

PIECING

The instructions below are for making the quilt
by the strip-piecing method. (See instructions
on page xvi). A diamond template (A) is
provided for those wishing to piece in the traditional manner. This quilt requires 57 pieced
diamonds to make all the stars and half stars.

1. Sew together four strips of the same color to
make one continuous strip approximately 176
inches long (a little more than the 4¹⁄₂ yards
necessary, but good for accommodating cutting
adjustments or errors). You will need two red,
six green, five yellow, and three white 4¹⁄₂-yard
strips. Press seams open.

2. Sew together four long strips in the color
combinations listed below, in the order
indicated, into a 9¹⁄₂-inch four-color band,
staggering each strip 3 inches as shown for
Band 1 in **Diagram 1**. Press seams open.

Band 1: Red, Yellow, White, Green
Band 2: Yellow, White, Green, Yellow
Band 3: White, Green, Yellow, Green
Band 4: Green, Yellow, Green, Red

BAND 1

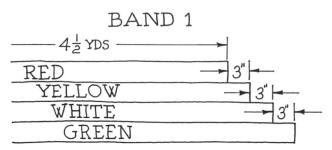

Diagram 1. Sew four strips together, staggering strips 3 inches as indicated

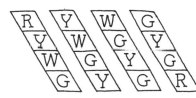

Diagram 2. Cut across strips at a 60-degree angle, 2 ¾ inches apart as shown

Diagram 3. Sew pieced strips together in the color order indicated

3. Mark cutting lines across strips, 2 ¾ inches apart and at a 60-degree angle, using the **Strip Cutting Guide**. Cut strips along marked lines (**Diagram 2**).

4. Matching seams at intersections, sew together four pieced strips (one each of the four color combinations) in order shown in **Diagram 3**, to make one pieced diamond. Press seams open. Repeat for a total of fifty-seven pieced diamonds.

5. Matching seams at intersections, sew together three pieced diamonds to create a half star (**Diagram 4**). Refer to color photograph as a guide to determine order of colors. Press seams open. Repeat for a total of eighteen half stars. Three pieced diamonds will be left over and used in step 11. Note the positioning of the diamonds when assembled into stars; in the star in the center of the quilt, the order of the colors is reversed.

6. Sew together two half stars, matching seams at intersections, to make a full star (**Diagram 4**). Press seams open. Repeat for a total of nine full stars.

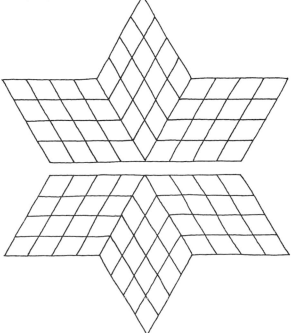

Diagram 4. Sew sets of diamonds together to create eighteen half stars. Sew half stars together, making nine full stars

7. Carefully draw a cutting line across the center of two full stars, from two opposite points and intersecting the center of the star as shown in **Diagram 5**. Cut the two stars in half along cutting line.

8. Sew one B (large white diamond) between two points of one full star (**Diagram 6**). To turn corners by machine when sewing B pieces between star points, leave needle down at point where corner is to be turned. Lift the presser foot and clip the seam allowance to the needle. With needle still down, align the next two sides, lower the presser foot, and continue sewing. Press seam away from pieced diamonds. Repeat for a total of six full stars.

Note: Because the seam allowance on the stars will be under B pieces after pressing, it may sometimes be necessary to trim so the darker colors do not show through.

9. Sew B pieces between points of half star (**Diagram 6**), turning in the same way. Press seams toward B pieces. Repeat for a total of two half stars.

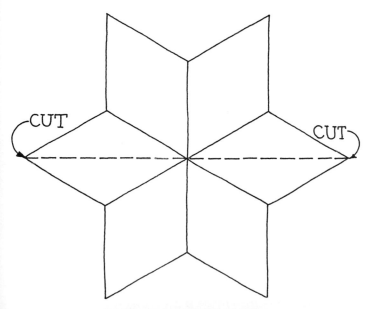

Diagram 5. Cut two stars in half, point to point as shown

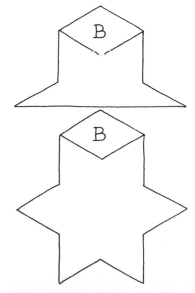

Diagram 6. Turning corners, sew one B piece between two points of full stars and half stars

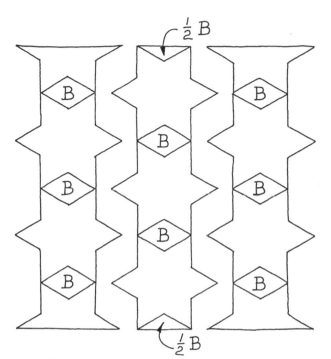

Diagram 7. Sew stars together in rows. Sew half stars to top and bottom of first and last rows. Sew half-diamond B pieces to top and bottom of center row

10. Sew the full and half stars together into rows, with B pieces between stars (**Diagram 7**). Sew the two half B pieces to top and bottom of center row. Press toward B pieces.

11. Sew additional B pieces, indicated by shaded areas, to sides of rows (**Diagram 8**). Press toward B pieces.

12. Cut three remaining pieced diamonds in half across width. Sew each one to a B piece as shown along the sides of the quilt (**Diagram 8**). Press seams toward B pieces. Sew these units into sides of quilt. Press seams open.

13. Sew rows together as shown in **Diagram 8**. Press seams toward B pieces.

Borders

14. Sew the 93¾-inch yellow borders to the right and left sides of the quilt (**Diagram 9**). Press seams toward borders.

15. Sew the 95-inch yellow borders to the top and bottom of the quilt (**Diagram 9**). Press seams toward borders.

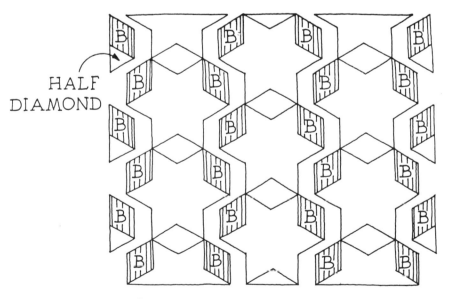

Diagram 8. Add more B pieces as indicated by shaded areas. Sew half pieced diamonds to B pieces as shown on sides of quilt

ASSEMBLY

16. Cut the 5½-yard length of fabric for the back in half across the width. Trim selvages. Sew the two pieces together along one side. Press seam open.

17. Proceed following instructions for assembling the quilt top, batting, and back, on page xx.

18. The quilt is bound with white bias binding. An alternate binding would be to fold backing fabric to front, turn under raw edge, and slip stitch in place.

QUILTING

19. Quilt as desired. The quilt shown was quilted with lines radiating from the center of each star, while the large white diamonds were quilted with a square grid pattern.

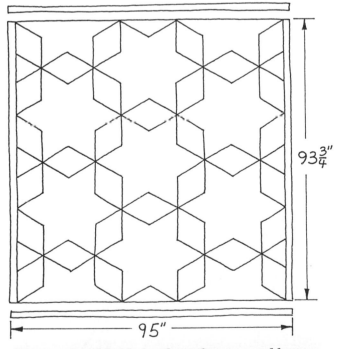

93¾"

95"

Diagram 9. Add side borders, then top and bottom borders.

Touching Stars

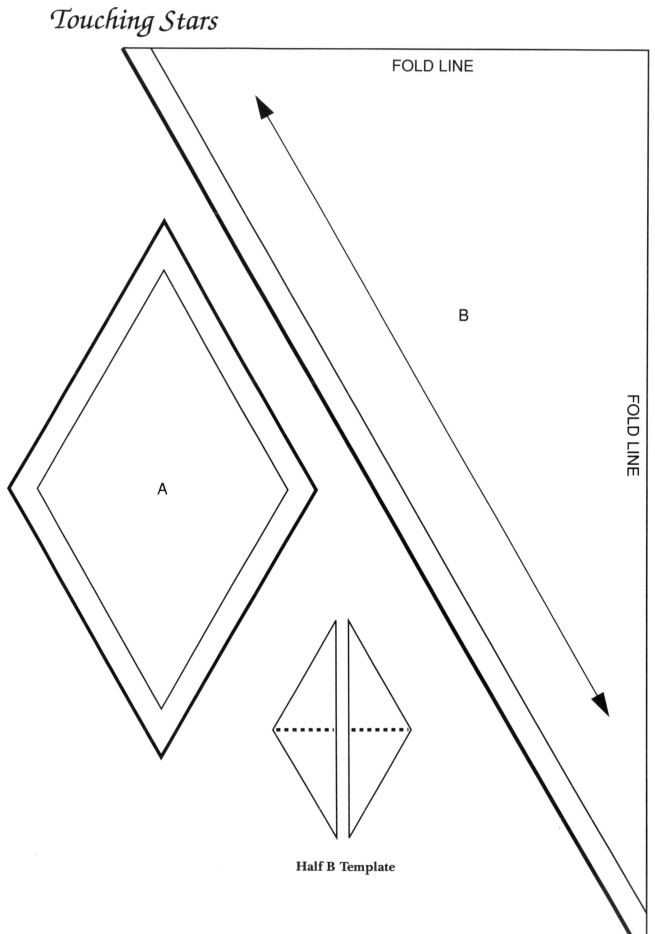

FOLD LINE

FOLD LINE

B

A

Half B Template

74

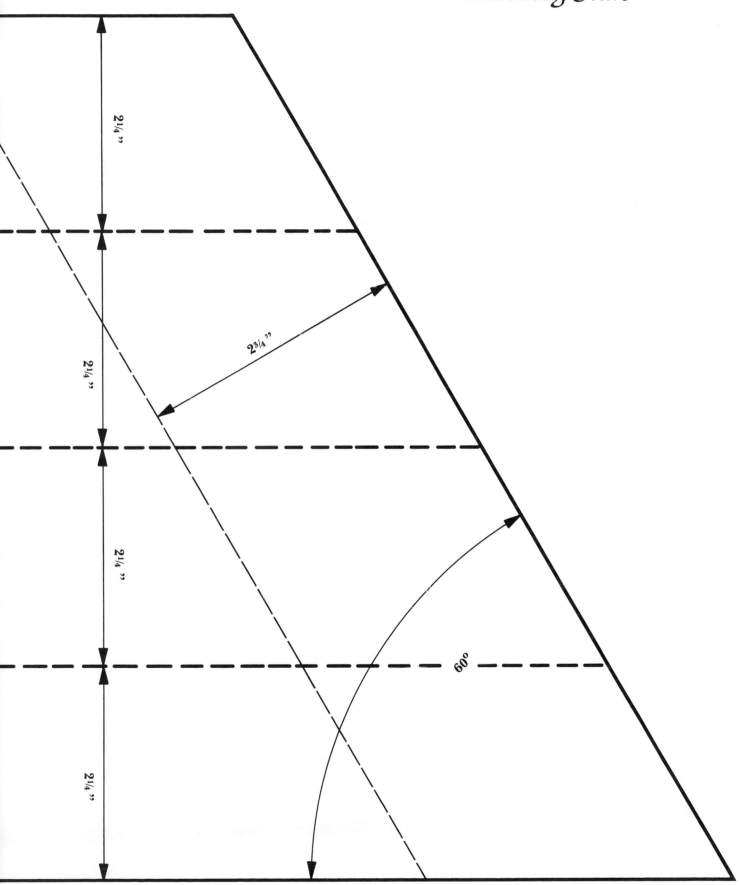

2¼"

2¼"

2¼"

2¼"

2³/₄"

60°

Strip Cutting Guide

LIGHT AND DARK
SQUARES QUILT

By Diane Rode Schneck

A kaleidoscope of colorful patches enclosed in a dramatic fabric frame
evokes images of a modern painting.

SIZE

The finished quilt is 62 x 72 inches

MATERIALS

This quilt is made of many scraps of print fabrics, so exact yardage requirements have been omitted. You will need a good selection of print scraps in light and dark shades totaling 4 to 5 yards.

- Assorted scraps for patchwork
- 2 ¼ yards red print for borders
- 4 yards fabric for back
- Twin-size batt

CUTTING

Pattern Piece	Number of Pieces
A	480 dark prints 480 light prints

Borders

Two strips red print 6½ x 62½ inches
Two strips red print 6½ x 72½ inches

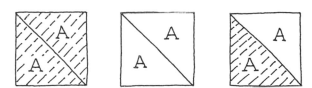

Diagram 1. Sew A's together to make squares

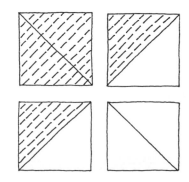

Diagram 2. Sew together four squares into one block

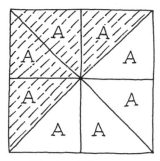

Piecing Diagram

PIECING

1. Sew together two A's to make each square in the following combinations: 120 squares with two dark triangles, 120 squares with two light triangles, and 240 squares with one light and one dark triangle **(Diagram 1)**. Press seams open.

2. Sew together four squares, arranged as shown **(Diagram 2)**, into one block. Repeat for a total of 120 four-square blocks. Press seams open.

3. Matching seams at intersections, sew blocks together into four-block units with light squares in the center, dark squares and triangles outside **(Diagram 3)**. Repeat for a total of 30 four-block units. Press seams open.

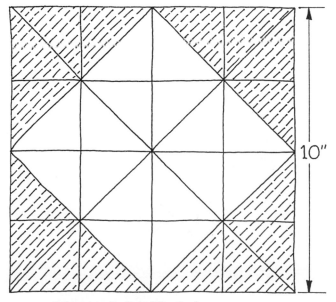

Diagram 3. Sew blocks into four-block units

ASSEMBLY

4. Matching seams at intersections, sew together five four-block units in a row (**Diagram 4**). Repeat for a total of six rows. Press seams open.

5. Matching seams at intersections, sew together rows to complete quilt top. Press seams open.

6. Sew 6½ x 72½-inch borders to sides of quilt top. Then sew 6½ x 62½-inch borders to top and bottom of quilt top (**Diagram 5**). Miter corners following instructions on page xix. Press seams open.

7. Proceed following instructions for assembling quilt, binding quilt with bias strips of contrasting fabric (see page xx).

QUILTING

8. Light and Dark Squares was quilted with simple outline quilting on the patchwork blocks. The borders were quilted in a scroll design made with a purchased stencil.

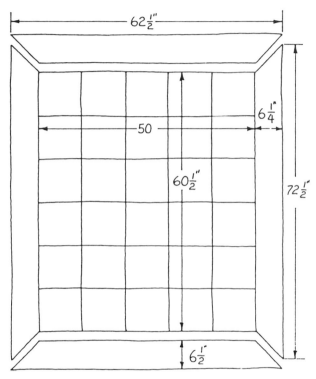

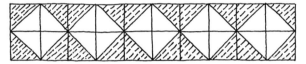

Diagram 4. Sew five four-block units together into a row

Diagram 5. Sew 6½ x 72½-inch borders to sides of quilt top and 6½ x 62½-inch borders to top and bottom

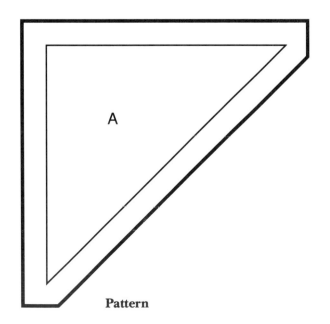

A

Pattern

STAR QUILT

By Loret Race

This design was inspired by a motif on a scarf the designer received as a gift. Because of the number of pieces, this quilt may appear daunting at first. But if you use a rotary cutter, preparing all the squares will be much less time-consuming. Assembling the quilt is as easy as sewing rows of these squares together. Just make sure you maintain a constant ¼-inch seam allowance and the pieces should fit.

SIZE

Each square is 1 x 1 inch

Star pattern is 57 x 57 inches

MATERIALS

Yardage given will complete only star portion of quilt.

- 2 yards dark fabric
- 2 yards medium fabric (print used in original quilt)
- 5 yards light fabric
- Any additional yardage for pieced or plain borders
- Fabric for quilt back and binding
- Batting

CUTTING

Cut 3,249 1½-inch squares using pattern

Colors	Number of Squares
light	1,629
medium	908
dark	712

Piecing Diagram: Bird Motif

Row Piecing Chart

Row	Light	Medium	Dark
1	0	57	0
2	55	2	0
3	7	18	32
4	34	8	15
5	15	27	15
6	31	12	14
7	28	17	12
8	32	15	10
9	30	16	11
10	35	11	11
11	31	13	13
12	33	1	13
13	32	12	13
14	38	10	9
15	28	14	15
16	31	14	12
17	34	11	12
18	39	10	8
19	39	10	8
20	25	17	15
21	15	20	22
22	25	17	15
23	33	12	12
24	23	18	16
25	25	17	15
26	31	16	10
27	25	19	13
28	18	25	14
29	45	10	2

Row Piecing Chart

PIECING & ASSEMBLY

The following directions refer to the center portion of the quilt. Add pieced or plain borders of your choice to achieve the desired size. Be sure to figure additional yardage accordingly.

Piecing directions are for the "square by square" manner in which the quilt was made. An alternate, time-saving method would be to strip-piece the quilt (see page xvi), substituting strips of fabric for long rows of squares of the same color. Quilting horizontal and vertical lines 1 inch apart would then give the illusion that the strips are made of individual squares.

It is helpful to make a copy of the **Row Piecing Chart** so that you can number and cross off each row as it is completed. It would also be helpful to attach pieces of paper or masking tape with a corresponding number to completed rows in order to avoid confusion when sewing rows together.

1. Referring to both the **Row Piecing Chart** and the **Piecing Diagram: Bird Motif**, sew squares together into rows. Make two each of rows 1 through 28; the top half of the star is exactly the same as the bottom half. Row 29 is the center row. Press all seams open.

2. To make left half of center portion, sew rows 1 through 29 together, matching all seams at intersections. Press seams open after each row is attached. Note: Sewing the rows together may be easier if they are done two at a time, then sewing those rows together two at a time instead of adding each row as you go.

3. To make right half of center portion, sew together rows 28 through 1, matching seams at intersections. Press seams open.

4. Sew row 28 of right half to center row 29, matching seams at intersections. Press seam open.

5. Add any borders at this time to achieve desired finished size. The quilter repeated the bird motif that she used between the north, south, east, and west points of the star in her top and bottom borders (see **Piecing Diagram: Bird Motif**).

6. Piece backing fabric and proceed following instructions for assembling the quilt top, batting, and back on page xx.

QUILTING

7. Part of the beauty of this quilt is the mosaic appearance created by the small squares and many seam lines. Quilt simply by following the seam lines of individual squares or, if strip-pieced, to create the look of individual squares.

Pattern

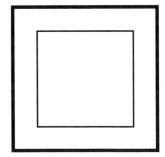

DIALOGUE

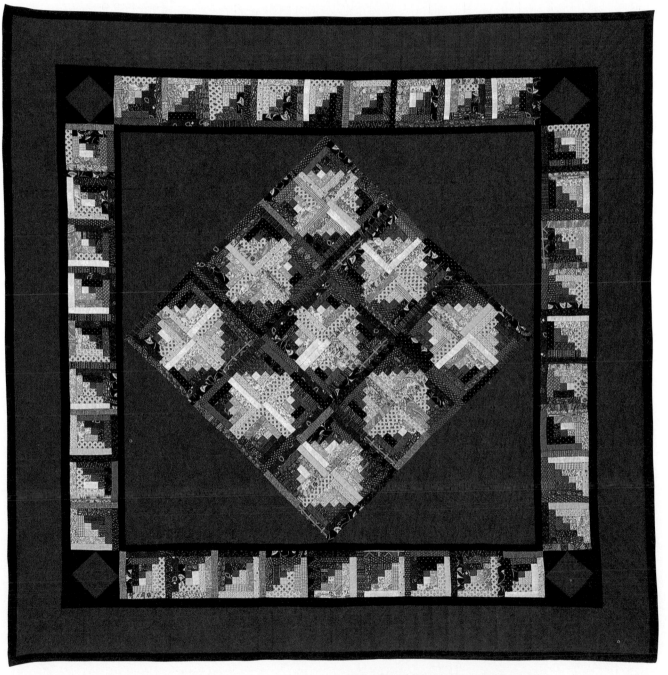

By Dee Danley-Brown

An Amish Diamond quilt was the inspiration for this unusual Log Cabin design. The quilting pattern was adapted from a book of traditional Japanese crests used in decorative design.

SIZE

Finished quilt is 70 inches square
Finished Log Cabin blocks are 5¼ inches square
Quilt requires 72 Log Cabin blocks

MATERIALS

- Assorted dark fabric scraps totaling 1¾ yards
- Assorted light fabric scraps totaling 1½ yards
- ¼ yard fabric for block centers *
- 3 yards red fabric
- 2¼ yards black fabric
- 4 yards fabric for quilt back
- Twin-size batt

* One strong color for the center square
of each block will create a striking effect.

CUTTING

As a shortcut when using purchased yardage, cut light and dark fabrics for Log Cabin blocks into 1¼-inch-wide strips across the width, then use patterns A through G to cut the strips into appropriate lengths.

To make full-size pattern for J, draw a 22¾-inch square on graph paper. Cut the square in half diagonally and use one of the resulting triangles as the pattern.

Pattern Piece	Number of Pieces
A	72 of one color for center squares 72 assorted light
B – F	72 assorted light 72 assorted dark
G	72 assorted dark
H	4 red
I	16 black
J	4 red

Borders

Four strips red 5½ x 70¼-inch for outer borders
Four strips black 1⅞ x 47¾-inch for inner black border
Four strips black 1½ x 60¼-inch for outer black border
Four strips black 2½ x 78-inch for binding (extra length allowed) or 8 yards of 2½-inch bias binding (see page xxiii).

PIECING

Note: Seams can be pressed open or to one side for the Log Cabin blocks (center square) as preferred, so the direction will not be specified below.

PIECING DIAGRAMS

Log Cabin Block

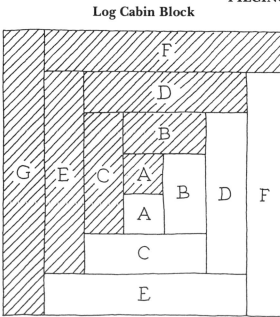

Corner Block

1. Sew together one center A and one light A (**Diagram 1**). Press seam.

2. Sew one light B to right side of the A unit (**Diagram 2**). Press seam. Sew one dark B to top of A-B unit and press seam.

3. Sew one dark C to the left side of the center unit (**Diagram 3**). Press seam. Sew one light C to the bottom of the center unit and press seam.

4. Sew one light D to the right side of the center unit (**Diagram 4**). Press seam. Sew one dark D to the top of the center unit and press seam.

5. Sew one dark E to the left side of the center unit (**Diagram 5**). Press seam. Sew one light E to the bottom of the center unit and press seam.

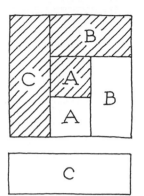

Diagram 3. Sew one dark C to the left side of the center unit. Sew one light C to the bottom

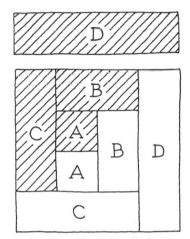

Diagram 4. Sew one light D to the right side of the center unit. Sew one dark D to the top

Diagram 1. Sew together two A's

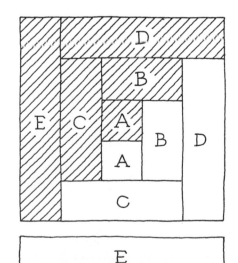

Diagram 5. Sew one dark E to the left side of the center unit. Sew one light E to the bottom

Diagram 2. Sew one light B to the right side of the A unit. Sew one dark B to top of A-B unit

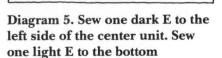

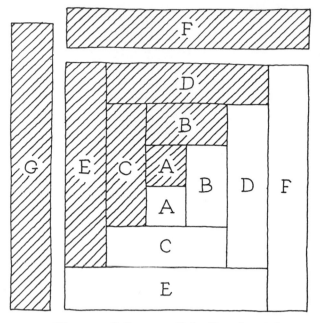

Diagram 6. Sew one light F to the right side of the center unit. Sew one dark F to the top. Sew one G to the left side.

6. Sew one light F to right side of center unit (**Diagram 6**). Press seam. Sew one dark F to the top of center unit and press seam.

7. Sew one G to the left side of the center unit (**Diagram 6**). Press seam.

8. Repeat steps 1 through 7, for a total of 72 Log Cabin blocks.

9. Sew I to opposite sides of H (**Diagram 7**). Press seams open. Sew I to remaining sides of H to make a square, and press seams open. Repeat for a total of four corner blocks.

ASSEMBLY

10. Sew together six Log Cabin blocks in a row, with lights and darks arranged as shown in **Diagram 8**. Press seams open. Repeat for a total of six rows.

11. Matching seams at intersections, sew together the six rows to make the central square of Log Cabin blocks. Press seams open.

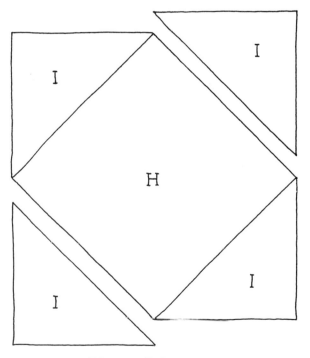

Diagram 7. Sew one I to opposite sides of each H

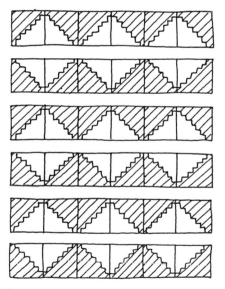

Diagram 8. Sew six blocks together in a row. Make six rows

12. Sew one J to each side of the center unit (**Diagram 9**). Press seams open. Adding the J pieces to the Log Cabin square will change its orientation in the quilt top. It will look like a diamond instead of a square, and the appearance of the Log Cabin blocks will be dramatically altered.

13. To make Log Cabin borders, sew together nine blocks in a row with lights and darks arranged in a sawtooth pattern as shown in **Diagram 10**. Press seams open. Repeat for a total of four borders.

14. Sew one 1 ⁷/₈ x 47 ³/₄-inch black border to each side of the quilt top (**Diagram 11**) and miter corners following instructions on page xix. Press seams open.

15. Sew a Log Cabin border to two opposite sides of the quilt top (**Diagram 11**). Press seams open.

16. Sew a corner block to each end of the remaining two Log Cabin borders (**Diagram 11**). Press seams open. Sew these borders to the top and bottom of the quilt top.

17. Sew one 1¹/₂ x 60 ¹/₄-inch outer black border to each side of the quilt top and miter corners (**Diagram 11**). Press seams open.

18. Sew one 5¹/₂ x 70¹/₄-inch red border to each side of the quilt top and miter corners (**Diagram 11**). Press seams open.

19. Proceed following instructions for assembling the quilt on page xx. Bind the quilt with the 2¹/₂-inch-wide strips of black fabric.

QUILTING

20. Quilt as desired.

Assembly Diagram

Diagram 11. Sew the 1 ⁷/₈ x 47 ³/₄-inch black borders to each side of the quilt top. Then add the log cabin borders. Follow with the 60 ¹/₄-inch black borders add the 70¹/₄-inch red borders

Diagram 9. Sew one J to each side of the center unit

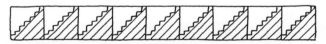

Diagram 10. Sew together nine blocks in a row

Dialogue

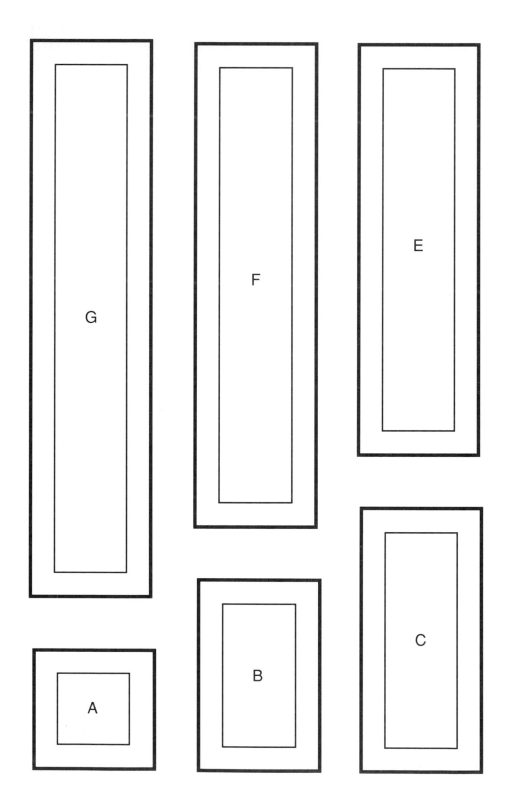

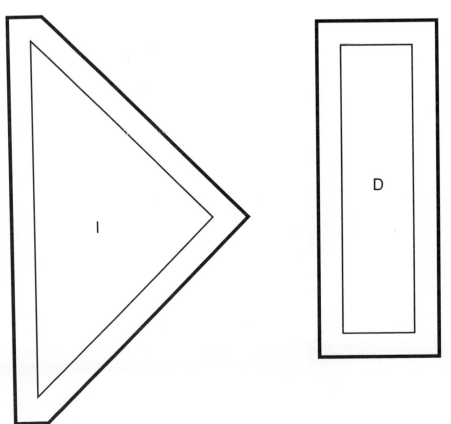

YOUNG MAN'S FANCY

By Sarah Barnett

This heirloom quilt was the second-prize winner in the 1940 Kansas State Fair. It is too small for today's beds, so we offer a revised version that is suitable for a double bed.

SIZE

Block is 15 inches square
Finished quilt is 83¼ x 91¾ inches

MATERIALS

- 3 yards red fabric
- 5 ⅝ yards white fabric
- 5½ yards fabric for quilt back
- Queen-size batt
- Templates for:
  F: 15½ inches square
  G: Right triangle made from 15½-inch
    square cut in half diagonally
  H: Right triangle made from 11⅛-inch
    square cut in half diagonally
  (All include seam allowance)

CUTTING

Blocks and Pieced Border

Pattern Piece	Number of Pieces
A	61 red
B	108 red 164 white
C	36 red 72 white
D	250 red 200 white
E	8 white
F	4 white
G	8 white
H	4 white

Piecing Diagram: 15-inch block

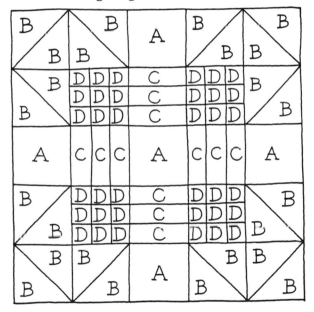

Borders

Two strips 2 x 77 inches, red
Two strips 2 x 68 inches, red
10½ yards of 1½-inch-wide red bias binding
Two strips 8½ x 92¼ inches, white
Two strips 8½ x 83¾ inches, white

Diagram 1. Sew together two B triangles

Diagram 2. Sew together 3 C's—a red between two whites

Diagram 3. Sew D pieces together in rows as shown

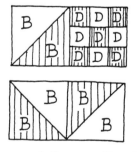

Diagram 4. Sew one B unit to one D unit. Sew together two B units. Sew together B-D unit and B-B unit to form square

PIECING

One Block

1. Sew one red B to one white B along the diagonal to form a square (**Diagram 1**). Repeat for a total of twelve squares. Press seams open.

2. Sew together two white C's and one red C as shown in **Diagram 2**. Repeat for a total of four C units. Press seams open.

3. Sew nine D's into three rows of three squares each, alternating red and white in rows as shown in **Diagram 3**. Matching seams at intersections, sew rows together to make a square. Repeat for a total of four D units. Press seams open.

4. Sew together one B unit and one D unit as shown in first row of **Diagram 4**. Sew together two B units as shown in second row of **Diagram 4**. Press seams open.

5. Matching seam intersections, sew together B-D unit and B-B unit to form a square (**Diagram 4**). Press seams open. Repeat steps 4 and 5 for a total of four squares.

Diagram 5. Sew one C unit to one A, making one C-A unit

Order of Assembly: Block

Diagram 6. Sew completed units together in rows as shown

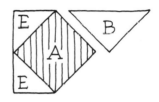

Diagram 7. Sew two E's and one B to A, making B-A-E unit

6. Sew one C unit to one red A as shown in **Diagram 5**. Press seams open. Repeat for a total of four C-A units.

7. Matching seams at intersections, sew together completed units in three rows following Order of Assembly as indicated in **Diagram 6**. Press seams open.

8. Sew the three rows together, matching seam intersections. Press seams open.

9. Repeat steps 1 through 8 for a total of nine blocks.

Pieced Border

10. To make end corners of border, sew diagonal sides of two E's to adjacent sides of A, pressing seams open after each step. Sew short side of one B to top right side of A (**Diagram 7**). Press seam open. Repeat for a total of four corner units.

11. Following instructions in step 3, make fourteen D units.

12. Sew short side of two B's to opposite sides of each D unit, and short side of two B's to opposite sides of twelve A's (**Diagram 8**). Press seams open.

13. Sew seven B-D-B and six B-A-B units together in a row, alternating units as shown in **Diagram 9**. Sew corner units to each end of border. Press seams open. Repeat for a total of two pieced borders.

ASSEMBLY

14. Sew together pieced blocks (**Diagram 6**) and F, G, and H pieces into rows, following **Piecing Diagram: Quilt Top**. Press seams open. Sew rows together, matching seams at intersections. Press seams open.

15. Sew one pieced border to top and bottom of quilt. Press seams open.

16. Center and sew one red 68-inch border to one white 83¾-inch border (**Order of Assembly: Quilt**). Repeat for another short border. Press seams open.

17. Leaving ¼-inch seam allowance free at beginning of each end, sew short borders to top and bottom of quilt, red strips next to pieced borders (**Order of Assembly: Quilt**).

18. Center and sew one red 77-inch border to one white 92¼-inch border. Repeat for another long border (**Order of Assembly: Quilt**).

19. Leaving ¼-inch seam allowances free at beginning of each end, sew long borders to sides of quilt, red strips next to G's and H's (**Order of Assembly: Quilt**).

20. Miter corners following directions on page xix.

21. Cut the 5½-yard length of fabric for the back in half across the width. Trim selvages. Sew the two pieces together along one side and press seam open.

22. Follow directions for assembling quilt top, batting and back on page xx.

23. Bind the quilt with the 10½ yards of bias binding.

QUILTING

24. Quilt as desired. The quilt maker stitched four touching hearts in each of the large plain blocks and overlapping hearts along the borders. Simple outline quilting on the pieced blocks completed the quilt.

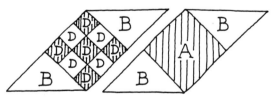

Diagram 8. Sew two B's to opposite sides of D unit, making B-D-B unit. Sew two B's to opposite sides of A, making B-A-B unit

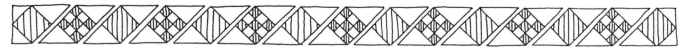

Diagram 9. Sew together a row of seven B-D-B units alternating with six B-A-B units. Sew corner units to each end of strip

Piecing Diagram: Quilt Top

Order of Assembly: Quilt

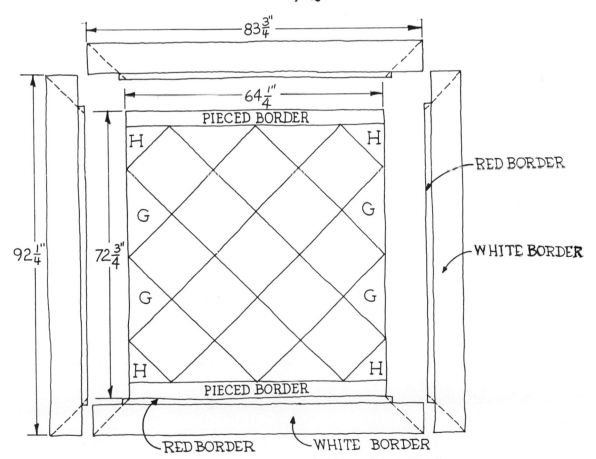

Young Man's Fancy

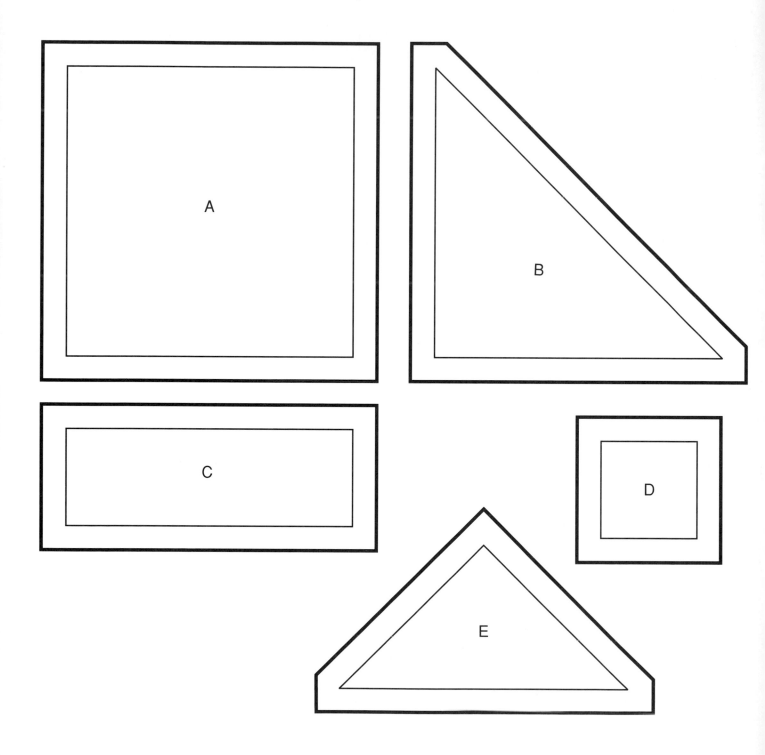

CELEBRATING
THE HOLIDAYS

VALENTINE QUILT

By Diane Rode Schneck

This delightful miniature quilt makes a wonderful Valentine's Day gift that
will become a cherished heirloom.

Appliqué Diagram

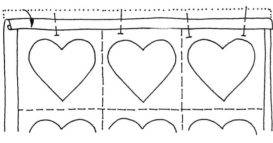

Diagram 1. Fold backing over to front to bind

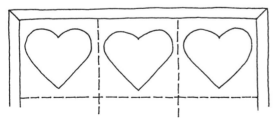

Diagram 2. Miter corners of binding

SIZE

Finished quilt is 12 x 16 inches

MATERIALS

- ³/₈ yard red fabric for background
- Twelve 5 x 5-inch scraps in assorted prints
- ³/₈ yard fabric for back
- Freezer paper
- 12 x 16-inch piece of batting

CUTTING

12½ x 16½-inch red rectangle for background

13½ x 17½-inch rectangle for backing

Twelve freezer-paper hearts using heart pattern without seam allowance

Twelve assorted print hearts

APPLIQUÉ

Freezer-paper appliqué is recommended for this quilt. See page xvii for instructions.

1. Mark a line ¼ inch in from all four edges of red background rectangle to indicate seam allowance. Divide the center area into twelve 4-inch squares (see **Appliqué Diagram**).

2. Appliqué one heart in the center of each 4-inch square.

ASSEMBLY

3. Assemble the quilt top, batting, and back according to instructions on page xx.

4. Quilt along dotted lines shown in **Appliqué Diagram**. You can also quilt around each heart.

5. To finish the edges of the quilt, fold the edges of the back over to the front, turn the edges under and pin in place (**Diagram 1**). Miter corners of binding (**Diagram 2**). Blindstitch binding to quilt top.

Heart Appliqué Pattern

SHAMROCK PILLOW

By Diane Rode Schneck

Easily strip-pieced with scraps of green, this engaging pillow will bring the luck of the Irish into your home.

SIZE

Finished pillow is 12 inches square

MATERIALS

- ⅜ yard muslin or white fabric
- Scraps of several shades of green prints
- 12-inch pillow form or stuffing

CUTTING

Cut green fabrics into different width strips
("strings")

Two 12½-inch squares muslin or white fabric
for pillow front and back

PIECING & APPLIQUÉ

1. The shamrock is made of "strings" of leftover scraps of green fabric. Sew together enough strings to make a piece of fabric about 12 inches square (**Diagram 1**). Press seams open.

2. Enlarge shamrock appliqué pattern to fit into a 10½-inch square. For instructions on enlarging pattern, see page xiv. Trace shamrock pattern onto right side of string patchwork (**Diagram 2**).

3. Machine stitch along tracing line and cut out ¼ inch beyond stitching line for seam allowance.

4. Center, pin, and appliqué shamrock to pillow front by turning under seam allowance just inside stitching line (**Diagram 3**). Press appliqué.

ASSEMBLY

5. Complete pillow following instructions for pillow assembly on page xxx.

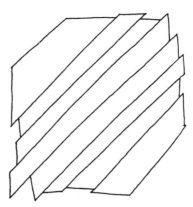

Diagram 1. Sew string scraps together to make 12-inch square

Diagram 2. Trace shamrock design onto right side of patchwork

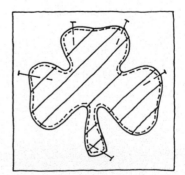

Diagram 3. Appliqué shamrock to pillow top

Shamrock Pillow

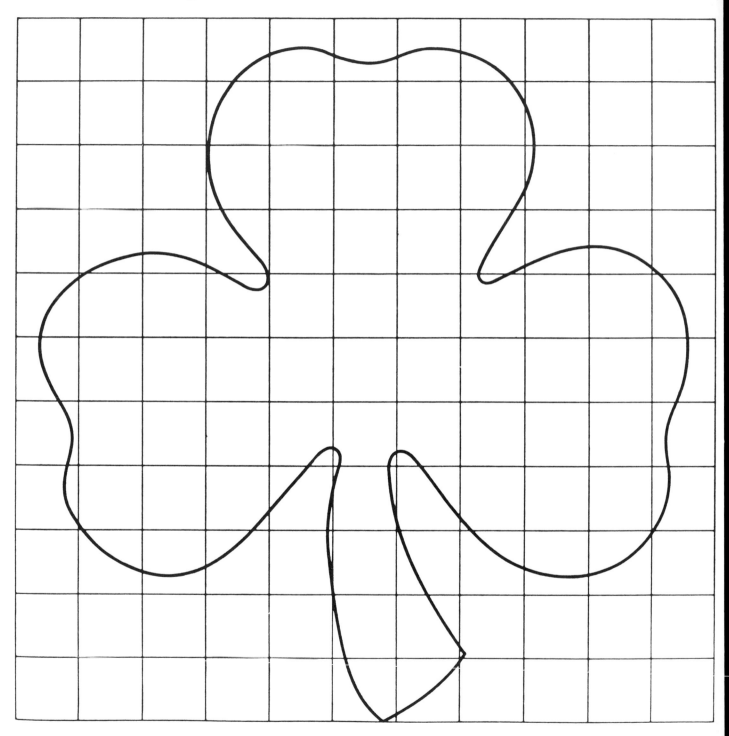

Appliqué Pattern: 1 square = 1 inch

EASTER BUNNY WALL HANGING

By Diane Rode Schneck

Appropriate as a holiday decoration or as a wall hanging in a child's room,
this appliquéd bunny and her eggs will make everyone smile.

SIZE
Finished wall hanging is 16 x 19 inches

MATERIALS
- ½ yard green and white print for background
- ⅛ yard green pindot for borders
- 5 x 16-inch scrap of green print for grass
- Scrap tan print for bunny
- Scrap white for tail
- Freezer paper
- Assorted scraps of bright solids for eggs
- Embroidery floss in brown, white, and black
- Small amount polyester filling for tail
- 2 yards bias binding
- 17 x 20-inch piece of batting or craft-size batt

CUTTING

Pattern Piece	Number of Pieces
Background 12 x 15 inches	1 white and green print
Grass 4¾ x 15 inches	1 green print
Bunny	1 tan print
Eggs	5 assorted bright solids
Tail	1 white

Borders

Two strips 2½ x 12 inches green solid
Two strips 2½ x 19 inches green solid

APPLIQUÉ

Freezer-paper appliqué is suggested for this quilt (see page xvii for instructions). Enlarge **Appliqué Pattern** following instructions on page xiv.

1. Trace entire appliqué design onto background fabric. Also trace each pattern piece onto dull side of freezer paper. Cut out each piece and iron, shiny side down, onto wrong side of fabric. Cut out each piece, adding ¼-inch seam allowance.

2. Machine appliqué grass to background fabric. Next, appliqué bunny, tucking tail under bunny. Appliqué tail, inserting small amounts of filling inside as you work. Lastly, appliqué eggs.

3. Using chain stitch, embroider details on the bunny: the eye, ear line, and leg line.

ASSEMBLY

4. Sew 12-inch borders to sides of center panel. Press seams open.

5. Sew 19-inch borders to top and bottom of center panel. Press seams open.

6. Proceed following instructions for assembling the quilt on page xx. Bind the quilt with bias binding and add loops for hanging, if desired.

QUILTING

7. Quilt as desired. Original was quilted simply by outlining the basic shapes.

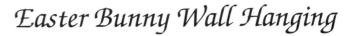

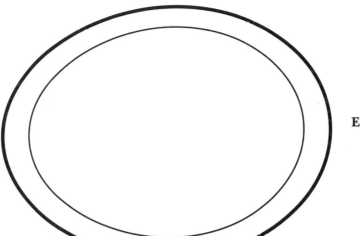

Egg Appliqué Pattern

Appliqué Pattern: 1 square = 1 inch

AMERICAN EAGLE

By Eugenia Mitchell

The quilter drew inspiration from a quilt, now in the Smithsonian Institution collection, made in 1854 by a woman traveling west with her husband in search of gold. Eighty-six-year-old Eugenia Mitchell added the date and designs of her own to create American Eagle.

SIZE
Finished quilt is 81 x 95 inches

MATERIALS

- 5½ yards muslin for quilt top
- 1 yard muslin for bias binding
- 1¼ yards blue for scallops
- 1¼ yards red for stars
- ⅔ yard brown for eagle
- 1 yard medium green for leaves
- ½ yard dark green for stems
- Scrap of gold for beak
- Scraps of red for numbers
- Scraps of brown for small branch and arrows
- Scraps of green for leaves of small branch
- 5½ yards fabric for back
- Full-size batt
- Embroidery floss (colors optional)
- Freezer paper

CUTTING

Enlarge eagle design to measure 20 x 30 inches following instructions for enlarging patterns on page xiv. Enlarge scallops. Make full-size patterns for other appliqué pieces. Make 4 to 4½ yards of 1-inch wide continuous bias binding from dark green for stems (see page xxiii). Make 10 yards of 2-inch muslin bias binding for quilt edges.

Freezer-paper appliqué is recommended for the small pieces in this quilt. See page xvii for instructions.

Pattern Piece	Number of Pieces
Eagle	1 brown
Corner scallops	2 blue
Full scallops	16 blue
Half scallops	2 blue
Stars	29 red
Leaves	53 medium green
Stems	6 dark green
Beak	1 gold
Small branch and arrows	4 brown
Leaves	3 green
Numbers (optional)	Your choice

PIECING

1. To make the background for appliqué top, remove selvages from the 5½-yard piece of muslin. Cut the muslin in half, making two 2 ¾-yard pieces. From one of these pieces cut two strips 19 inches wide and 2 ¾ yards (99 inches) long. Sew one strip to each long side of the remaining piece. Press seams open. This piece, the quilt top, should now measure 81 x 99 inches.

2. Trim top and bottom of quilt to measure 81 x 95 inches.

Star Appliqué Pattern

Wreath Leaf Appliqué Pattern

APPLIQUÉ

3. To locate placement for eagle, measure 42 inches down from top of quilt, and 40 inches in from one side and mark for center top of eagle's head. Baste eagle, small branch and leaves, and arrows in place, then appliqué all pieces in place.

4. Using photograph of finished quilt as a guide, appliqué numbers, stems, wreath leaves, and stars around eagle.

5. To locate placement for top leaf design, measure 18 inches down from top of quilt and 40 inches in from one side, and mark. This mark is the center where the two stems will cross.

6. Appliqué top stems and leaves. Appliqué three stars above the stems and leaves.

7. Arrange half, full, and corner scallops around outer edge of quilt. Pin in place and appliqué.

8. Center a star above each scallop, with the exception of the top two, and appliqué.

9. Embroider message or history if desired.

ASSEMBLY

10. Proceed following instructions for assembling the quilt on page xx. The quilt is bound with 2-inch continuous bias binding.

QUILTING

11. Quilt as desired. The original was quilted with a clamshell design in the central portion of the quilt. The outer edges were quilted with straight lines, and radiating lines were quilted at the corners.

American Eagle

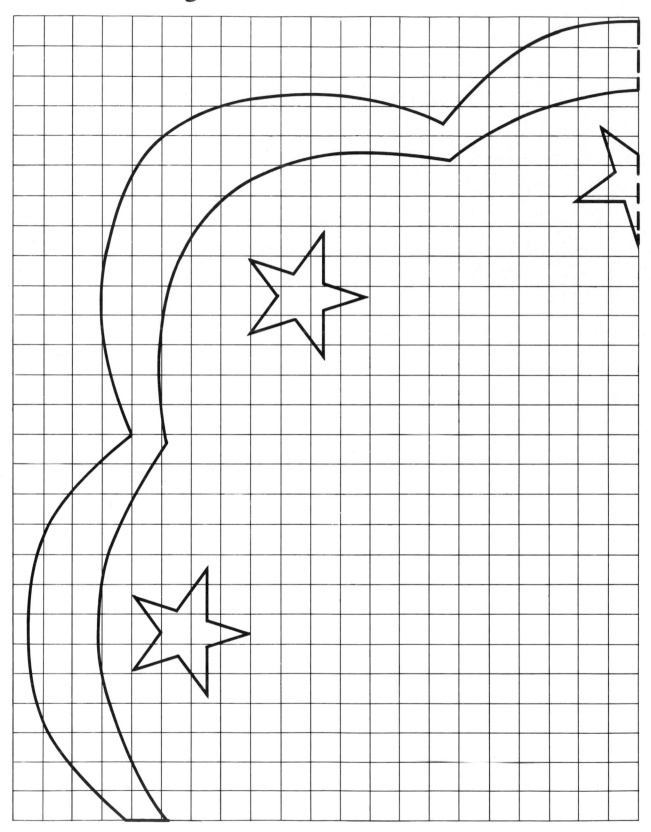

Scallop Appliqué Pattern: 1 square = 1 inch

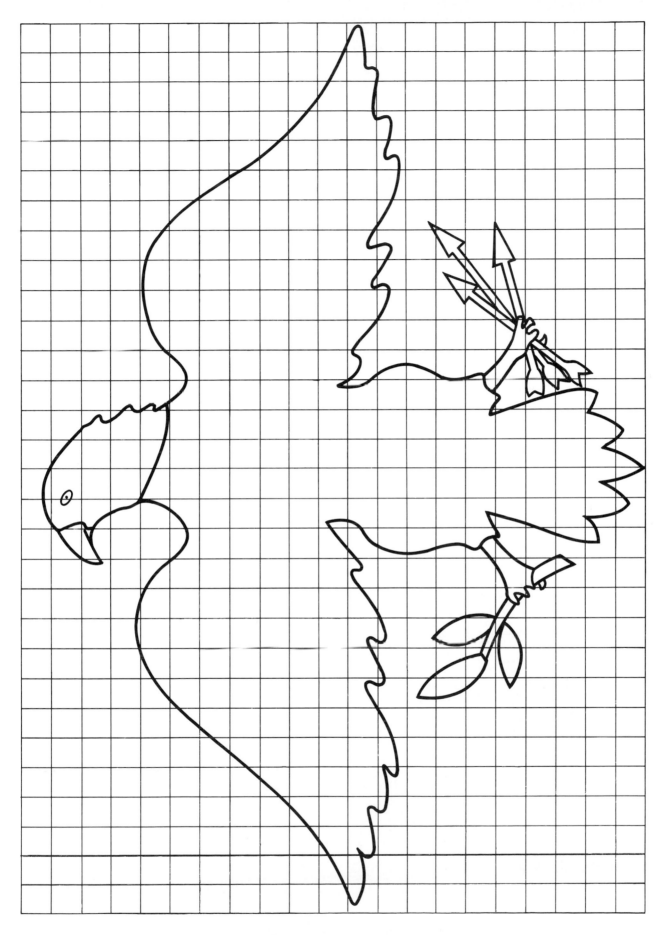

Center Appliqué Pattern: 1 square = 1 inch

TRICK OR TREAT
BAG

By Diane Rode Schneck

Little ghoulies and ghosties and long-legged beasties will enjoy stuffing their Halloween treats into this appliquéd jolly jack-o'-lantern bag.

SIZE

The finished bag measures 10 inches high,
9 inches wide, and 4 inches deep

MATERIALS

- ⅜ yard prequilted muslin
- 1 yard orange print for pumpkin appliqué,
  handle, and binding
- Scrap of green
- Black embroidery floss
- Fusible webbing
- Dressmaker's carbon

Appliqué and Assembly Diagram

CUTTING

Patterns are not provided for A, B, and C. Mark
the measurements directly on the fabric and
cut. Machine appliqué with fusible webbing (see
page xviii) is suggested for pumpkin and stem.
Iron fusible webbing to wrong side of orange
print and green print before cutting out
pumpkin and stem.

Pattern Piece	Number of Pieces
A 9½ x 10½ inches	**2 muslin** **(front and back)**
B 4½ x 9½ inches	**1 muslin (bottom)**
C 4½ x 10½ inches	**2 muslin (sides)**
Handle 2½ x 14 inches	**1 orange print**
Pumpkin	**1 orange print**
Stem	**1 green print**

Binding

One-yard strip of 3-inch-wide bias binding
from orange print (see page xxiii)

APPLIQUÉ & EMBROIDERY

1. Using dressmaker's carbon, transfer face
details to pumpkin fabric.

2. Fuse and machine appliqué pumpkin to bag
front (A), using a wide satin stitch (**Diagram 1**).
Fuse and appliqué pumpkin stem in the same
manner.

3. Embroider pumpkin details and letters with
black embroidery floss, using outline or stem
stitch.

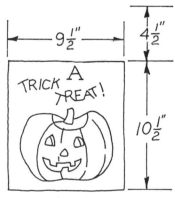

**Diagram 1. Fuse and
appliqué pumpkin and
stem to A**

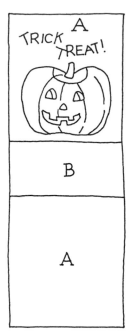

Diagram 2. Sew B between the two A's

4. With right sides together, sew B to bottom of appliquéd A, then sew remaining A to bottom of B **(Diagram 2)**. Machine zigzag stitch over raw edges of seams.

5. With right sides together, sew C to each side of the bag by stitching down one side, across bottom and up the other side **(Diagram 3)**. Zigzag over raw seam edges.

6. Finish raw edge of top of bag with 3-inch-wide bias binding.

7. To make handle, fold 2½ x 14-inch strip of orange print in half lengthwise, right sides together, and stitch long edge. Turn right side out and press. Fold each end under 1 inch and machine stitch handle to bag sides as shown in **Appliqué and Assembly Diagram.**

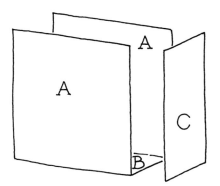

Diagram 3. Sew one C to each side of the bag

Appliqué Pattern

THANKSGIVING BANNER

By Diane Rode Schneck

A wall hanging featuring a harvest basket filled with appliquéd fruits and vegetables is a fitting way to welcome guests to the holiday table.

SIZE
Finished banner is 20 x 28 inches

MATERIALS
- ¹/₂ yard tan fabric for background and corners
- ¹/₂ yard plaid fabric for basket
- ¹/₂ yard dark brown fabric for borders
- Assorted fabric scraps for fruit, vegetables, and leaves (see cutting chart for suggested colors)
- ³/₄ yard fabric for quilt back
- Embroidery floss in shades of brown and purple
- Dressmaker's carbon
- Freezer paper

Appliqué and Assembly Diagram

CUTTING

Enlarge center panel design to measure 14 x 22 inches. Patterns are not provided for A, B, C, and D. Mark the measurements directly on the fabric and cut, or make templates for B, C, and D.

Pattern Piece	Number of Pieces
A 14¹/₂ x 22¹/₂ inches	1 tan
B 3¹/₂ x 14¹/₂ inches	2 dark brown
C 3¹/₂ x 22¹/₂ inches	2 dark brown
D 3¹/₂-inch square	4 tan
Quilt back 20¹/₂ x 28¹/₂ inches	1 backing fabric
Basket	1 plaid
Basket handle	1-inch-wide bias strip of plaid
Apple	7 red
Apple leaves	2 green
Pumpkin	1 rust
Pumpkin stem	1 brownish green
Corn	2 gold plaid
Bunch of Grapes	1 dusty purple
Squash (under grapes)	1 dark green print
Corn husks	2 light and 3 dark green
Autumn leaves	1 brown and 2 rust

APPLIQUÉ

Freezer paper appliqué technique is suggested for the appliqué portions of this banner (see page xvii).

1. Enlarge **Appliqué Pattern** onto paper with grid of 1-inch squares (see page xiv).

2. Tape enlargement to window or light box with right side down (to reverse design).

3. Place freezer paper, shiny side down, over each shape, and trace on dull side and cut out. Iron each shape, shiny side down, on wrong side of appropriate piece of fabric.

4. For placement of appliqué pieces, turn enlargement right side up and trace drawing on right side of A.

5. Appliqué fruits, vegetables, leaves, and basket to background A **(Diagram 1)**. Also refer to photograph for placement.

6. Using two strands of floss and outline or stem stitch, embroider details on fruits, vegetables, and leaves, using photograph as a guide.

Diagram 1. Appliqué fruits, vegetables, leaves, and basket to A

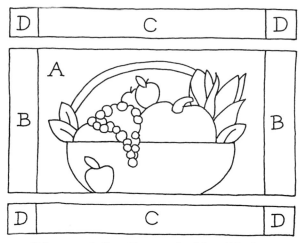

Diagram 2. Sew B to each side of A. Sew one D to each end of C

ASSEMBLY

7. Sew one B to each side of A (**Diagram 2**). Press seams open.

8. Appliqué one apple to each D.

9. Sew one D to each end of both pieces, as shown in **Diagram 2**. Press seams open.

10. Matching seams at intersections, sew C-D border units to top and bottom of center unit. Press seams open.

11. Using dressmaker's carbon, transfer lettering to lower border. Embroider lettering using outline or stem stitch and three strands of floss.

12. With right sides facing, sew finished top to back around all sides, leaving an opening for turning. Turn right side out, press, and slip stitch opening closed.

13. This piece can be used as a table runner or banner. If using as a banner, attach loops or a casing to the back to hang.

Appliqué Pattern: 1 square = 1 inch

MINI PATCHWORK ORNAMENTS

By Margit Echols

Traditional quilt patterns can be reduced to make miniature patchwork pillows for Christmas ornaments. They can also be sewn together into mini quilts.

SIZE

Each finished ornament is 4 x 4 inches

MATERIALS (for each pillow)

- Scraps of fabric for patchwork
- 1/2 yard of 1/2 -inch gathered lace edging
- 1/4-inch-wide ribbon for hanging loops
- Polyester filling
- One 4 1/2-inch square of fabric for back

AMISH SQUARE

CUTTING

Pattern Piece	Number of Pieces
A	1
B	4
C	4
D	4
E	4
F	4

Amish Square Piecing Diagram

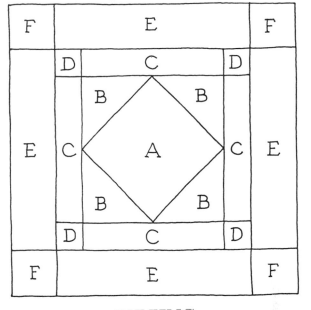

PIECING

1. Sew one B to opposite sides of A **(Diagram 1)**. Press seams open. Sew one B to the other two sides of A, forming center unit. Press seams open.

2. Sew one C to opposite sides of center unit **(Diagram 2)**. Press seams open.

3. Sew one D to each end of the two remaining C's **(Diagram 2)**. Press seams open.

4. Matching seams at intersections, sew C-D units to top and bottom of center unit. Press seams open.

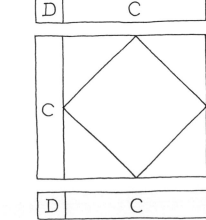

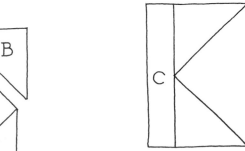

Diagram 1. Sew one B to opposite sides of A

Diagram 2. Sew one C to opposite sides of center unit. Sew one D to each end of remaining C's

5. Sew one E to opposite sides of center unit (**Diagram 3**). Press seams open.

6. Sew one F to each end of the two remaining E's (**Diagram 3**). Press seams open.

7. Matching seams at intersections, sew E-F units to top and bottom of center unit. Press seams open.

8. To finish, scc directions under Assembly.

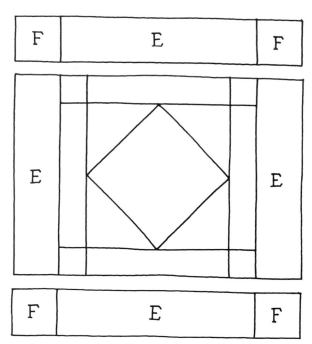

Diagram 3. Sew one E to opposite sides of center unit. Sew one F to each end of remaining two E's

MONKEY WRENCH

CUTTING

Pattern Piece	Number of Pieces
A	2 light, 2 dark
B	2 light, 2 dark
C	2 light, 2 dark
D	2 light, 2 dark
E	2 light, 2 dark
F	2 light, 2 dark
G	2 light, 2 dark

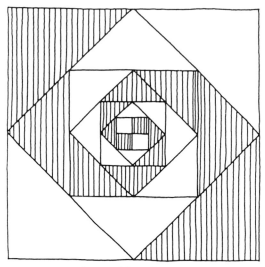

Assembly Diagram

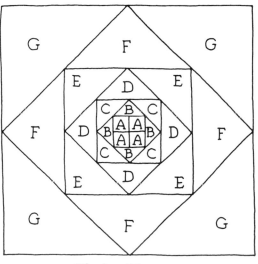

Piecing Diagram

PIECING

Because of the size of the pieces in this block most seams should be pressed to one side, rather than open.

1. Sew one dark A to one light A (**Diagram 1**). Repeat. Press seams open.

2. Reversing the position of light and dark pieces and matching seams at intersections, sew together the A pieces to form a square. Press seams open.

3. Sew one dark B to opposite sides of A unit (**Diagram 2**). Press seam away from center. Sew one light B to top and bottom of A unit. Press seams away from center.

4. Sew one dark C to upper left and lower right sides of center unit (**Diagram 3**). Press seams away from center. Sew one light C to upper right and lower left sides of center unit. Press seams away from center.

5. Sew one dark D to top and bottom of center unit (**Diagram 4**). Press seams away from center. Sew one light D to each side of center unit. Press seams away from center.

6. Sew one dark E to upper right and lower left sides of center unit (**Diagram 5**). Press seams away from center. Sew one light E to upper left and lower right sides of center unit. Press seams away from center.

7. Sew one dark F to each side of center unit (**Piecing and Assembly Diagrams**). Sew one light F to top and bottom of center unit. Press seams away from center.

8. Sew one dark G to upper left and lower right sides of center unit (**Piecing and Assembly Diagrams**). Press seam away from center. Sew one light G to upper right and lower left sides of center unit. Press seams away from center.

9. To finish, see directions under Assembly.

Diagram 1. Sew one dark A to one light A. Repeat

Diagram 2. Sew one dark B to opposite sides of A unit. Sew one light B to top and bottom

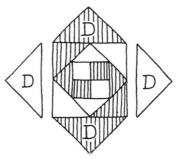

Diagram 3. Sew one dark C to upper left and lower right. Sew one light C to upper right and lower left

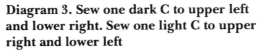

Diagram 4. Sew one dark D to top and bottom of center unit. Sew one light D to each side

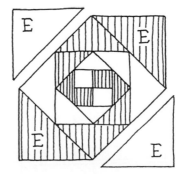

Diagram 5. Sew one dark E to upper right and lower left sides of center unit. Sew one light E to upper left and lower right

BOW TIE

CUTTING

Pattern Piece	Number of Pieces
A	**4 dark**
B	**8 light** **8 medium**

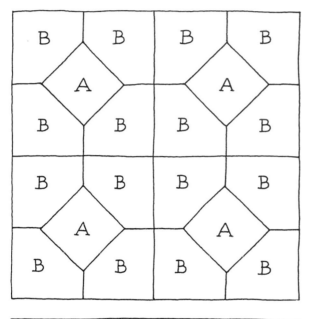

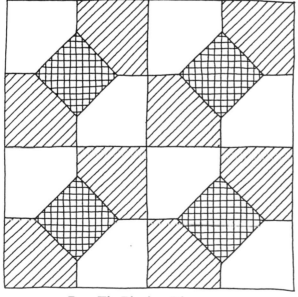

Bow Tie Piecing Diagrams

PIECING

1. Matching notches, sew the diagonal side of one medium B to one side of A (**Diagram 1**). Press seam open.

2. Sew light B piece to medium B piece along one short side, stopping at seam line (**Diagram 2**). Note: Light B is shown underneath medium B in the diagram. Leave needle down at dot, lift presser foot and clip stitching to dot as shown to release corner for turning.

3. Rotate notched side of light B (underneath) to align with notch on A, lower presser foot and continue sewing (**Diagram 3**). Press seams open.

4. Repeat steps 2 and 3 to sew third B (medium) in place (**Diagram 4**). Press seams open.

5. Sew fourth B (light) to the last side of A in the same manner, turning corners in two places between first and third B pieces (**Diagram 5**). Press seams open.

6. Repeating steps 1 through 5, make a total of four bow tie units.

7. Matching seams at intersections, sew together bow tie units in two sets of two (**Diagram 6**), then sew together sets to form complete bow tie block. Press seams open.

8. To finish, see directions under Assembly.

ASSEMBLY
(for all three designs)

To make mini pillow ornaments, piece each patchwork design. To make a loop for hanging, fold a 1½-inch piece of ¼-inch ribbon in half and pin in place in one corner. Sew lace around edges of patchwork block then assemble using hand-stitched closing, page xxx. Stuff ornaments with polyester filling.

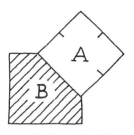

Diagram 1. Sew the diagonal side of one medium B to one side of A, matching notches

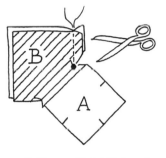

Diagram 2. Sew a light B (underneath) to the first B and stop at seam line. Clip stitching to dot

Diagram 3. Rotate notched side of light B to match notch on A and continue sewing

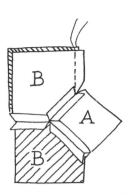

Diagram 4. Repeat procedure for third B

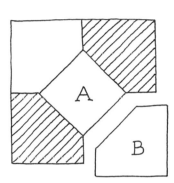

Diagram 5. Repeat procedure for fourth B, turning corners in two places

☐ LIGHT
▨ MEDIUM
▦ DARK

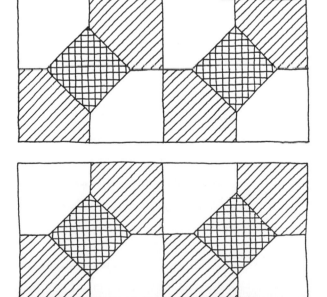

Diagram 6. Sew completed units together into two sets of two

Amish Square

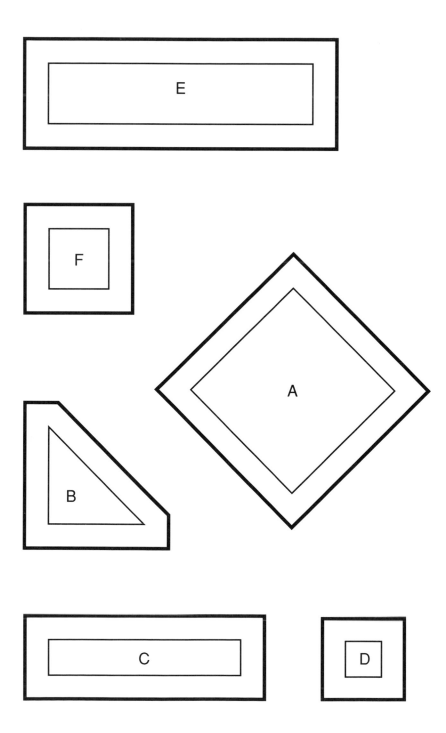

Monkey Wrench

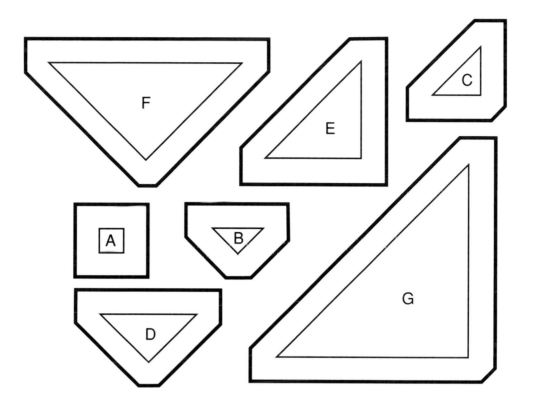

Bow Tie

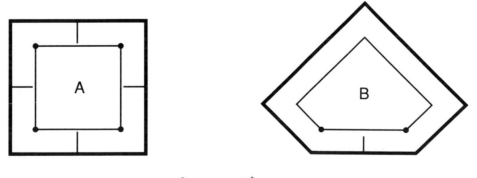

PATCHWORK & LACE CHRISTMAS TREE SKIRT

By Doris J. Carmack

Biscuit quilting with triangles instead of squares creates a festive star design for a unique tree skirt. After you've made one for yourself, there are probably some people on your Christmas list who would love one, too!

SIZE

Biscuit is a 5½-inch triangle
Finished tree skirt is 40 inches in diameter

MATERIALS

- ½ yard each of three Christmas prints
- 1¼ yards muslin
- 1⅛ yards fabric for back
- 1¼ yards fabric for ruffle
- 3 yards 3-inch-wide ruffled lace
- Polyester filling

CUTTING

Pattern Piece	Number of Pieces
7-inch triangle (top)	18 each of three prints
6-inch triangle (base)	54 muslin

Ruffle

Five strips fabric, each 8 x 45 inches

PIECING & ASSEMBLY

1. Similar to the directions for Basic Biscuit Block, page 145, this triangular block is made with a 6-inch muslin triangle on the bottom and a 7-inch triangle on top. Sew two sides of the triangle with a pleat in each side. Stuff and sew the third side closed in the same manner. Repeat to make a total of 54 triangle biscuits.

2. Sew together the biscuits in six large triangles of nine biscuits each (**Diagram 1**).

3. Sew together large triangles to form a hexagon, leaving one seam open (**Diagram 2**).

4. With the gathers facing toward the center, sew lace to the outer edge of tree skirt.

5. To make ruffle, sew together the 8 x 45-inch strips end to end to make a continuous loop. Press seams open. Fold the loop in half lengthwise, right side out, and press. Using two rows of stitching, machine baste along raw edge. Gather ruffle and fit to edge of skirt right on top of lace. With the ruffle facing toward the center, machine baste the outside edge of the tree skirt on top of the lace.

6. Using the tree skirt as a pattern, cut a piece of fabric for the back and mark the center. Cut from one corner straight to the center mark. Right sides together, sew tree skirt back to biscuit top, leaving an opening for turning. Turn and slip stitch opening closed.

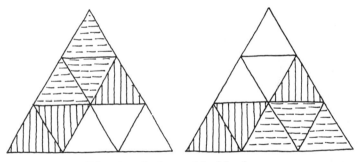

Diagram 1. Assemble blocks into 9-block triangles

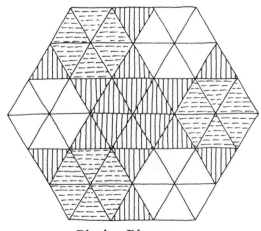

Piecing Diagram

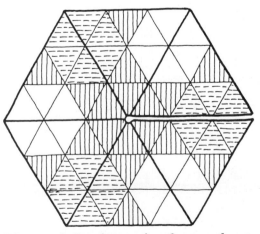

Diagram 2. Sew large triangles together to form hexagon, leaving one seam open

Patchwork & Lace Christmas Tree Skirt

Biscuit Base

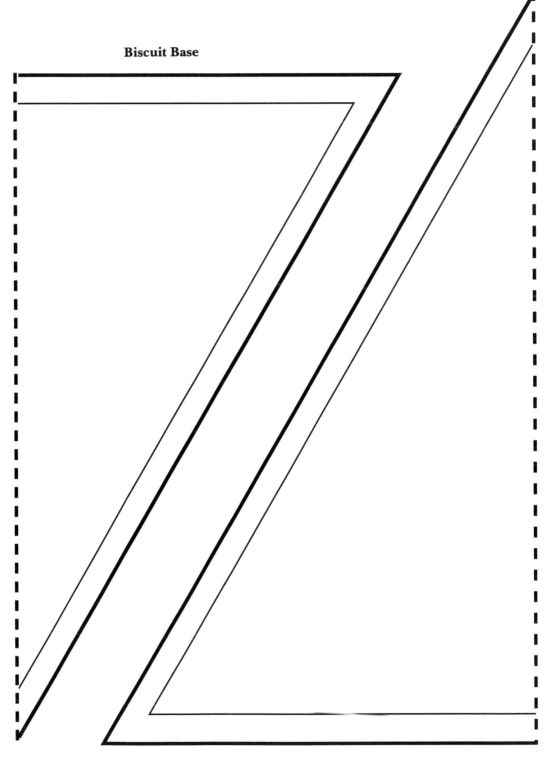

Biscuit Top

COZY KITCHEN COMPANIONS

COTTAGE TEA COZY

Design by Barbara Macaulay

The second cup of tea will be just as comforting as the first when poured from a pot kept warm under this charming cozy.

SIZE

Finished tea cozy is 13 inches high by 16 inches wide

MATERIALS

- ½ yard fine blue print for tea cozy front and back
- ½ yard fabric for lining
- ⅛ yard green fabric for grass
- Scraps of fabric for appliqué
- 18-inch square fusible webbing
- ½ yard high-loft batting

CUTTING

Enlarge pattern for tea cozy front, back, and lining following instructions on page xiv.

To make appliqué shapes, trace patterns onto paper side of fusible webbing (see page xviii). Fuse to wrong side of appropriate fabrics and cut without seam allowance. When ready to appliqué, remove paper and fuse to background fabric.

One front and one back piece from blue print
Two lining pieces for front and back pieces
One 4½ x 17-inch green strip for grass appliqué
One 3 x 5-inch strip blue print for loop
Appliqué pieces from assorted scraps

APPLIQUÉ & ASSEMBLY

1. Match bottom edge of grass appliqué to bottom edge of cozy front. Fuse and machine appliqué top edge of grass strip using a wide satin stitch (**Diagram 1**).

2. Using photograph and **Appliqué Diagram** as guides, arrange appliqué pieces on grass/sky section.

3. When pleased with arrangement, fuse appliqué pieces to background and machine appliqué around all pieces, matching thread to fabric. Satin stitch roof and window lines.

4. To make loop, press under ¼ inch on both long edges of 3 x 5-inch strip. Fold strip in half lengthwise, wrong sides together, and topstitch ⅛ inch from each long edge. Fold to make loop (**Diagram 2**). Pin loop to right side of front at center top, matching raw edges (**Diagram 2**) and stitch.

5. With right sides facing, pin and sew together front and back along outside edge, using a ⅝-inch seam allowance. Trim seam and clip curve, then turn right side out.

6. Using the tea cozy as a pattern, cut out two pieces of batting. Pin together the two batting pieces and sew outside seam ⅝ inch from edge. Trim seam close to stitching. Do not turn right side out.

Appliqué Diagram

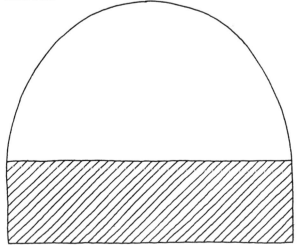

Diagram 1. Sew grass to cozy front

7. Pin together lining pieces with right sides facing. Starting at bottom edge, sew up each side about 12 inches and backstitch to secure, using a ⅝-inch seam allowance. There will be an opening of about 12 inches at the top middle of the lining (**Diagram 3**). Do not turn right side out.

8. Slip batting inside tea cozy, fitting smoothly. Pin batting and cozy together and trim excess batting at bottom.

9. Slip lining over top of cozy, right sides together (**Diagram 4**). Matching lower raw edges, pin and sew around bottom ⅝ inch from edge.

10. Pull cozy through opening in lining and stitch opening closed. Push lining up into cozy. Carefully smooth and pin extra lining that extends at bottom and topstitch along seam line to form binding.

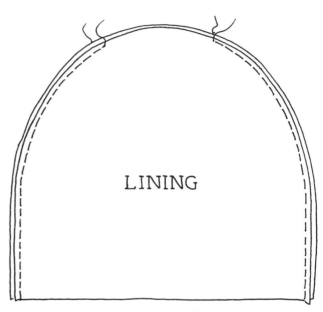

Diagram 3. Sew sides of lining together

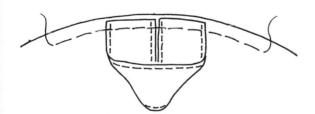

Diagram 2. Fold loop as shown and pin to right side of front at center top and stitch

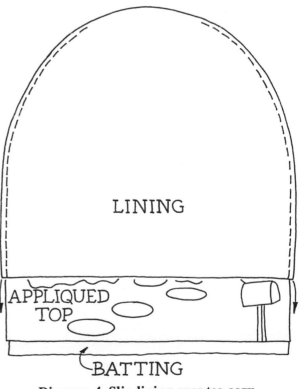

Diagram 4. Slip lining over tea cozy

Cottage Tea Cozy

Appliqué Pattern

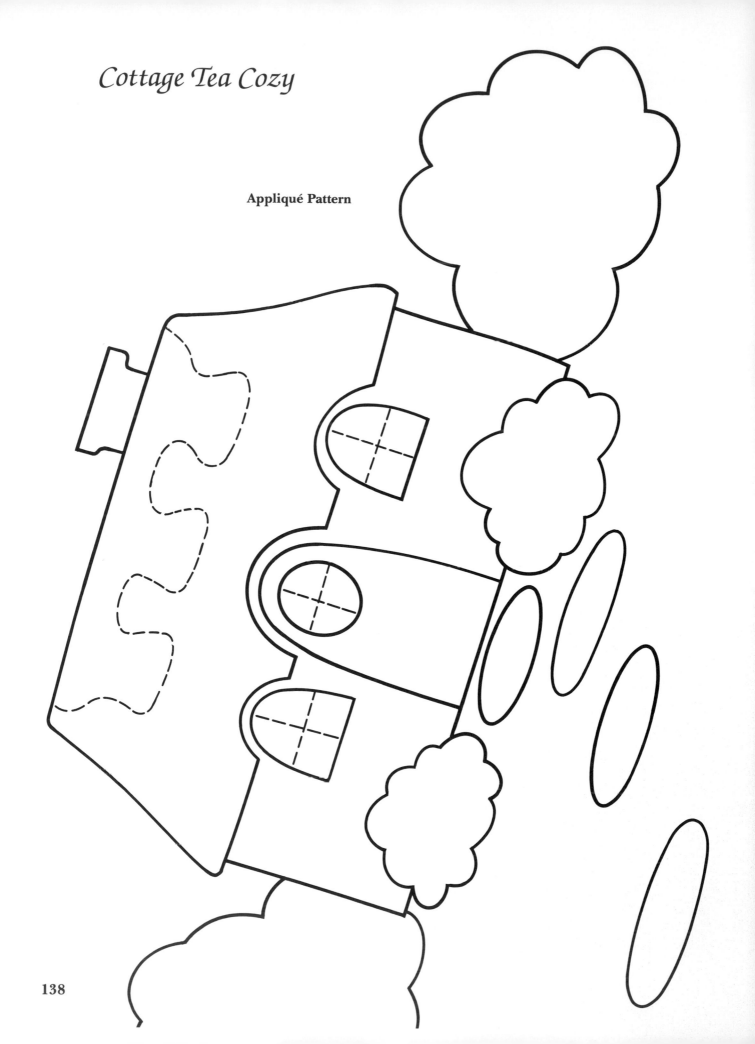

138

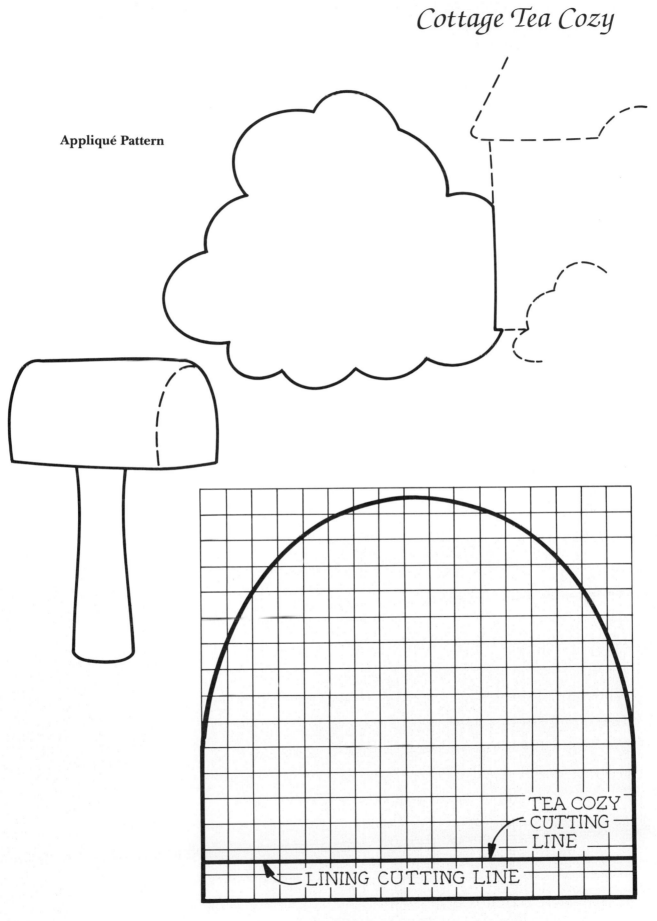

Cottage Tea Cozy

Appliqué Pattern

TEA COZY
CUTTING
LINE

LINING CUTTING LINE

Tea Cozy Pattern: 1 square = 1 inch

139

SPICED TEA MAT

By Sheri Kawahara-Fisher

Set your teapot on this homey tea mat and the warmth will release the inviting aroma of cinnamon and cloves.

SIZE
Finished mat is 8½ inches square

MATERIALS
- ¼ yard print fabric for borders, backing, and pocket
- Scrap of muslin
- Scrap of print for appliqué
- Scrap of fusible webbing
- Heavyweight fusible interfacing
- High-loft batting
- 4 ounces mixed ground spices: cinnamon, cloves, allspice, ginger and/or mint

CUTTING

Pattern Piece	Number of Pieces
A	1 muslin
B	2 print fabric
C	2 print fabric

One 8½ x 9-inch piece print fabric for pocket
One heart appliqué piece
One 6 x 12-inch piece heavyweight fusible interfacing
Two 9-inch squares batting

APPLIQUÉ & ASSEMBLY

1. Sew B to opposite sides of A (**Diagram 1**). Press seams open.

2. Sew C to top and bottom of A-B unit (**Diagram 1**). Press seams open.

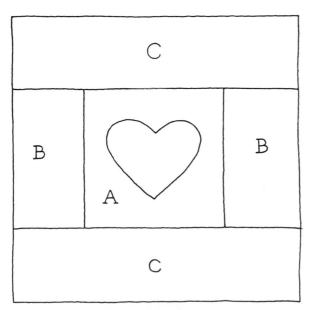

Piecing Diagram

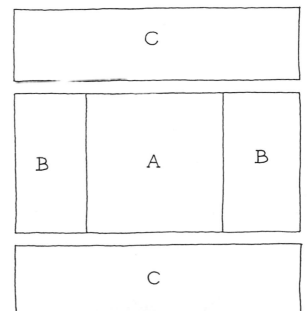

Diagram 1. Sew B to right and left sides of A. Sew C to top and bottom of A-B unit

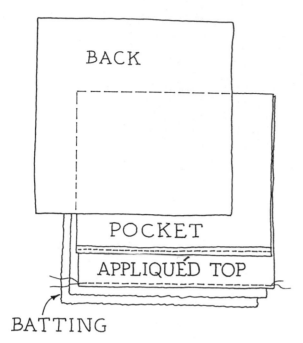

Diagram 2. Layer batting and appliquéd top. Stitch lower edge. Then add pocket and back

3. Trace heart appliqué motif to paper side of fusible webbing. Fuse to wrong side of print scrap and cut out heart without seam allowance.

4. Center heart appliqué on muslin square, remove paper, and fuse. Machine appliqué around heart using wide satin stitch.

5. To make pocket, turn under ¼ inch along one long edge of 8½ x 9-inch piece of print fabric and press. Turn same edge under ¼ inch again. Press and topstitch.

6. Layer two squares of batting, and heart appliqué square (right side up). Sew through all layers across bottom edge, just outside seamline. Add pocket, and back on top of pocket (right side down), align edges and sew around all sides, leaving a 5-inch opening at the bottom for turning **(Diagram 2)**.

7. Trim corners and batting. Turn right side out, with pocket over front, and stitch opening closed. Turn pocket to back.

8. To make spice bag, fold heavyweight interfacing in half crosswise (fusible sides together) to make a 6-inch square. Press to seal ¼-inch seam along two edges. Fill with spices and press to seal opening closed.

9. Slip spice bag into mat pocket. Remove spice bag for laundering.

Heart Appliqué Pattern

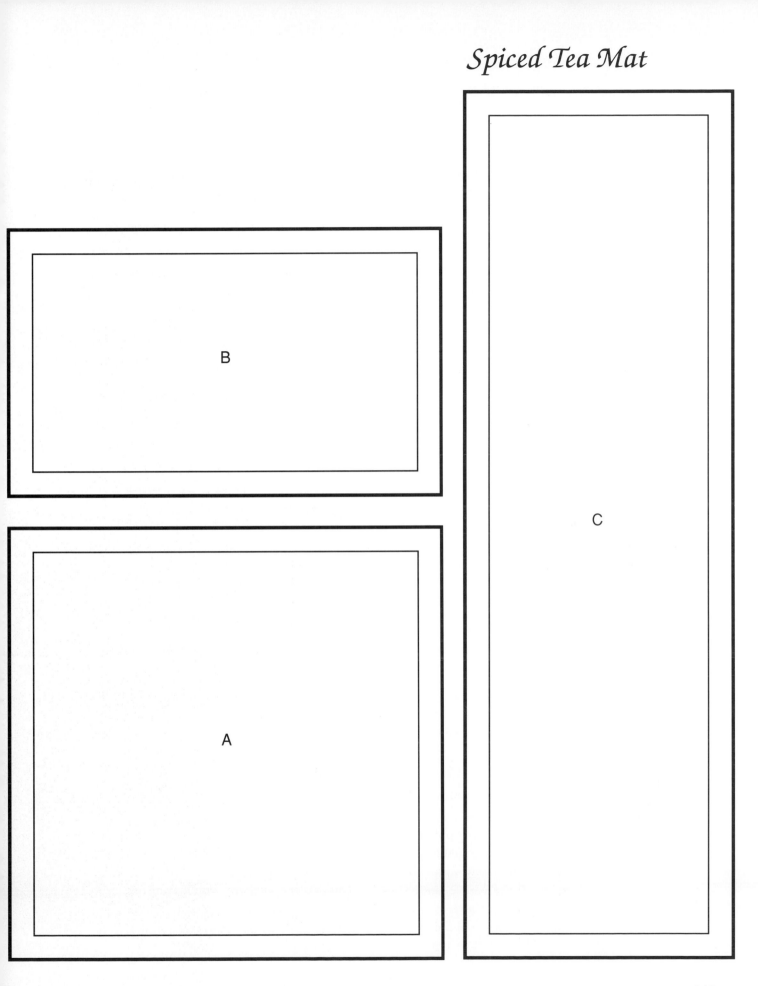

B

C

A

KITCHEN BISCUITS

By Doris J. Carmack

Biscuit blocks are easy to make and lend themselves to a whole range of wonderful quilting projects. This technique is done entirely by machine so the projects go together quickly. The basic directions for biscuit blocks are given here, along with two projects, potholders and a decorative bulletin board. Once you've made these "biscuits for the kitchen," you'll want to turn to Extra Batch of Biscuits on page 236, where more biscuit projects for the rest of the house are given.

DIRECTIONS FOR BASIC BISCUIT BLOCK

Biscuits are made with just two pieces of fabric, one $\frac{1}{2}$ inch larger than the other, in the shapes of squares, rectangles, or triangles. For example, a 4-inch-square top stitched to a $3\frac{1}{2}$-inch-square bottom makes a finished 3-inch biscuit block. The smaller square can be lightweight muslin, as it will not show in the finished project.

1. To make one biscuit, sew larger square to muslin square, wrong sides together using a $\frac{1}{8}$-inch seam allowance. Begin at one corner, sew a few stitches, make a pleat, match opposite corners and continue sewing to corner. Turn and repeat, making a pleat folded toward you in the center of each of three sides (**Diagram 1**).

2. Without cutting thread, sew the next block around three sides in the same manner as in step 1. Continue sewing blocks together in the colors indicated by your pattern, making a string of blocks for each row (**Diagram 2**). For some biscuit projects, you may wish to pin a number on each row as you finish it.

3. Lightly fill each block with a small amount of polyester stuffing.

4. After all blocks in a row have been stuffed, sew the fourth sides closed, pleating as before. Do not cut the blocks apart.

5. Working across each row, sew blocks together (with pleated sides together) using a $\frac{1}{4}$-inch seam allowance (**Diagram 3**).

6. Sew rows together, opening seams and matching them at intersections (**Diagram 3**).

To determine size for backing fabric, lay project on a flat surface and measure the width and length, without stretching. If the project is made of twelve rows of fourteen 3-inch blocks, it should measure 36 x 42 inches. However, it may contract and be slightly smaller, so the backing should be cut to actual measurement.

After all biscuits for a project have been sewn together, sew front to backing fabric with right sides together, leaving an opening for turning. Turn right side out and slip stitch the opening closed.

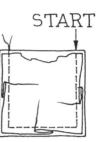

Diagram 1. Sew large square to small square making a pleat in center of each of three sides

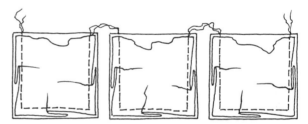

Diagram 2. Continue sewing blocks together into rows, leaving one side open on each block

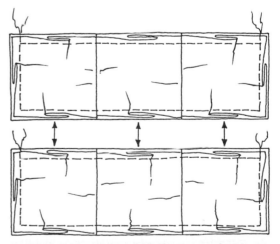

Diagram 3. Sew rows together, opening seams at each intersection

POTHOLDERS

SIZE

Potholder is 7½ inches square
Block size is 1½ inches square

MATERIALS

- Fabric scraps for blocks
- ¼ yard muslin
- 8-inch square fabric for backing
- 8-inch square batting
- Polyester filling
- 4-inch piece of 1½-inch ribbon or fabric strip for loop

CUTTING

Pattern Piece	Number of Pieces
2½-inch squares fabric scraps	25
2-inch squares muslin	25

PIECING & ASSEMBLY

1. Make twenty-five biscuits in desired fabrics, according to directions for Basic Biscuit Block, page 145.

2. Sew blocks together in five rows of five blocks.

3. Lay backing fabric right side up on batting square. Place biscuit block on top, right side down.

4. Use a piece of ribbon for loop. Or, fold long sides of 4 x 1½-inch fabric strip into the center so raw edges meet in the middle, and press. Fold lengthwise in half and topstitch close to edge. Fold fabric or ribbon loop in half and pin inside one corner between block and back.

5. Sew around outer edge of block leaving an opening for turning. Turn and slipstitch opening closed.

BULLETIN BOARD

SIZE

Bulletin board is 12 x 18 inches
Block size is 1½ inches square

MATERIALS

- Purchased bulletin board 12 x 18 inches
- Fabric scraps for blocks and butterflies
- ¼ yard muslin
- 1½ yards decorative trim
- 2 yards bias tape
- 12 inches ⅛-inch-wide ribbon
- Silk flowers
- White glue
- Polyester stuffing
- Polyester fleece

CUTTING

Pattern Piece	Number of Pieces
2½-inch squares fabric scraps	36
2-inch squares muslin	36
A	1 fabric 1 fleece
B	2 fabric
C	1 fabric 1 fleece
D	2 fabric

PIECING & ASSEMBLY

1. Make 36 biscuit blocks in one long row according to directions for Basic Biscuit Block, page 145.

2. Arrange the row of blocks in the shape of the frame, marking each corner block with a pin. There should be eight blocks across the top and bottom **(Diagram 1)**, and ten blocks on each side. Sew the blocks together.

3. Sew bias tape across top and bottom outside edges and trim even with outside edge of biscuit block frame. Sew bias tape to each side and trim even with outside edge of bias tape on top and bottom **(Diagram 2)**.

4. Starting at one corner, sew decorative trim to inside edge of biscuit block frame, mitering each corner (see page xix). To finish, fold under end of trim at beginning corner **(Diagram 3)**.

5. Position biscuit block frame on bulletin board. Fold bias tape over to back, miter each corner and glue (or staple if bulletin board has wooden back) in place. Reinforce with staples if necessary. Glue decorative trim to bulletin board, carefully folding and mitering inner corners.

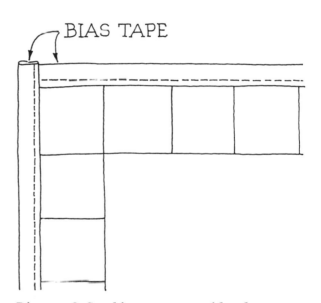

Diagram 2. Sew bias tape to outside edges

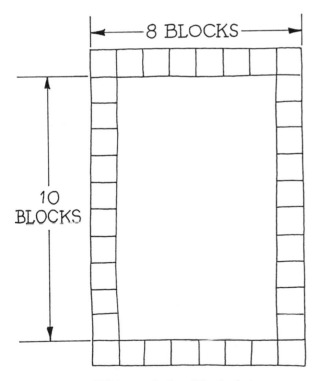

Diagram 1. Sew blocks into frame with eight blocks at top and bottom

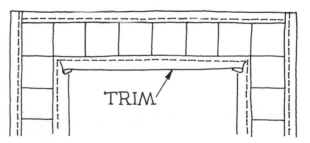

Diagram 3. Add decorative trim to inside edges, mitering corners

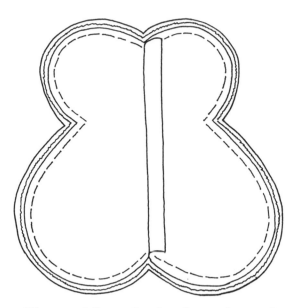

Diagram 4. Layer batting, front piece and back pieces, then sew around outside edges

6. To make small butterfly, place A right side up on butterfly fleece (A). Fold over center back seam allowance on one B and lay right side down on top of A. Lay remaining B right side down on top of A and sew around outside edge of butterfly **(Diagram 4)**. Trim seam, turn right side out and topstitch around butterfly ¼ inch from edge. With A on the outside, fold butterfly in half and topstitch ¼ inch from center fold **(Diagram 5)**. Repeat for large butterfly C and D.

7. Arrange and glue butterflies in corners and decorate with silk flowers. Use ⅛-inch ribbon to make antennae for butterflies.

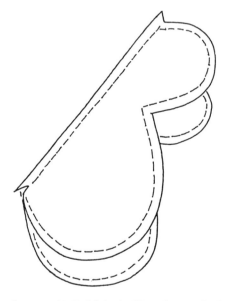

Diagram 5. Fold in half and topstitch center fold

SMALL BUTTERFLY BACK

Cut 2 fabric

A

SMALL BUTTERFLY FRONT

Cut 1 fabric
Cut 1 fleece

B

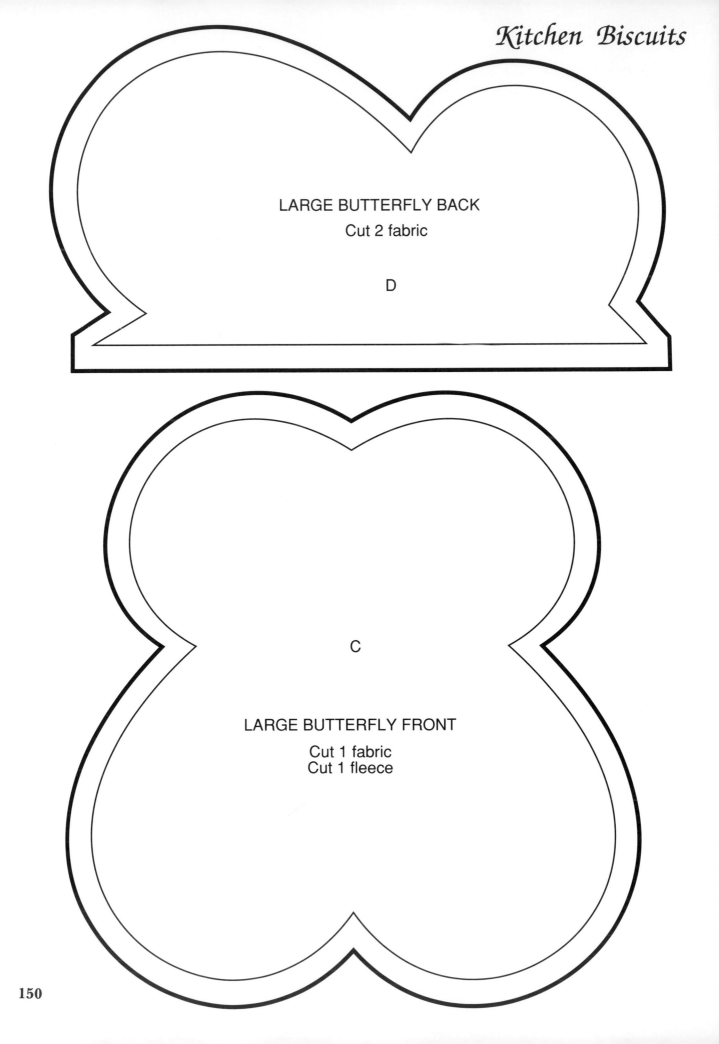

LARGE BUTTERFLY BACK
Cut 2 fabric

D

C

LARGE BUTTERFLY FRONT

Cut 1 fabric
Cut 1 fleece

APPLIQUÉD COASTERS & NAPKIN RINGS

By Sheri Kawahara-Fisher

Easy-to-make coasters and napkin rings are dressed up with appliquéd hearts, but any simple design motif of your choice would work as well.

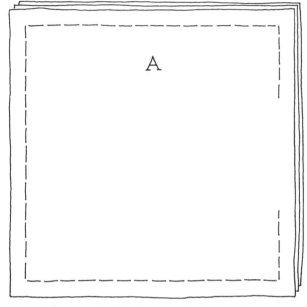

Diagram 1. Stitch around sides of coaster, leaving an opening for turning

SET OF FOUR COASTERS

SIZE

Each finished coaster measures 4 inches square

MATERIALS

- 4½ x 18-inch piece print fabric
- 4½ x 18-inch piece coordinating fabric for lining
- 4½ x 18-inch piece polyester fleece
- Scraps red fabric for appliquéd hearts

CUTTING

Coasters

Pattern Piece	Number of Pieces
A	4 print 4 lining 4 fleece
B	4 red

ASSEMBLY

1. Layer each coaster as follows: polyester fleece; print fabric, right side up; then lining fabric, right side down. Pin together all layers.

2. Sew around all sides of coaster, leaving an opening for turning (**Diagram 1**).

3. Trim corners.

4. Turn coaster right side out and press lightly. Slipstitch opening closed.

5. Topstitch through all layers ⅜ inch from outside edges.

6. Machine appliqué heart design (or any other motif) in the center of each coaster, zigzag stitching through all layers (**Diagram 2**).

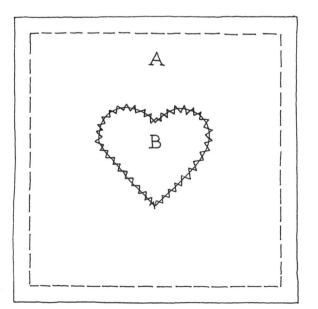

Diagram 2. Topstitch edges and zigzag-stitch heart to center of coaster

NAPKIN RINGS

SIZE

Each napkin ring is 1¾ inches wide and approximately 1¼ inches in diameter

MATERIALS

- 5 x 9-inch piece print fabric
- 5 x 9-inch piece lining fabric
- 5 x 9-inch piece fusible interfacing
- Scraps red fabric for appliquéd hearts

CUTTING

Napkin Rings

Pattern Piece	Number of Pieces
A	1 print 1 lining 1 interfacing
B	4 red

ASSEMBLY

1. Iron fusible interfacing to wrong side of print fabric.

2. With fabric marking pen, mark all seam lines and cutting lines for four napkin rings onto wrong side of lining fabric, as shown in **Napkin Ring Pattern and Marking Diagram**.

3. Right sides together, match and pin together interfaced print fabric and lining fabric.

4. Using ¼-inch seam allowance, sew horizontal seams, backstitching at beginning and end to secure seams.

5. Cut napkin rings apart on horizontal cutting lines and turn right side out. Press napkin rings flat.

6. Machine appliqué heart design (or any other motif) to the center of each napkin ring **(Diagram 1)**.

7. For each napkin ring, bring right sides together, pin together print fabric only at ½-inch seam lines. Sew ½-inch seam, making sure that lining is not caught in stitching **(Diagram 2)**.

8. Trim seam and finger-press open. Fold ends of lining inside and slipstitch opening closed.

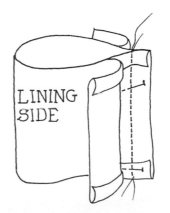

Diagram 1. Machine appliqué heart to center of each napkin ring

Diagram 2. Fold back lining at ends and stitch right sides of print fabric together

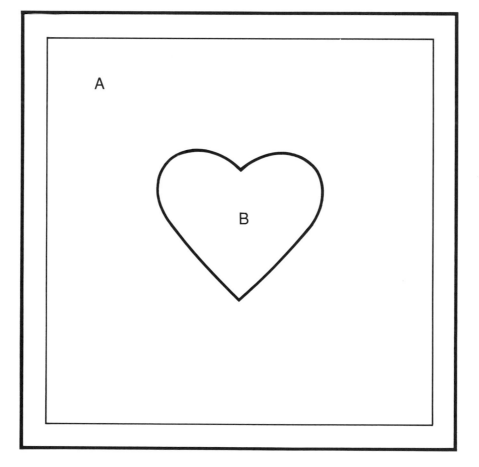

Coaster Pattern

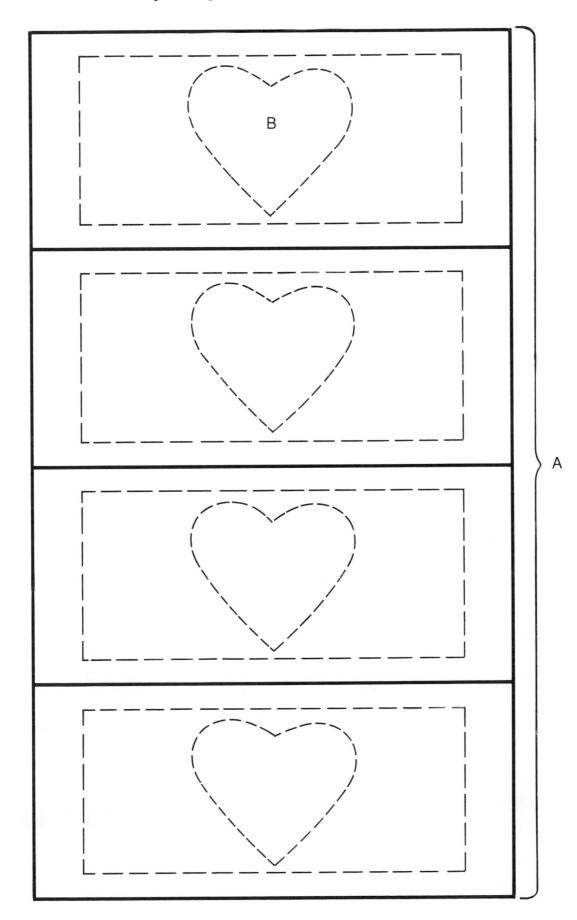

COUNTRY PLACEMATS ENSEMBLE

By Barbara Clayton

Traditional Dutch delftware was the inspiration for this set of placemats, matching napkins with bow-tie rings, and bun warmer.

SIZES

Napkins are 15 inches square
Placemats are 13½ x 23 inches
Bun warmer is 16 inches square

MATERIALS

Materials listed are for all three projects

- 2½ yards muslin
- ½ yard dark print
- ¼ yard medium print
- ¼ yard light print
- ⅞ yard very light print
- 1¼ yards polyester fleece or batting
- Fusible webbing
- Basket measuring 9 x 13 x 2 inches

CUTTING

NAPKINS

Four 16-inch squares of muslin
Four strips 2 x 25-inch dark print
Flowers and leaves appliqué pieces from dark
and medium print

PLACEMATS (For four placemats)

Pattern Piece	Number of Pieces
A	16 dark print 16 medium print 16 light print 16 very light print
B	8 very light print

Four muslin rectangles 13½ x 23 inches for
   backing
Four batting rectangles 13½ x 23 inches
Flowers and leaves appliqué pieces from dark
   and medium print
2-inch-wide continuous bias binding from
   remaining muslin

BUN WARMER

Two 16-inch squares very light print
One 16-inch square batting
Flowers and leaves appliqué pieces
Two strips 2 x 45-inch dark print

PIECING, APPLIQUÉ & ASSEMBLY

General Appliqué Tips

To make flowers and leaves appliqué pieces, see
page xviii for fusible webbing technique. Fuse to
wrong side of appropriate dark or medium
print fabric (see photo of finished items).

NAPKINS

1. To make hemmed edge, turn under all sides
¼ inch and press. Turn under all sides ¼ inch
again and machine stitch hem.

2. Trace appliqué design about 1¼ inch in from
the edge of one corner of the napkin. Arrange
appliqué pieces on the tracing and fuse in place.

3. Machine appliqué around each flower and
leaf piece, using a wide satin stitch. Satin stitch
along the stem line.

4. To make ties, fold each 2 x 25-inch dark print
strip in half lengthwise with right sides together.
Stitch ¼ inch from raw edges (stitch ends as
well), leaving a 2-inch opening in center of strip
for turning. Clip corners, turn, and press. Slip
stitch opening closed.

5. Fold napkin as desired and tie with strips.

Piecing Diagram

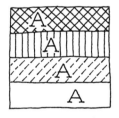

Diagram 1. Arranging colors from dark to light, sew together

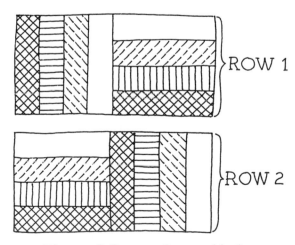

Diagram 2. Sew together two blocks as shown in Row 1. Sew together remaining two blocks as in Row 2

PLACEMATS

1. Arranging colors from dark to light, sew together four A pieces (**Diagram 1**) to make a square. Repeat for a total of four completed A blocks. Press seams open.

2. Sew together two A blocks with stripes arranged vertically and horizontally as shown in **Diagram 2**, Row 1. Sew together remaining blocks, arranged as in Row 2 of diagram. Press seams open.

3. Matching seams at intersections, sew together Row 1 and Row 2 with stripes arranged as shown (**Diagram 2**). Press seam open.

4. Sew B pieces to opposite sides of central A block as shown in **Piecing Diagram**. Press seams open.

5. Trace flowers and leaves border design onto B pieces (**Diagram 3**).

6. Arrange flowers and leaves appliqué pieces on the tracing and fuse in place.

7. Machine appliqué around all flower and leaf pieces using a wide satin stitch. Satin stitch over stem lines.

8. Layer finished placemat top, batting rectangle, and muslin backing and stitch around outside edge of top. Trim batting and backing to match top.

9. Bind placemat with bias strips. Fold back beginning end of bias strip, match edge of strip to edge of mat, and sew around mat ⅜ inch from edge. Fold remaining edge of binding to back of mat, turn edge under, and blindstitch.

Diagram 3. Trace flowers and leaves border design onto B pieces

BUN WARMER

1. Trace center flower motif from placemat design onto opposite corners of each 16-inch fabric square.

2. Arrange flowers and leaves appliqué pieces on tracing and fuse to fabric.

3. Machine appliqué around flower and leaf pieces using wide satin stitch.

4. Mark one appliquéd square with horizontal and vertical lines, 1 inch apart, across the entire surface of the square, making a grid design.

5. Layer unmarked square (wrong side up), batting, and marked square (right side up). Place top fabric square so that appliquéd designs are in opposite corners of those on the bottom square.

6. Hand quilt around flower designs on top and bottom squares, then hand quilt the grid design.

7. To make ties, starting at one corner, sew the first 2 x 45-inch dark strip to the edge of warmer, ⅜ inch from edge, leaving a 6-inch tail. Sew to next corner, miter corner, and sew to the mid-way point of the next side. With the second strip, start at original starting point, sew to next corner. Miter corner and sew to next corner **(Diagram 1)**.

8. Fold second binding strip over the edge of warmer, turn edge under, and pin to the back. Continue sewing first binding from midway point to end, sewing across second binding at corner.

9. Fold edge of first binding to back, turn edge under and pin. Seam allowances on tie ends should also be folded in and pinned. Machine stitch ⅛ inch in from edge of binding, through all layers, around all sides of warmer, and along edges of ties.

10. Tie into bow and place in basket.

Diagram 1. Sew two strips of binding around opposite sides for binding and ties

Country Placemats Ensemble

B

Napkin Appliqué Pattern

A

DOWN THE GARDEN PATH

CALICO CUPBOARD TULIP WALL QUILT

By Janet Page Kessler

Make a garden of appliquéd tulips and surround it with a picket fence. Hang baskets in the corners and get a head start on spring. Calico Cupboard refers to a specific line of fabrics, but feel free to substitute fabrics of your own choice.

Tulip Block

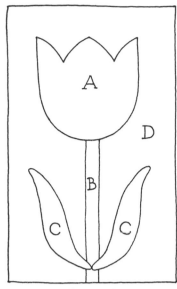

Appliqué Diagram

SIZE

Tulip block is 6 x 10 inches
Basket block is 6¾ inches square
Finished quilt is 49 x 52 inches

MATERIALS

- 2 yards white fabric
- ½ yard each of seven calicoes for tulips and pieced border strips.
- ¼ yard green fabric for leaves and stems
- ⅝ yard fabric for sashes, baskets, and binding
- 3 yards fabric for quilt back (also for pieced border strips)
- Template 6½ x 10½ inches (includes seam allowance) for rectangle D
- 55-inch square of batting or twin-size batt

CUTTING

Tulip Blocks

Pattern Piece	Number of Pieces
*A	18 in assorted calicoes
B	18 stems
C	36 leaves, green (18 pattern and 18 reverse pattern)
D	18 white

Corner Baskets

Pattern Piece	Number of Pieces
* E	8 white 28 in assorted calicoes
* F	4 basket block corners
G	4 white basket handles

* Specific colors are not listed as any colors of your choice will be appropriate.

Sashes and Narrow Borders

Six strips 2 x 36½ inches for horizontal sashes, top, bottom, and side borders

Pieced Borders

Top and Bottom Borders:
    Twelve strips 2 x 13½ inches, calicoes in
        assorted colors
    Eleven strips 2 x 13½ inches, white
    Two strips 2 ¾ x 13½ inches, white
    Two strips 1½ x 39½ inches, white
Side Borders:
    Eleven strips 2 x 13½ inches, calicoes in
        assorted colors
    Ten strips 2 x 13½ inches, white
    Two strips 2 ¾ x 13½ inches, white
    Two strips 1½ x 36½ inches, white

PIECING

Appliquéd Tulip Block

Note: The tulip blocks for this quilt were machine appliquéd. They could be hand appliquéd using the same templates, but you will have to add ¼-inch seam allowance. Fusible webbing could also be used.

1. Referring to **Tulip Block Appliqué Diagram** for placement, appliqué tulips, stems, and leaves (A, B, and C) to white background rectangles (D). Press finished blocks.

CORNER BASKET

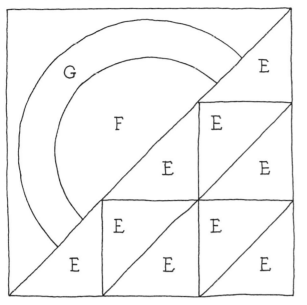

Piecing Diagram

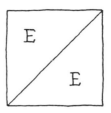

Diagram 1. Sew two triangles together to make a square

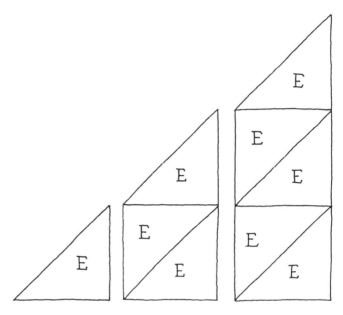

Diagram 2. Sew squares and triangles together in rows

Corner Basket

2. Referring to photograph of finished quilt as a guide to color placement, sew two small triangles (E) together to make a square as in **Diagram 1**. Press seam open. Repeat for a total of three squares.

3. Sew squares (E units) and triangles (E) together into rows as shown in **Diagram 2**. Press seams open. Matching seams at intersections, sew rows together to make basket base. Press seams open.

4. Appliqué basket handle (G) to large corner triangle (F) as in **Diagram 3**. Sew section with basket handle to basket base. Press seam open.

5. Repeat steps 2 through 4 for a total of four corner basket blocks.

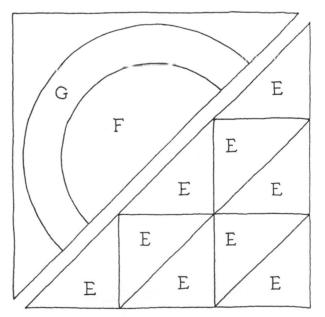

Diagram 3. Appliqué basket handle to F. Sew F to basket base

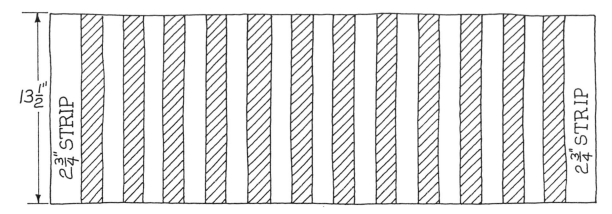

Diagram 4. For top and bottom borders sew 2 x 13½-inch strips together alternating twelve calico with eleven white. For side borders alternate eleven calico with ten white. Add 2 ¾ x 13½-inch white strips to each end of all border sections

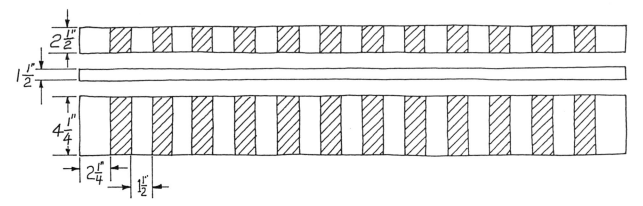

Diagram 5. Cut both top and side border strips across into two 2½-inch and two 4¼-inch sections. Sew 1½-inch white strip between sections

Pieced Borders

6. To make top and bottom borders, sew together 2 x 13½-inch strips, alternating twelve calico strips with eleven white strips **(Diagram 4)**. Press seams open.

7. Sew 2 ¾ x 13½-inch white strips to each end of border section. Press seams open.

8. To make side borders, sew together 2 x 13½-inch strips, alternating eleven calico strips with ten white strips. Sew 2 ¾ x 13½-inch white strips to each end of border strip. Press seams open.

9. Cut top/bottom border section into two 2½-inch sections and two 4¼-inch sections, cutting across strips as shown in **Diagram 5**. In the same manner, cut side border section into two 2½-inch strips and two 4¼-inch strips.

10. To complete top and bottom borders, sew 1½ x 39½-inch white strips between 2½-inch section and 4¼-inch section **(Diagram 5)**. Press seams open.

11. To complete side border sections, sew 1½ x 36½-inch white strips between 2½-inch section and 4¼-inch section **(Diagram 5)**. Press seams open.

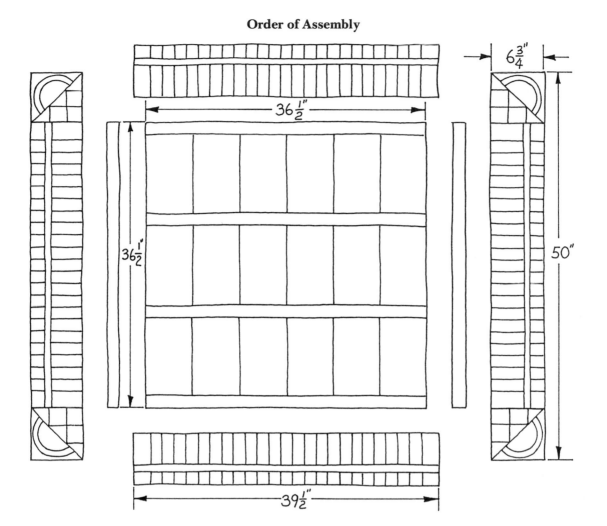

ASSEMBLY

12. Sew appliquéd tulip blocks together into three rows of six blocks as shown in **Order of Assembly**. Press seams open.

13. Sew two 2 x 36½-inch sashes between rows of tulip blocks. Press seams open.

14. Sew one 2 x 36½-inch sash to top and bottom of tulip section. Press seams open.

15. Sew remaining 2 x 36½-inch sashes to opposite sides of tulip section. Press seams open.

16. Sew the 39½-inch-long pieced border sections to the top and bottom of the quilt. Press seams away from borders.

17. Sew corner basket blocks to opposite ends of both 36½-inch side border sections, making sure that basket bases point toward the center of the quilt. Press seams open.

18. Sew side borders to opposite sides of quilt top, matching seam intersections at corner basket blocks. Press seams away from borders.

19. For instructions in assembling the quilt top, batting, and back, see page xx. Trim selvages from the 3-yard piece of fabric for the back. Cut the fabric into two 1½-yard pieces and sew them together along the long sides.

QUILTING

20. Quilt "in the ditch" or as desired.

Calico Cupboard Tulip Wall Quilt

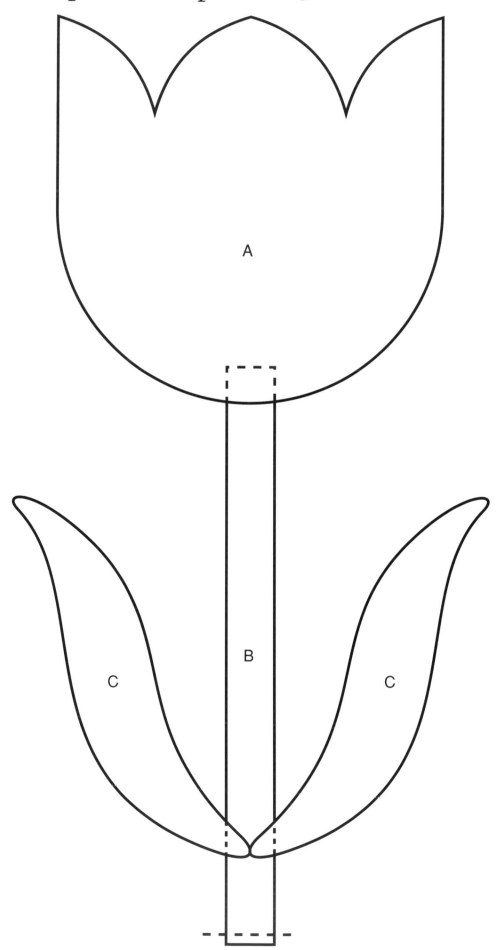

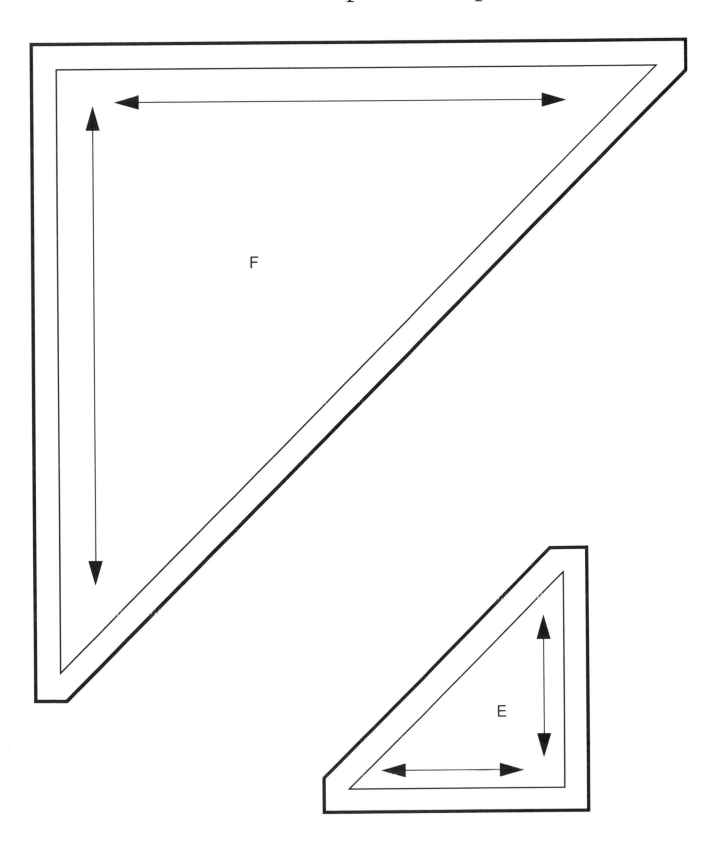

F

E

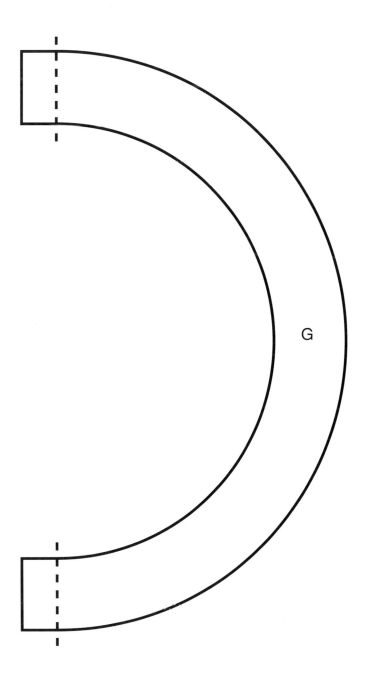

G

WINDBLOWN TULIP

By Kathy Patrick

The illusion of motion is created by bending the stems and leaves of the outer flowers of these rotating Windblown Tulip blocks. The border tulips also sway in the spring wind.

SIZE

Block is 17½ inches square
Finished quilt is 72 x 89½ inches

MATERIALS

- 7 yards white
- 3 yards yellow
- 2 ¼ yards orange
- 2 ⅔ yards light green
- 2 yards medium green
- 6 yards fabric for quilt back
- 1 yard fabric for bias binding
- Twin-size batt

CUTTING

This quilt can be made using the freezer-paper appliqué technique (see page xvii). Therefore, the patterns given were drawn without seam allowances. For patterns, trace A, B, C, and D found on full-size placement guides.

Appliqué Pieces

Pattern Piece	Number of Pieces
A	96 yellow 132 orange
B	96 green
C	14 green
C reversed	14 green
D	8 green

Bias Tulip Stems

From light green fabric, make 22 yards of ¼-inch bias by cutting 1-inch-wide bias strips (see page xxiii). Fold strip in half, wrong sides together, and machine stitch ¼ inch from folded edge. Trim seam allowance close to stitching. Press strip flat so that stitching is centered on underneath side of strip. From this light green ¼-inch bias, cut:

Pattern Piece	Number of Pieces
3-inch strips	144 stems for blocks
2-inch strips	8 stems for border
9-inch strips	28 stems for border

Blocks and Borders

Eighteen squares 18 x 18 inches, white
Two strips 5 x 68 inches, white
Two strips 5 x 85½ inches, white
Two strips 2 x 56 inches, yellow
Two strips 2 x 73½ inches, yellow
Two strips 2 x 59 inches, orange
Two strips 2 x 76½ inches, orange
Two strips 2 ¾ x 72½ inches, green
Two strips 2 ¾ x 90 inches, green

Appliqué Block Diagram

APPLIQUÉ

Tulip Blocks

1. To make guidelines for centering appliqué design, finger-crease 18-inch white square by folding square in half lengthwise, widthwise, and diagonally from corner to corner **(Diagram 1)**.

2. The **Tulip Block Placement Guide** (one-fourth of the full design) may be traced onto the 18-inch square, centered on the crease lines. Or it may be used only as a reference for placement of appliqué pieces.

3. Crisscross four 3-inch stems in a star design and appliqué them to the center of the square, using finger creases as a guide **(Diagram 2)**.

4. Place and appliqué eight outer 3-inch stems so that ends will be hidden under the tulips **(Diagram 3)**.

5. Appliqué leaf (B) to right side of each outer stem so that leaf end will be hidden under tulip **(Diagram 3)**.

6. Appliqué eight yellow inner tulips (A) to square **(Diagram 3)**, making sure that ends of stems and leaves are hidden under the tulips.

7. Appliqué eight orange outer tulips (A) to square **(Diagram 3),** making sure that ends of stems are hidden under tulip. Press the square.

8. Repeat steps 1 through 7 for a total of twelve Tulip Blocks.

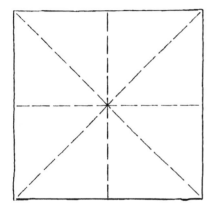

Diagram 1. Finger-crease 18-inch square as shown

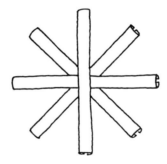

Diagram 2. Overlap four 3-inch bias stem strips in a star over finger creases and appliqué to center of square

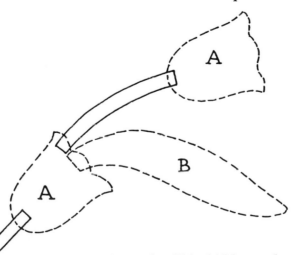

Diagram 3. Appliqué the outer stems so that ends will be hidden under tulips. Appliqué leaves, then inner and outer tulips

Borders

9. Referring to the **Quilt Assembly Diagram** for position, appliqué a 2-inch stem to the center of one 5-inch-wide white border. Appliqué leaf (D) and orange tulip (A) so that they cover the stem ends as shown in the **Border Tulip I Placement Guide**. Repeat, appliquéing stems, leaves, and orange tulips to the center of remaining 5-inch-wide borders for a total of four white borders.

10. Refer to **Border Tulip II Placement Guide** and appliqué 9-inch stems, leaves (C), and orange tulips (A) to top, bottom, and side borders. Position tulips as shown in the **Quilt Assembly Diagram**. Press borders. (Corner tulips are added after borders are attached and mitered.)

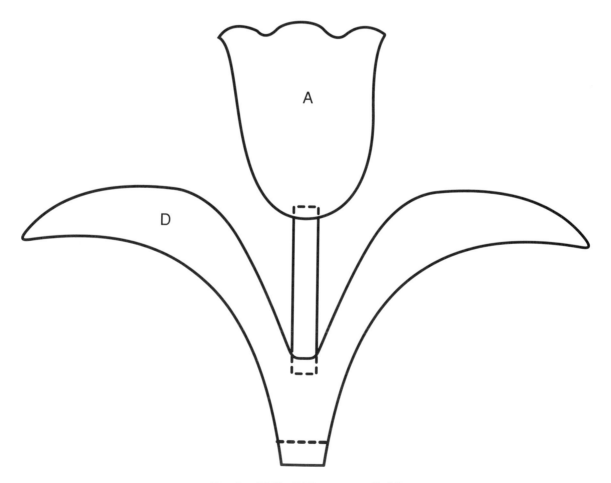

Border Tulip I Placement Guide

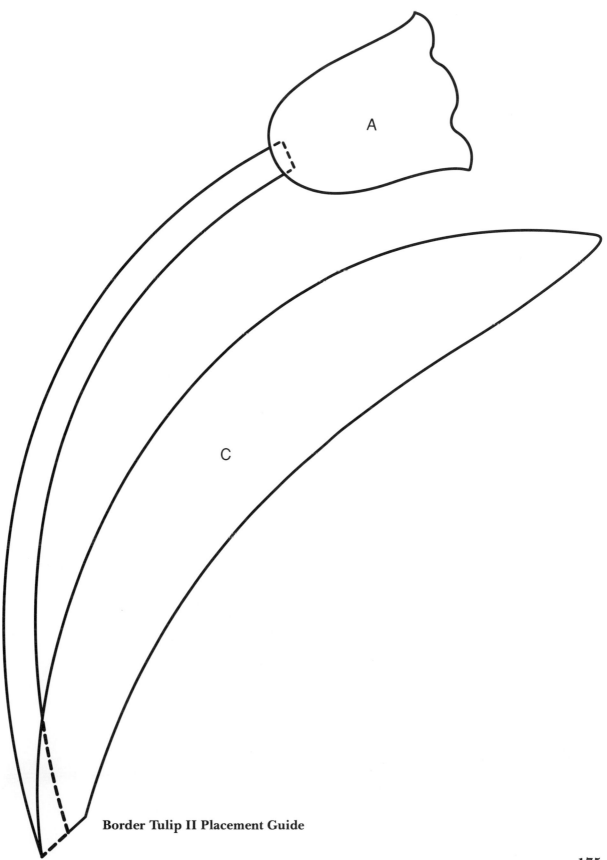

A

C

Border Tulip II Placement Guide

Windblown Tulip

A

B

Tulip Block Placement Guide (one-fourth of block design)

ASSEMBLY

11. Sew together three blocks. Press seams open. Repeat, making four rows of three blocks (**Diagram 4**). Press seams open.

12. Sew rows together, matching seams at intersections. Press seams open.

13. To assemble side borders, mark the center of one 2 x 73½-inch yellow strip, one 2 x 76½-inch orange strip, one 5 x 85½-inch white strip, and one 2 ¾ x 90-inch green strip. Sew strips together in order shown in **Diagram 5**, aligning center mark of each strip with center mark of next strip. Repeat for a total of two side borders. Press seams open. Note: Uneven ends of strips will be trimmed when border corners are mitered.

14. Assemble top and bottom borders in the same manner as side borders, marking centers and sewing together remaining yellow, orange, white, and green strips as shown (**Diagram 5**). Press seams open.

15. Beginning and ending ¼ inch from corners, sew top border to quilt with yellow strip next to tulip blocks. Press seam open. Repeat, sewing bottom border to bottom of quilt.

16. Beginning and ending ¼ inch from corners, sew side borders to opposite sides of quilt in same fashion as above. Press seams open.

17. Miter corners of borders by following directions for mitering on page xix. Take extra care to match seam lines of individual borders. Press seams open.

18. Appliqué Border Tulips I over diagonal seam in each corner of the quilt as shown in **Quilt Assembly Diagram**.

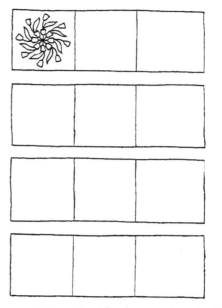

Diagram 4. Sew the blocks together in four rows of three blocks as shown

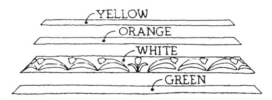

Diagram 5: Mark center of all border strips, align center marks, and sew strips together in order shown

19. Proceed following instructions for assembling quilt top, batting, and back on page xx. Bind quilt with bias binding.

QUILTING

20. The quilt shown was outline-quilted, following the shapes of tulips, leaves, and stems in the blocks and borders. The inner circle of tulips on the **Tulip Block Placement Guide** can be quilted in the white areas. Straight lines of quilting were used to enhance borders.

Quilt Assembly Diagram

ROSE FEVER

By Janet Page Kessler

Pretty chintz fabric has become synonymous with the romantic country look. Inspired by April Wreath from *Scrap Quilts* by Judy Martin, this stylish floral wall hanging uses coordinating borders, stripes, and medallions in an original way to create a lovely design that adds a touch of country to your home.

SIZE

Finished wall hanging is 41 inches square

MATERIALS

- 1 22-inch-square printed center medallion, or pieced or plain fabric
- 1 yard floral fabric for border*
- 1 yard stripe fabric for border*
- ½ yard fabric for inner and outer borders
- 1¼ yards fabric for quilt back
- 1¼ yards batting or craft-size batt
- ½ yard fabric for bias binding
- Template for 9 x 9 x 12 ¾-inch right triangle B (includes seam allowance)

*Allow extra yardage for matching large prints and stripes.

CUTTING

Pattern Piece	Number of Pieces
Center Medallion A	22 x 22-inch square
B	8 floral 12 stripe

Borders

Inner Border:

Two strips 1½ x 22 inches

Two strips 1½ x 24 inches

Outer Border:

Two strips 2½ x 36 inches

Two strips 2½ x 39½ inches

Binding

4 ⅔ yards of 1½-inch-wide bias binding

PIECING

1. Scw 1½ x 22-inch borders to the right and left sides of the medallion (**Diagram 1**). Press seams open.

2. Sew 1½ x 24-inch borders to top and bottom of the medallion (**Diagram 1**). Press seams open.

Piecing Diagram

3. Sew one floral B to one striped B along short side (**Diagram 2**). Press seams open. Repeat for a total of eight B-B units.

4. To make pieced borders, sew together two B-B units in a row as shown in **Diagram 3**, joining striped and floral B pieces. Sew fifth B piece (striped) to end of row. Press seams open. Repeat for a total of four pieced borders.

5. Beginning and ending ¼ inch from corners, sew a pieced border to the right and left sides of quilt top (**Diagram 4**). Press seams open. Sew remaining pieced borders to top and bottom of quilt, again beginning and ending ¼ inch from corners. Press seams open.

6. Matching stripes, sew the four diagonal corner seams. Press seams open.

7. Sew 2½ x 36-inch outer borders to the right and left sides of quilt top (**Diagram 5**). Press seams open.

8. Sew 2½ x 39½-inch outer borders to top and bottom of quilt top (**Diagram 5**). Press seams open.

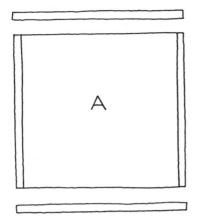

Diagram 1. Sew 1½ x 22-inch borders to right and left sides of medallion. Sew 1½ x 24-inch borders to top and bottom

Diagram 2. Sew two contrasting B pieces together along short sides

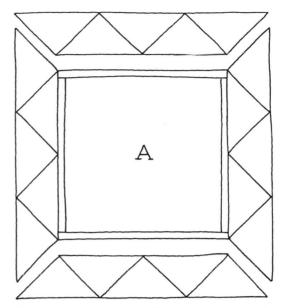

Diagram 4. Sew pieced borders to left and right sides of quilt top. Sew remaining pieced borders to top and bottom of quilt

Diagram 3. Sew B-B units together, joining striped and floral B pieces. Sew fifth B piece to the end of the row

9. Proceed following directions for assembling quilt top, batting, and back on page xx.

10. Bind quilt with bias binding when quilting is complete (See page xxiii).

QUILTING

11. Quilt as desired. The wall hanging shown was machine quilted "in the ditch."

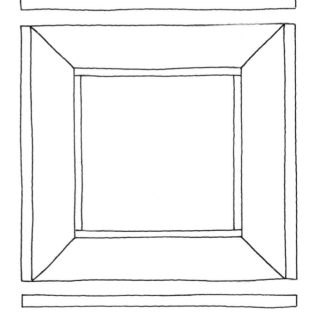

Diagram 5. Sew 2½ x 36-inch borders to left and right sides of quilt. Sew 2½ x 39½-inch borders to top and bottom of quilt

IRIS MEDALLION

**Mary Gomez, designer and co-founder
of Schoolhouse Quilters Guild
Made by the Wandering Foot Quilt Guild**

An appliquéd Iris Block combines with two patchwork blocks, Nine-Patch
and Pine Tree, and circles around a central kaleidoscope of appliquéd irises
in a celebration of spring. This is a good project for the experienced quilter
to showcase her appliqué and piecing skills.

SIZE

Center block is 24 inches square
Other blocks are 12 inches square
Finished quilt is 84 x 108 inches

MATERIALS

- 1 yard blue print (Nine-Patch)
- ¾ yard rose print (Nine-Patch)
- 1 yard light green print (Pine Tree)
- 1 yard dark green print (Pine Tree)
- 1¾ yards purple solid (iris, inner border)
- 2½ yards purple print (iris, outer border)
- Scrap yellow (iris)
- 1 yard medium green print (iris leaves, stems)
- ¼ yard dark green solid (leaves, medallion)
- 1 yard light green mini dot (iris blocks)
- 5 yards white
- 1¼ yards binding fabric (410 inches of 2-inch bias binding)
- 7½ yards fabric for quilt back
- Freezer paper
- Queen-size batt
- Templates for:
  G: 12½ x 12½ x 17¾-inch right triangle (includes seam allowance)
  N: 24½-inch square (includes seam allowance)

CUTTING

This quilt can be made using the freezer-paper appliqué technique (see page xvii). The patterns given are drawn without seam allowances.

Nine-Patch Blocks

Pattern Piece	Number of Pieces
A	100 blue print 80 rose print
B	80 white

Pine Tree Blocks

Pattern Piece	Number of Pieces
B	12 dark green print
C	120 light green print 120 white
D	12 white 12 dark green print
E	12 dark green print
F	24 white

Iris Blocks

Pattern Piece	Number of Pieces
G	12 white 12 light green mini dot
H	12 purple solid
I	12 purple print
J	12 purple print
K	12 purple print
L	12 green print
M	12 yellow

Center Medallion

Pattern Piece	Number of Pieces
B	4 light green mini dot
H	8 purple solid
I	8 purple print
J	8 purple print
K	8 purple print
M	8 yellow
N	1 white
O	8 dark green solid
P	8 medium green print

▦ BLUE

▨ LIGHT GREEN

▧ DARK GREEN

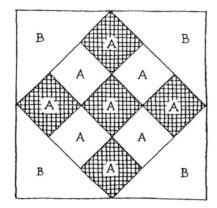

Piecing Diagram: Nine Patch

Bias Stems

Cut 1¼-inch bias strips from medium green print. Fold strips in half lengthwise, wrong sides together, and machine stitch ¼ inch from folded edge. Trim raw edges close to stitching and press strips so that seam is centered along back of stem. Cut stem sections as specified for each block:

> Four 2¾-inch strips ⅜-inch bias for diagonal stems
> Four 4¾-inch strips ⅜-inch bias for horizontal and vertical stems
> Twelve 6-inch strips of ⅜-inch bias for iris block stems

Borders

Inner Border:
> Two strips 2½ x 76½ inches purple solid
> Two strips 2½ x 96½ inches purple solid

Outer Border:
> Two strips 4½ x 84½ inches purple print
> Two strips 4½ x 100½ inches purple print

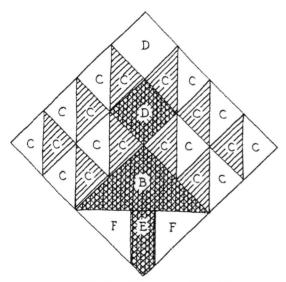

Piecing Diagram: Pine Tree

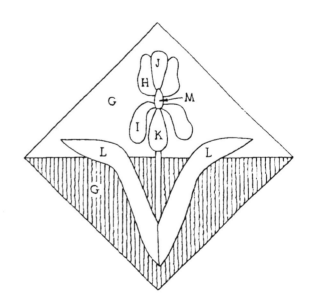

Appliqué Diagram: Iris Block

PIECING

Nine-Patch Block

1. Alternating blue and rose, sew together three rows of three A's (**Diagram 1**). Press seams open. Matching seams at intersections, sew rows together to make A unit. Press seams open.

2. Sew one B to upper left and one B to lower right sides of the A unit (**Diagram 2**). Press seams open. Sew one B to upper right and one B to lower left of A unit. Press seams open.

3. Repeat steps 1 and 2 for a total of twenty Nine-Patch blocks.

Pine Tree Block

4. Sew together one white C and one light green C to form a square (**Diagram 3**). Repeat for a total of ten C units. Press seams open.

5. Sew together the C units in two rows of three squares and two rows of two squares (**Diagram 4**). Make sure that rows are constructed so that triangles face in opposite directions as shown in the diagram. Press seams open.

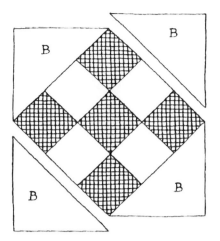

Diagram 2. Sew one B to the upper left and lower right sides of the A unit. Sew one B to upper right and lower left of A unit

Diagram 3. Sew together one white C and one colored C to form square

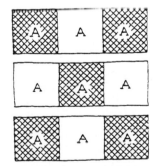

Diagram 1. Alternating blue and rose, sew three rows of three A pieces. Sew rows together

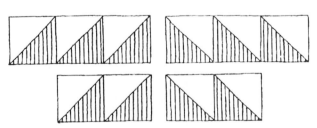

Diagram 4. Sew the C squares together in two rows of three and two rows of two, with the triangles facing in opposite directions as shown

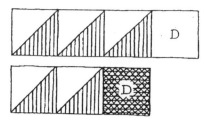

Diagram 5. Sew one white D to the right end of left-hand row of three C squares. Sew one dark green to right end of the row of two C squares

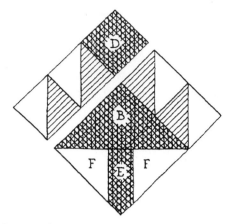

Diagram 7. Sew remaining row of two C squares to the right side of B-E-F unit. Sew C-D row to the left side of B-E-F unit

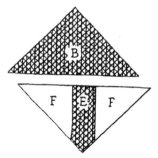

Diagram 6. Sew one F to the right and left sides of E. Sew dark B to top of E-F unit

Diagram 8. Sew the right-hand row of three C squares to the right side of the tree. Sew the remaining C-D unit to the left side of the tree

6. Sew one white D to right end of left-hand row of three C squares. Sew one dark green D to right end of left-hand row of two C squares **(Diagram 5)**. Press seams open.

7. Sew one F to the right and left sides of each E **(Diagram 6)**. Press seams open. Sew one dark B to the top of E-F unit. Press seams open.

8. Sew the remaining row of two C squares to the right side of the B-E-F unit. Press seam open. Matching seams at intersections, sew the C-D row to the left side of B-E-F unit **(Diagram 7)**. Press seams open.

9. Sew the right-hand row of three C squares (shown on right side in **Diagram 4**) to right side of tree, matching seams at intersections. Sew remaining C-D unit to left side of tree **(Diagram 8)**. Press seams open.

10. Repeat steps 4 through 9, for a total of twelve Pine Tree blocks.

APPLIQUÉ

Iris Block

11. Sew together one white G and one green mini-dot G to form a square. Press seam open.

12. Appliqué H and I and one 6-inch stem to G square (**Diagram 9**).

13. Appliqué pieces J, K, and L to the square. Appliqué M last (**Diagram 10**). Press square.

14. Repeat steps 11 through 13 for a total of twelve Iris blocks.

Center Medallion

15. Sew one green mini-dot B to each corner of N. Fold and finger-crease block lengthwise, widthwise, and diagonally (**Diagram 11**) to aid in flower placement.

16. Using **Diagram 12** as a guide, appliqué O leaves to block.

17. Appliqué 4¾-inch stems along horizontal and vertical creases. Align and appliqué 2¾-inch stems along diagonal creases, then appliqué P leaves (**Diagram12**).

18. Referring to **Appliqué Diagram: Center Medallion** on next page, appliqué iris flowers following procedure in Iris block section. Press block.

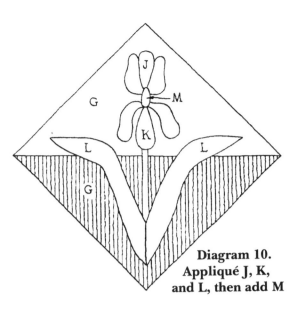

**Diagram 10.
Appliqué J, K,
and L, then add M**

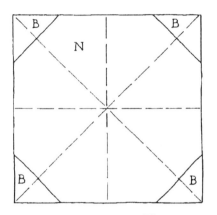

Diagram 11. Sew green B's to corners of N. Fold and crease N, as shown by dotted lines, to aid in placement

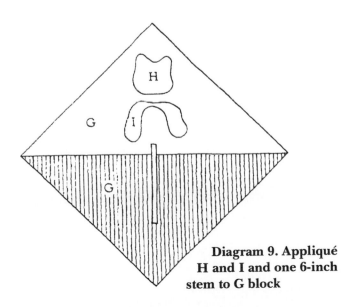

**Diagram 9. Appliqué
H and I and one 6-inch
stem to G block**

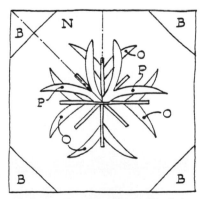

**Diagram 12. Appliqué O pieces
first, then stems, then P's**

Appliqué Diagram: Center Medallion

ASSEMBLY

19. Following **Order of Assembly Diagram**, sew together Nine-Patch blocks, Pine Tree blocks, Iris blocks, and Center Medallion in rows, matching seams at intersections. Press seams open. Matching seams at intersections, sew rows together. Press seams open.

20. Sew 96½-inch purple solid inner border strips to sides of quilt. Press seam toward border. Sew 76½-inch purple solid inner border strips to top and bottom of quilt. Press seams open.

21. Sew 100½-inch purple print outer border strips to sides of quilt. Press seams open. Sew 84½-inch purple print outer border strips to top and bottom of quilt.

22. Cut backing fabric lengthwise into three 90-inch sections. Trim selvages and sew sections together horizontally. Press seams open.

23. Proceed following directions for assembling the quilt top, batting, and back on page xx. Quilt is bound with bias binding.

QUILTING

24. The makers of this complex quilt enhanced its beauty with simple quilting "in the ditch" on the pieced and appliquéd blocks, and quilting straight lines in the borders.

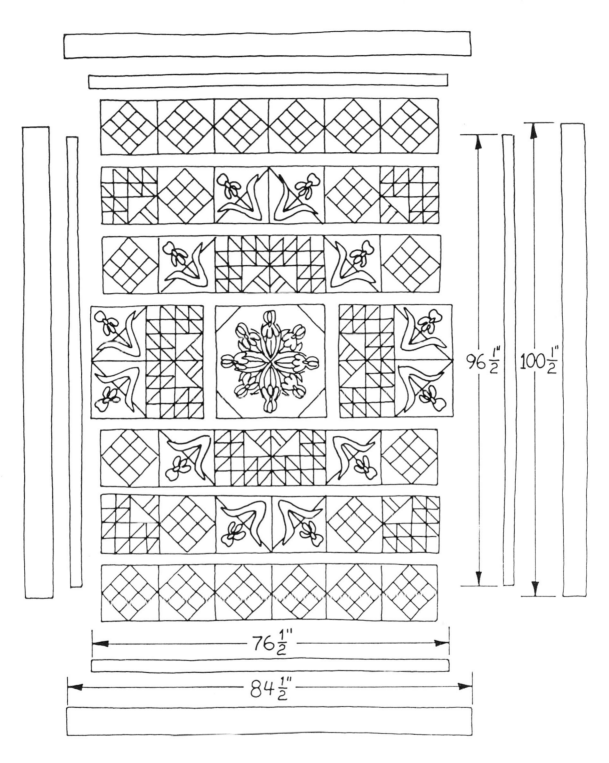

Order of Assembly Diagram

Iris Medallion

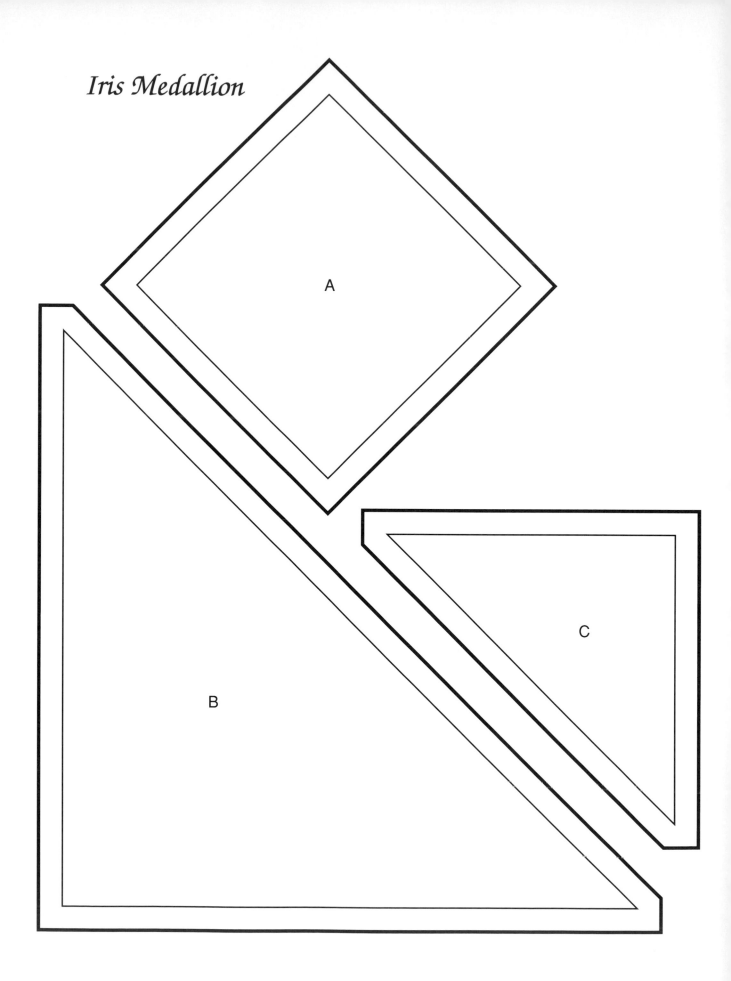

A

B

C

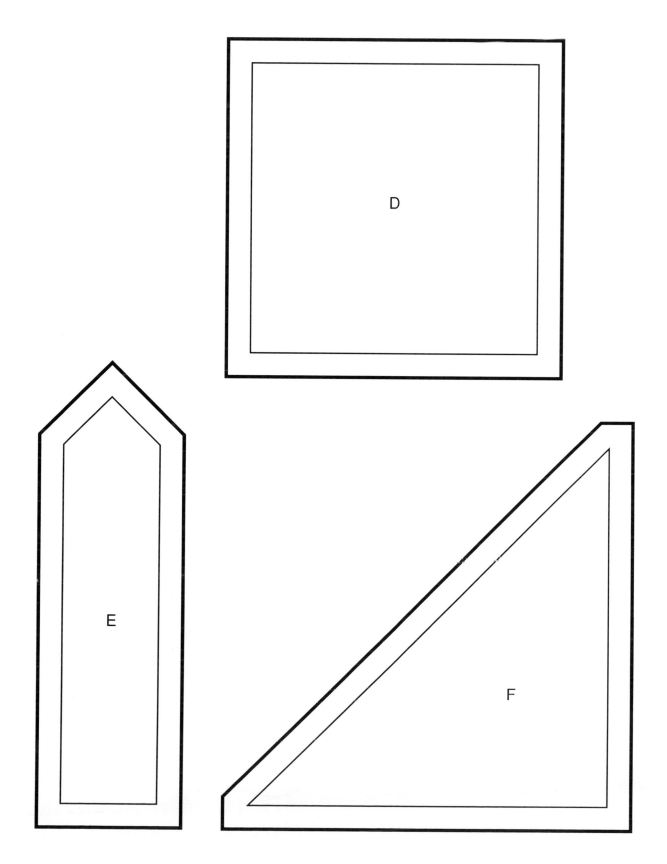

Iris Medallion

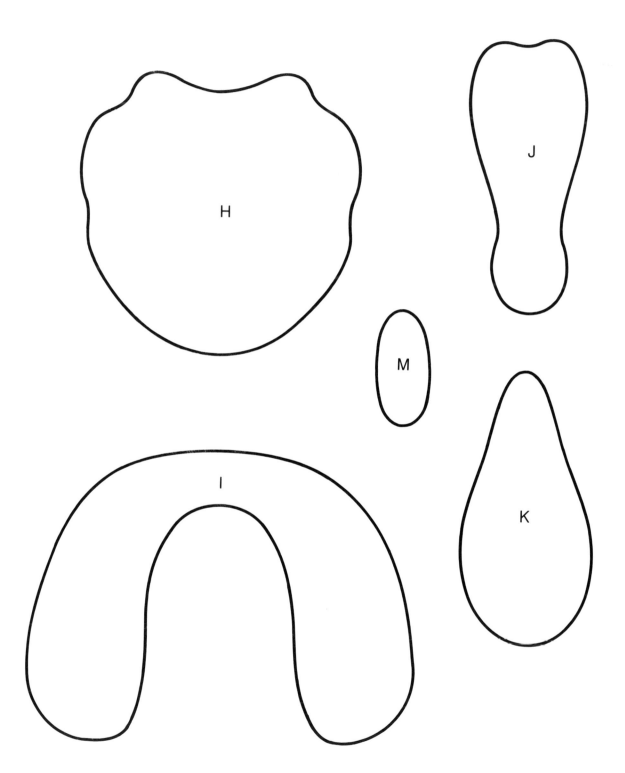

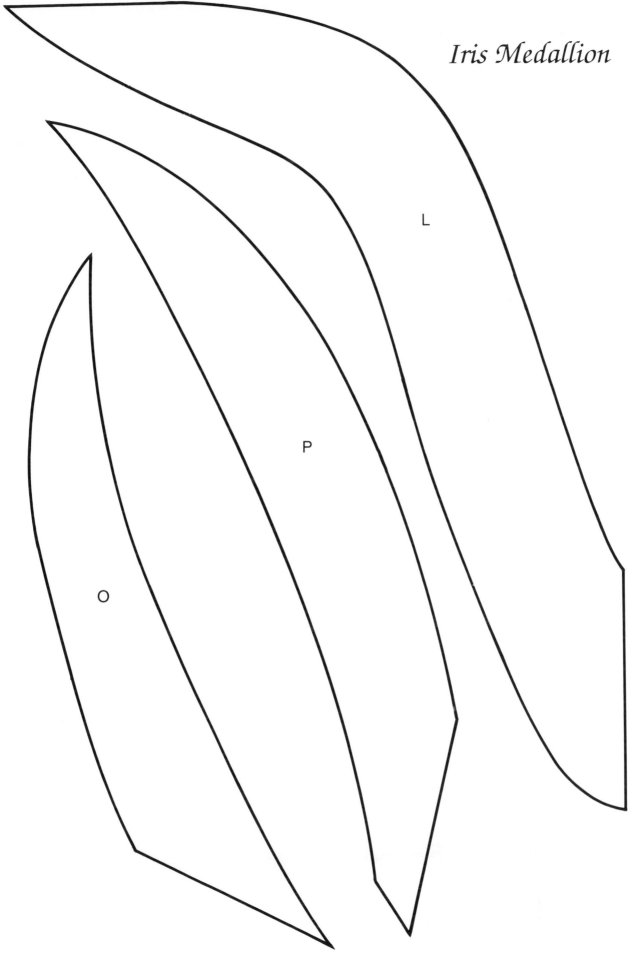

Iris Medallion

L

P

O

FARMER'S MARKET

COUNTRY VILLAGE

By Cheri Tamm Raymond

The richness and depth of 100 percent wool give this earthy wall hanging its subtle colors, texture, and dimension. For a different effect, feel free to choose other fabrics.

SIZE

• Finished wall hanging is 19 x 35 inches

MATERIALS

• ½ yard dark green for outer border
• ½ yard rust for inner borders, binding,
  chimney, and ground
• ½ yard pale green for background
• Scraps of white and other colors of choice for
  church, houses, windows, doors, and roofs
• 20 x 36-inch batt
• ⅔ yard fabric for back

CUTTING

Houses and Church: Cut from assorted scraps. The house chart below is for one house only because you may want to use different colors for the second house.

One House

Pattern Piece	Number of Pieces
A	1 background
B	2 (chimney)
C	2 background
D	1 background
E*	2 background
F	1 (roof)
G	1 (roof)
H	1 (roof)
I	1 (door)
J	1 (house)
K	2 (house)
L	1 (house) 2 (window)
M	2 (house)
N	1 (house)
O	1 (house)
P	1 (house)
Q	1 (house)
R	1 (ground)

Church

Pattern Piece	Number of Pieces
C	1 background
E*	2 background
F	1 (roof)
G	1 (roof)
H	1 (roof)
I	1 (door)
J	1 (church)
K	2 (church)
N	2 (church)
P	1 (church)
Q	1 (church)
R	1 (ground)
S	1 background
T	1 (steeple)
U	1 background
V	1 (steeple)
W	1 background
X	1 (church) 2 (window)
Y	2 (church)

* Cut E pieces from folded fabric so pieces face
in opposite directions.

Outer Borders

Two strips dark green 3½ x 35½ inches
Two strips dark green 3½ x 13½ inches

Inner Borders

Two strips rust 1 x 29½ inches
Two strips rust 1 x 12½ inches

Sashes

Two strips pale green 1½ x 28½ inches
Four strips pale green 1½ x 10½ inches

Chimney Section

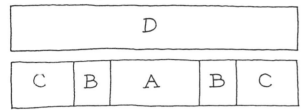

**Diagram 1. Sew together A, B, and C
in a row. Sew D to top of unit**

Roof Section

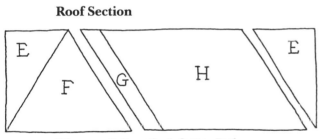

**Diagram 2. Sew the left E to F, then sew
together G, H, and the right E in a row**

Door Section

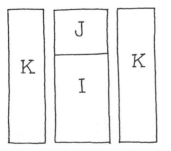

**Diagram 3. Sew together I and J.
Sew K to each side**

PIECING

Note: The chimney sections for the houses were pieced differently in the photograph than shown in the Piecing Diagram. Please use patterns provided and follow instructions and Piecing Diagram (which match each other) and results will look the same.

House

The quilter decided to make the house on the left with one chimney instead of two. She also positioned the pieces so the house would face right instead of left. This was done by flipping patterns G and H when cutting out the fabric.

1. To piece chimney section, sew together A, B, and C pieces in a row as shown **(Diagram 1)**. Press seams open. Sew D to top of the A-B-C unit. Press seam open.

2. To piece the roof, sew left E to F, then sew G, H, and right E together **(Diagram 2)**. Press seams open. Sew both sections together to make roof. Press seam open.

3. Piece door by sewing together I and J **(Diagram 3)**. Press seam open. Sew a K to each side of I-J unit. Press seams open.

4. Piece window section by sewing together L and M pieces in a row as shown in **Diagram 4**. Press seams open. Sew N to top of L-M unit. Sew O to bottom of L-M unit. Press seams open.

Window Section

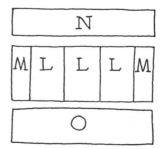

**Diagram 4. Sew together L and M
in a row. Add N and O**

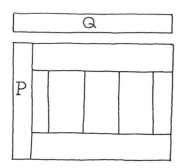

Diagram 5. Sew P to left side and Q to top of window section

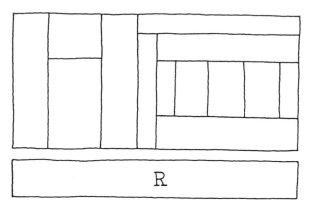

Diagram 6. Sew the door and window sections together

5. Sew P to left side of windows, then sew Q to top (**Diagram 5**). Press seams open after each step.

6. Sew door section to left side of window section (**Diagram 6**). Press seams open. Sew R to bottom. Press seams open.

7. Referring to **House Piecing Diagram**, sew roof to top of door-window unit. Press seam open. Sew chimney to top of roof. Press seam open.

8. Repeat steps 1 through 7 to complete second house block. You may decide to reverse the position of the second house and eliminate one chimney, as was done on the quilt in the photograph.

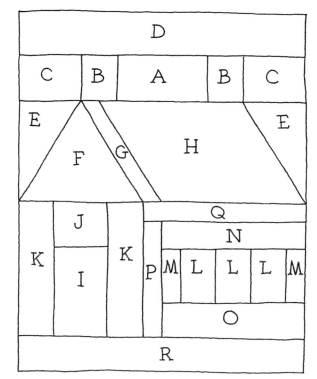

House Piecing Diagram

Church

9. To piece steeple, sew S to left side of T, then U to right side of T to make a row **(Diagram 7)**. Press seams open after each step.

10. Sew C to one side of V and W to opposite side of V to make second row of steeple section **(Diagram 8)**. Press seams open.

11. Sew S-T-U unit to top of C-V-W unit to make steeple section **(Diagram 9)**. Press seam open.

12. To make roof, sew together E, F, G, and H in the same manner as for house roof in step 2.

13. To make door, follow instructions for house door, sewing together I, J, and K as in step 3.

14. Piece window section by sewing together Y and X pieces in a row as shown in **Diagram 10**. Press seams open. Sew one N to top of X-Y unit and one N to bottom. Press seams open.

15. Sew P to left side of window. Press seam open. Sew Q to top of window **(Diagram 11)**. Press seam open.

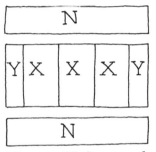

Diagram 9. Sew together S-T-U and C-V-W units

Window Section

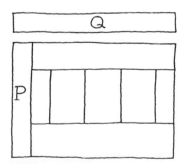

Diagram 10. Sew together X's and Y's in a row. Add N's to top and bottom

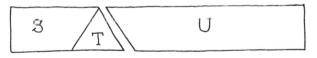

Diagram 7. Sew together S, T, and U in a row

Diagram 8. Sew together C, V, and W in a row

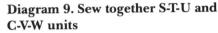

Diagram 11. Sew P to the left side and Q to the top of the window section

16. Referring to **Church Piecing Diagram**, sew door section to left side of window. Press seam open. Sew R to bottom of door-window unit. Press seam open.

17. Referring to **Church Piecing Diagram**, sew roof to top of door-window unit, then sew steeple section to top of roof. Press seams open.

ASSEMBLY

18. Sew a 1½ x 10½-inch sash between the blocks to make a row of house-church blocks. Sew one 1½ x 10½-inch sash to each end of the house-church row as shown in **Diagram 12**. Press seams open. Sew 1½ x 28½-inch sashes to top and bottom of blocks. Press seams open.

19. Sew short inner borders, 1 x 12½ inches, to opposite sides of center section. Press seams open. Then sew long inner borders, 1 x 29½ inches, to top and bottom of center section. Press seams open (**Diagram12**).

20. Sew short outer borders, 3½ x 13½ inches, to opposite sides of center section. Press seams open. Sew long outer borders, 3½ x 35½ inches, to top and bottom of center section to complete. Press seams open (**Diagram 12**).

21. Proceed following instructions for assembling the quilt, on page xx. The wall hanging is bound with 2-inch wide strips of rust fabric (see page xxiii).

QUILTING

22. Quilt as desired. Country Village was quilted with simple outline quilting on the church and house blocks. Outer borders were quilted with hearts, vines, and leaves.

Church Piecing Diagram

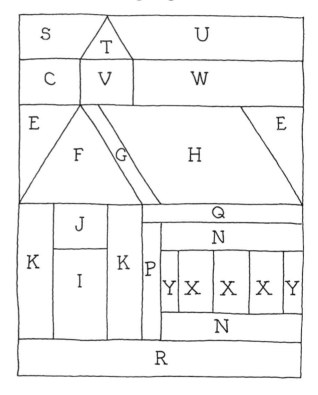

Diagram 12. Sew small sashes between the house and church blocks and on both ends of the row. Sew long sashes to top and bottom of the house-church row. Add inner and outer borders

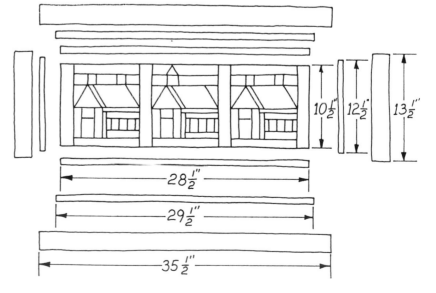

Country Village

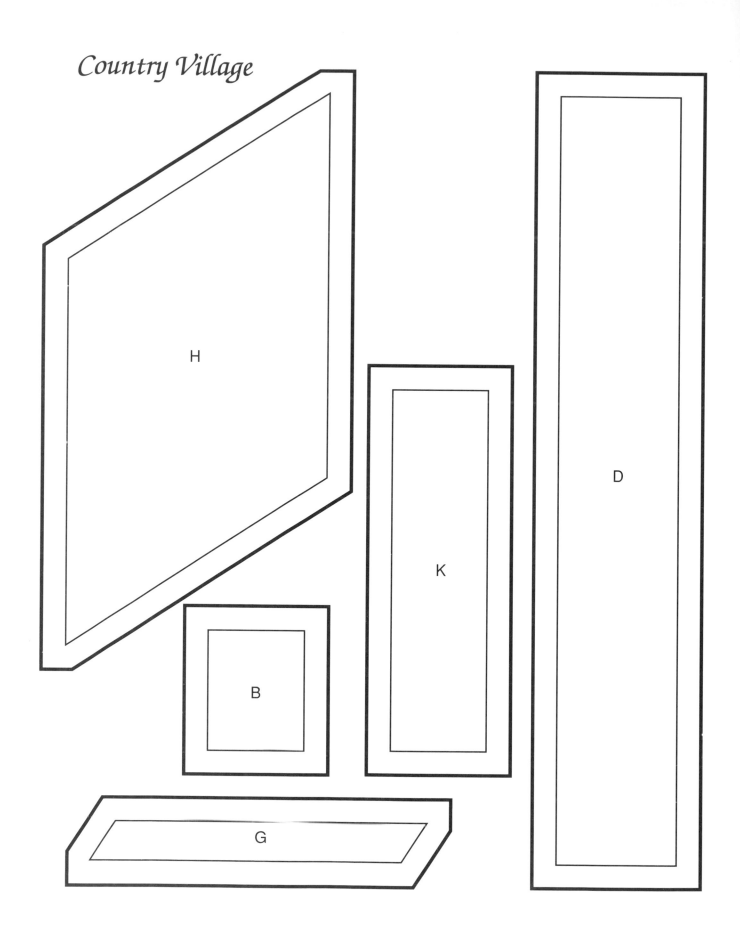

H

D

K

B

G

204

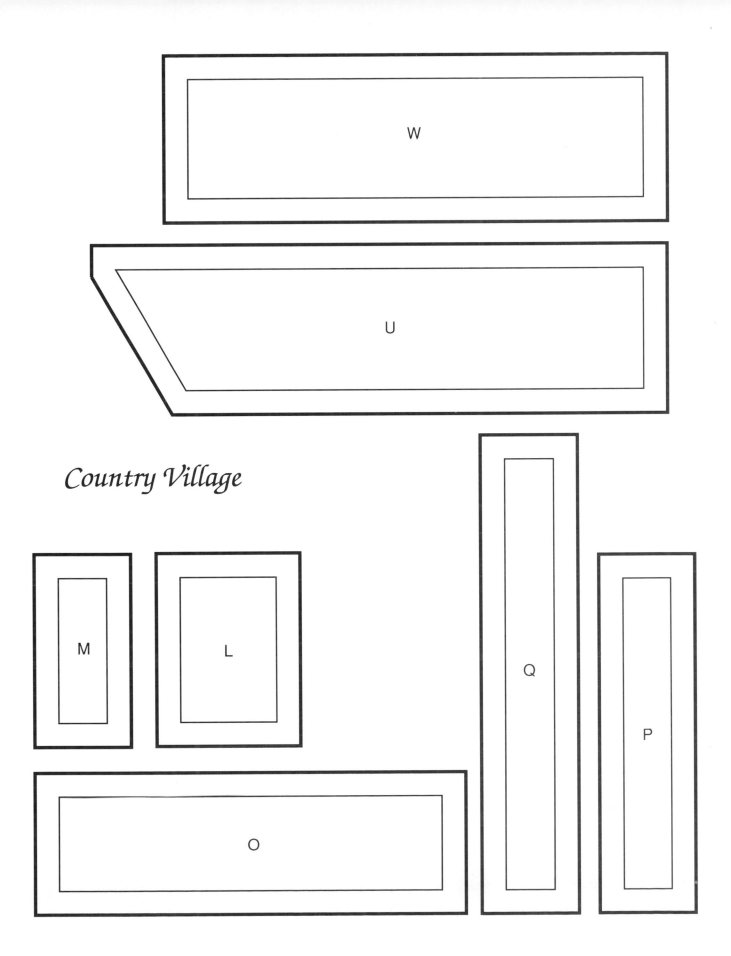

Country Village

Country Village

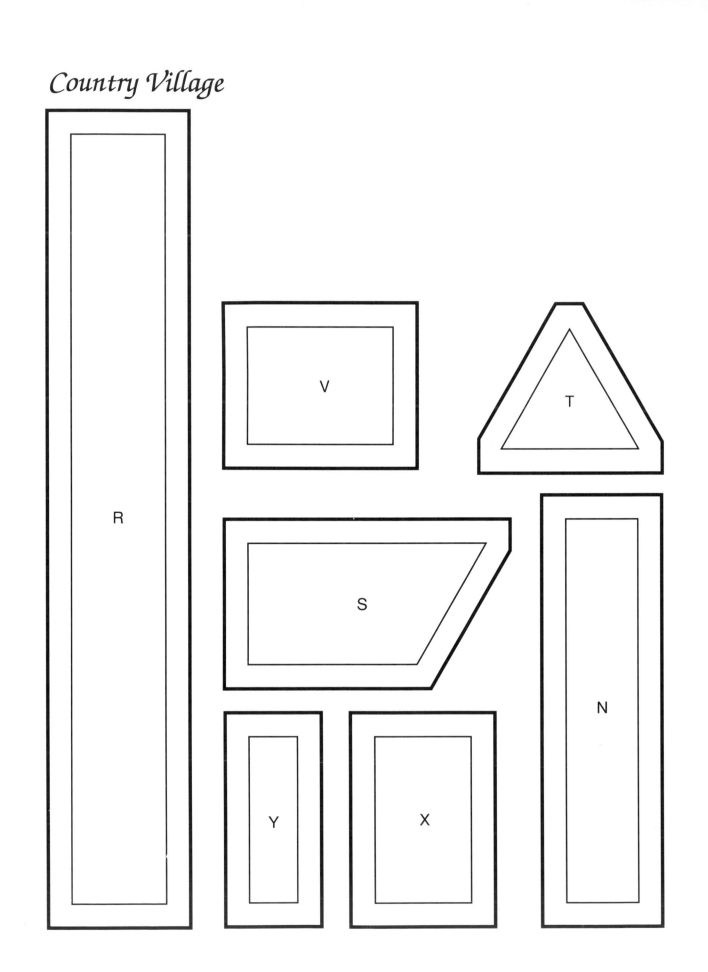

QUILTED BEDSIDE POCKET

By Anna Mae Schack

Here's a bedside pocket you can make to hold a book or a small needlework project. It slips between the mattress and springs and puts your book or needlework within easy reach. Make it in colors that match your decor or in any color scheme you fancy, since the pocket is hidden when the bed is made.

There are two versions for you to choose from, one with a sunrise pattern, the other with an appliquéd heart and leaves motif. If you can't decide between the two, make one for yourself and the other as a gift.

Piecing Diagrams

Sunrise   Heart and Leaves

SIZE
The finished piece is 10 x 22 inches; the pocket section is 7 x 10 inches

MATERIALS
- Scraps of assorted colors
- ⅔ yard background fabric
- 2 ¼ yards of 2-inch bias strip in same or contrasting color for each bedside pocket design
- One 10½ x 22½-inch and one 7½ x 10½-inch piece of batting for each design
- 10-inch length of brown 4-ply yarn for Heart and Leaves design
- Freezer paper for Heart and Leaves appliqués

CUTTING: SUNRISE

Pattern Piece	Number of Pieces
A	1 gold
B,C,D,E,F	1 of each in assorted colors

One 7½ x 10½-inch rectangle of background color

Two 10½ x 22½-inch rectangles of background color

CUTTING : HEART AND LEAVES

The heart and leaves are cut using the freezer paper appliqué method (see page xvii). The heart can be cut from previously pieced patchwork.

Pattern Piece	Number of Pieces
A	1 color (or piece of patchwork)
B	4 green

Two 7½ x 10½-inch rectangles of background color

Two 10½ x 22½-inch rectangles of background color

SUNRISE PIECING

1. Sew pieces B, C, D, E, and F together so they fan out in the order indicated in the **Piecing Diagram**. Press seams open.

2. Pin the curved edge of A to the inside curve of section B-C-D-E-F completed above so the notches on A match the seams between B, C, D, E, and F. To help ease the curves when sewing them together, clip the seam allowance between the notches on the inside curve of the B-C-D-E-F section up to, but not through, the seam line. Sew the two curves together, turning the work as you go. Carefully press the seam away from A.

SUNRISE ASSEMBLY

3. Lay out the 7½ x 10½-inch fabric rectangle with the right side down. Place the piece of batting of the same size on top. With the right side up, place the Sunrise section on top of the batting. Pin and stitch the three layers together ⅛ inch from the outside edge.

4. Using a ½-inch seam, sew a 7½-inch piece of 2-inch bias strip to the right side of the top edge of the Sunrise. Fold the binding over to the back, turn under ½ inch, and hand stitch the binding to the back with a blind stitch **(Diagram 1)**.

5. Lay out one of the 10½ x 22½-inch fabric rectangles with the right side down. Place the piece of batting of the same size on top. With the right side up, place the second rectangle on top of the batting. Pin the three layers together

around the outside edge. Quilt the three layers together by hand or machine, using rows of stitching in straight lines or in a grid pattern of squares or diamonds.

6. Place the Sunrise section at one end and on top of the larger rectangle. Line up the bottom and side edges of both pieces so they match. Pin the Sunrise section to the bottom end of the larger rectangle. Trim all four corners to round them off. Sew both sections together as you sew around the entire edge of the larger rectangle **(Diagram 2)**.

7. Using a ½-inch seam, sew the remaining piece of bias binding to the right side and around the entire edge of the finished piece. Fold the binding over to the back, turn under ½ inch, and hand stitch the binding to the back with a blind stitch.

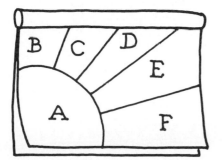

Diagram 1. Sew bias binding to top edge of pocket

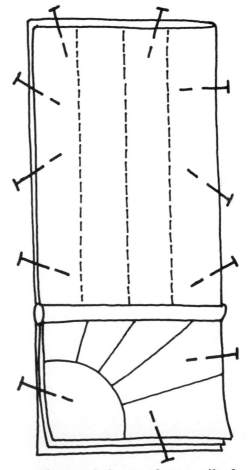

Diagram 2. Sew pocket to quilted rectangle

Diagram 3. Use couching stitch to create stems

Couching

HEART AND LEAVES APPLIQUÉ

1. Using the **Piecing Diagram** as a guide, place the heart and leaves patterns in position on the right side of one 7½ x 10½-inch rectangle. Lightly trace around them with a pencil and remove.

2. To make the stems, cut the yarn into two even pieces and pin them in place on the right side of the rectangle, referring to **Piecing Diagram** for placement. Allow the ends to extend over the pencil lines marking the edges of the leaves and heart. Couch the stems in place using thread of same or contrasting color **(Diagram 3)**.

3. With the right side up, pin the heart in place in the center of the rectangle so it covers the ends of the stems. Clip the seam allowance at the center-top of heart up to the freezer paper. Turning the edges under as you go, stitch the heart in place by hand using a blind stitch.

4. Sew the leaves in place in the same way and so the top leaves cover the other ends of the stems.

5. To finish the Heart and Leaves design, proceed with step 3 of the Sunrise design. Use the 7½ x 10½-inch rectangle appliquéd with heart and leaves in place of the Sunrise section in those steps.

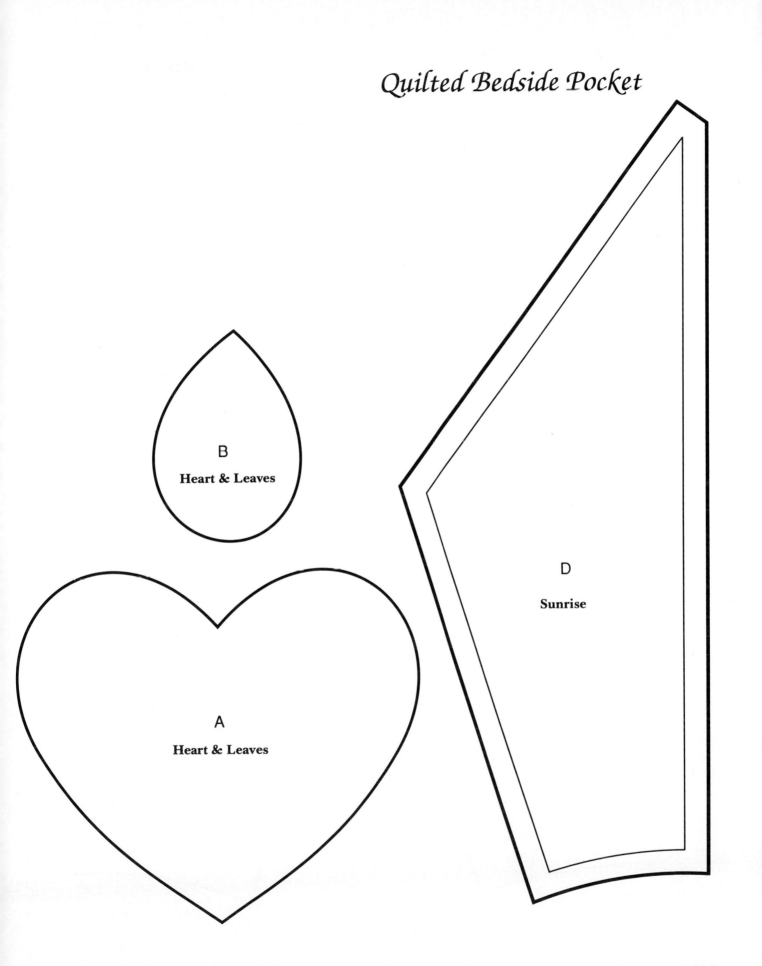

B

Heart & Leaves

D

Sunrise

A

Heart & Leaves

Quilted Bedside Pocket

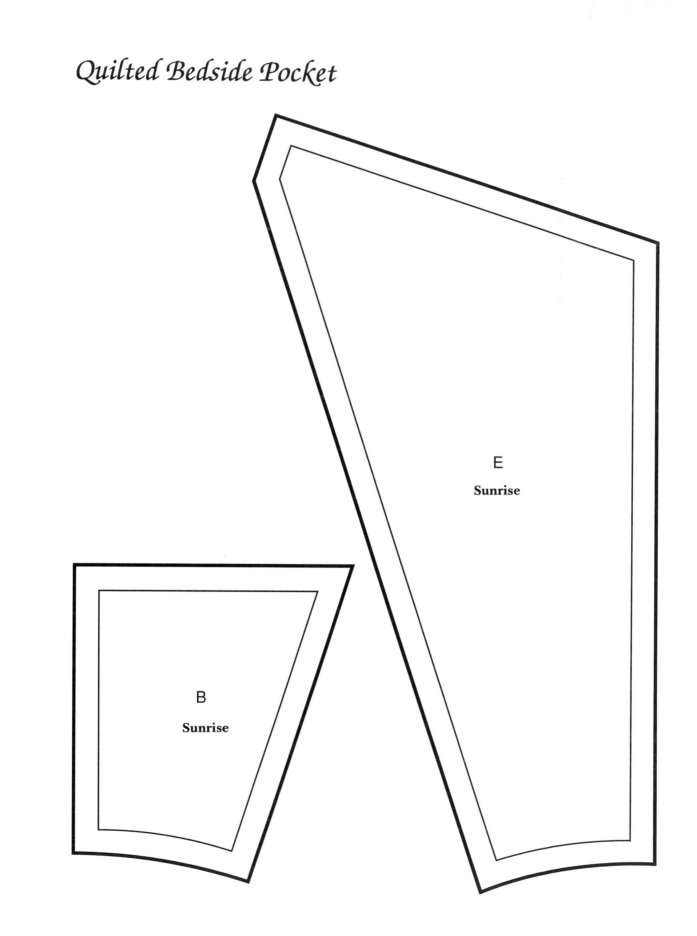

E

Sunrise

B

Sunrise

Quilted Bedside Pocket

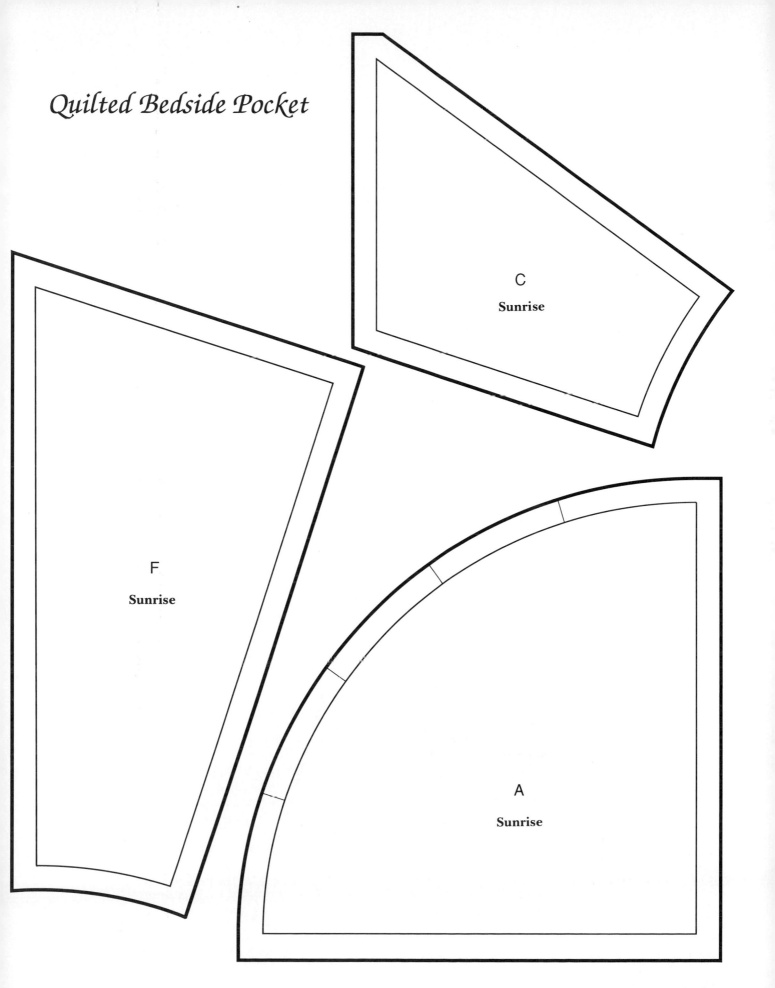

C
Sunrise

F
Sunrise

A
Sunrise

CRAZY CAT

By Dee Danley-Brown

This favorite folk art critter will nestle cozily in the corner of a couch, on the bed, or in a baby's crib.

SIZE

Finished cat is 16 inches tall by 11 inches wide

MATERIALS

- ½ yard muslin
- ½ yard print fabric for back, head, and base
- Scraps of print fabrics for crazy patches and heart
- Fusible webbing
- Fabric pens or embroidery floss for face
- One package piping in coordinating color
- Stuffing
- 1 yard ribbon

CUTTING

Pattern Piece	Number of Pieces
Cat body and head	1 muslin
Cat head	1 print
Cat base*	1 print
Heart	1 print
Crazy patches**	assorted prints
Cat back	1 print (cut after completing cat front)

*Note: Fold fabric in half two times, align fold lines on pattern with fold lines on fabric, and cut.

**Note: See step 3 before cutting crazy patches. Use odd, irregular patch shapes, varying from 1 to 3 inches in size.

PIECING AND APPLIQUÉ

1. Make body pattern for muslin foundation by drawing a 10 x 11-inch rectangle on graph paper (**Diagram 1**). Mark 5½ inches up on left side and 6 inches in from top right corner, then draw curve between the two marks as shown. Add ¼ inch seam allowance to all sides, except neckline. Trace cat head pattern without neckline seam allowance and tape to cat body, matching necklines, and cut out pattern (**Diagram 2**).

2. Cut one full cat shape out of muslin for body foundation.

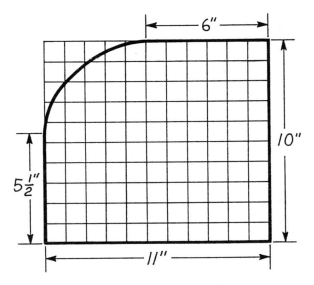

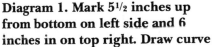

Diagram 1. Mark 5½ inches up from bottom on left side and 6 inches in on top right. Draw curve

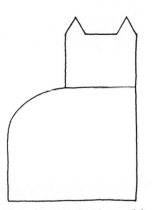

Diagram 2. Join body and head pattern, matching seamlines at neck

3. Apply fusible webbing to wrong side of assorted fabric scraps for crazy patches. Arrange scraps in a crazy-quilt design over the muslin body foundation of the cat to the neckline (**Diagram 3**). Patches should be cut so that they overlap a fraction of an inch on all sides. When all patches are in place, fuse to muslin foundation.

4. Embroider or satin stitch, by hand or machine, over all edges where patches meet. Fuse and appliqué heart to front.

5. Place print cat head on muslin foundation, so that neckline covers neckline on body. Satin stitch over neckline (**Diagram 4**).

6. Trace oval face and features onto a piece of muslin, then embroider or draw features. Apply fusible webbing to wrong side and cut out oval. Fuse to cat head and embroider or satin stitch by machine around the edge of the oval (**Diagram 5**).

7. Make two small fabric circles for cheeks, fuse to face, and satin stitch around edges.

ASSEMBLY

8. Place finished cat front right side up on wrong side of backing fabric. Cut out cat back to match front.

9. Starting at right bottom corner, sewing across bottom and up left side, sew piping around outside edge of cat front on right side. Leave enough piping to go across bottom back (**Diagram 6**). Clip curves where necessary to turn corners.

10. With right sides facing, sew front and back together, working from one bottom corner up one side, across top, and down to other corner.

11. Sew the base to the bottom front and back, inserting piping as you sew. Leave an opening for stuffing. Clip curves and trim where necessary.

12. Turn cat right side out, stuff, and slipstitch opening closed. Tie ribbon around the neck.

Diagram 5. Fuse and appliqué oval face onto print head

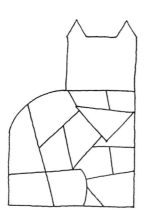

Diagram 3. Add crazy patches up to neckline on muslin foundation

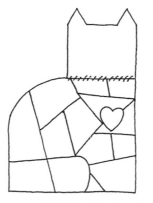

Diagram 4. Add print for head and satin stitch over neckline

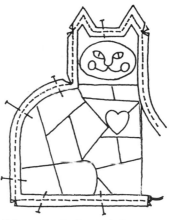

Diagram 6. Sew piping to outside edges, leaving enough to go across bottom back

Crazy Cat

Fold Line

Base

Fold Line

PATCHWORK BOXES

By Cheri Tamm Raymond

These beautiful covered boxes are easy to make and a delight to use. You'll want to make boxes of various sizes to give as gifts or to store your trinkets and desktop paraphernalia. Other patchwork or appliquéd squares may be substituted for the box tops shown here.

SIZE

Maple Leaf and Churn Dash boxes are
   5 x 5 x 3 inches high

Log Cabin box is 5 x 5 x 5 inches high

MATERIALS (for each box)

- ¼ yard fabric for outer box
- ¼ yard fabric for box lining
- ⅜ yard polyester fleece
- Scraps of fabric for patchwork (see Cutting for three different box top designs)
- 12 x 18-inch piece heavy cardboard (mat board weight)
- 12 x 18-inch piece light cardboard (poster weight)
- White craft glue
- Scrap of ½-inch ribbon for tab
- Masking tape

CUTTING

MAPLE LEAF

Pattern Piece	Number of Pieces
A	4 light 4 dark
B	1 light 3 dark
C	2 light
D	1 dark
E	2 of outer box fabric
F	2 of outer box fabric

CHURN DASH

Pattern Piece	Number of Pieces
A	1 light
B	4 light 4 dark
C	4 light 4 dark
D	2 of outer box fabric
E	2 of outer box fabric

(Maple Leaf and Churn Dash Cutting continued)

Heavy cardboard for outer box sections
    Two 5-inch squares
    Four 5 x 3-inch rectangles

Light cardboard for lining sections
    Two 4 ¾-inch squares
    Four 2 ¾ x 4 ¾-inch rectangles

Outer box fabric
    One 6-inch square
    One 4 ¾ x 21½-inch rectangle

Box lining fabric
    Two 6-inch squares
    Four 4 x 6-inch rectangles

Assorted scraps as necessary for patchwork design

LOG CABIN

Pattern Piece	Number of Pieces
A	1
B	1
C	2
D	1
E	1
F	2
G	1

Heavy Cardboard for outer box sections
    Six 5-inch squares

Light cardboard for lining sections
    Six 4 ¾-inch squares

Outer box fabric
    One 6-inch square (box bottom)

Box lining fabric
    Six 6-inch squares

Assorted fabrics to make five Log Cabin blocks

MAPLE LEAF BOX TOP

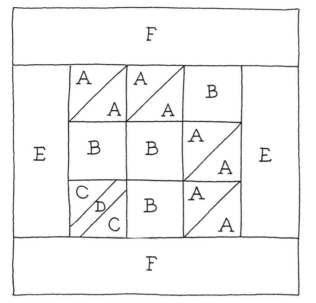

Piecing Diagram

**Diagram 1. Sew together one light
A and one dark A to make a square**

PIECING

Maple Leaf Box Top

1. Sew together one light A and one dark A to make a square (**Diagram 1**). Repeat for a total of four A squares. Press seams open.

2. Sew together two squares for top of leaf (**Diagram 2**). Press seams open.

3. Sew one C to each side of D to make a square (**Diagram 3**). Press seams open.

4. Sew A, B, and C-D squares together into rows as shown (**Diagram 4**). Press seams open.

5. Matching seams at intersections, sew together rows to make Maple Leaf block. Press seams open.

6. Referring to **Piecing Diagram**, sew E's to opposite sides of Maple Leaf block. Press seams open.

7. Referring to **Piecing Diagram** sew F's to top and bottom of Maple Leaf block. Press seams open.

8. Proceed to Box Assembly section.

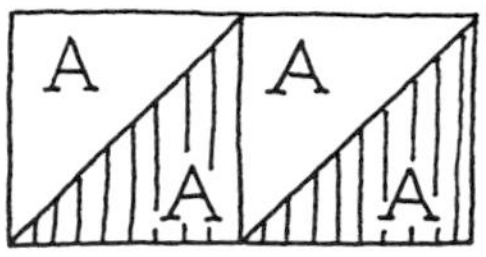

**Diagram 2. Sew together two
A squares for each side of leaf**

**Diagram 3. Sew one
C to each side of D**

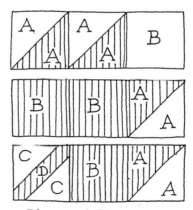

**Diagram 4. Sew squares
together into rows**

CHURN DASH BOX TOP

1. Sew together one light B and one dark B to make a square (**Diagram 1**). Repeat for a total of four B units. Press seams open.

2. Sew together one light C and one dark C to make a square (**Diagram 2**). Repeat for a total of four C units. Press seams open.

3. With A in the center of middle row, sew together B squares and C squares to make three rows as shown (**Diagram 3**). Press seams open.

4. Matching seams at intersections, sew the rows together to make the Churn Dash block. Press seams open.

5. Referring to **Piecing Diagram** sew D's to top and bottom of Churn Dash block. Press seams open.

6. Referring to **Piecing Diagram**, sew E's to opposite sides of Churn Dash block. Press seams open.

7. Proceed to Box Assembly section.

Diagram 1. Sew together one light B and one dark B to make a square

Diagram 2. Sew together one light C and one dark C to make a square

CHURN DASH BOX

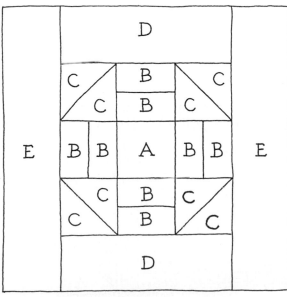

Piecing Diagram

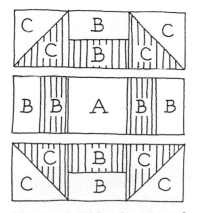

Diagram 3. With A in center of middle row, sew together squares as shown to make three rows

LOG CABIN

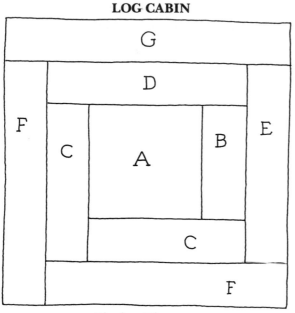

Piecing Diagram

Following instructions, make five Log Cabin blocks.

1. Sew one B to right side of A (**Diagram 1**). Press seam open.

2. Sew one C to bottom of A-B unit, then second C to left side of A-B-C unit (**Diagram 2**). Press each seam open before sewing next piece to unit.

3. Referring to the **Piecing Diagram**, continue sewing D, E, F, and G pieces to the block in the same manner, pressing seams open as you work.

4. After completing five Log Cabin blocks, sew together four Log Cabin blocks, using 1/2-inch seam allowance, to make box sides section (**Diagram 3**). Press seams open.

5. Proceed to Box Assembly section.

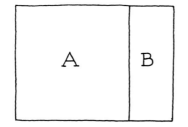

Diagram 1. Sew B to right side of A

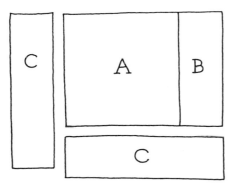

Diagram 2. Sew one C to bottom of A-B unit, then second C to left side of A-B-C unit

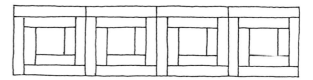

Diagram 3. Sew together four blocks as shown, using 1/2-inch seam allowance

BOX ASSEMBLY

Note: Each box is actually a box within a box. The inner box serves as a lining and provides a finished look to the inside.

Basic Box Preparation

Spread a thin layer of white glue on one side of all cut-out cardboard pieces and place, glue side down, on polyester fleece. When dry, cut out, following cardboard edges. For each box, cut one extra 5-inch square of fleece to double-pad the box top, but do not glue.

Small Boxes

1. To make outer box sides, lay out heavy cardboard rectangles or squares with fleece-padding side down and short edges touching. Tape edges together with a 3-inch piece of masking tape. Place box sides, padding side down, on wrong side of 4¾ x 21½-inch fabric rectangle (**Diagram 1**).

2. Fold in and glue down corners of fabric to the cardboard. Fold in and glue down top, bottom, and sides, mitering all corners (**Diagram 2**). Set aside to dry.

3. To make outer box bottom, place 5-inch heavy cardboard square, fleece-padding side down, on wrong side of 6-inch fabric square, fold over and glue down all sides, mitering corners.

4. To make outer box top, smooth extra 5-inch padding square on top of glued padding. Place double-padded side down on wrong side of patchwork square, centering patchwork design. Fold in and glue down all sides, mitering corners.

Box Lining

To make lining, use lightweight cardboard pieces for box top, bottom, and sides and cover each piece separately with box lining fabric. Mitering corners, fold edges over to other side and glue (**Diagram 3**).

5. Center and glue side lining pieces, right sides up, to the inside of box sides. Leave ⅛-inch space between each lining piece. Set aside to dry.

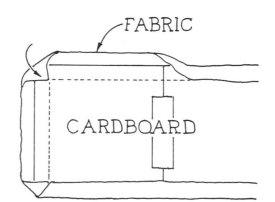

Diagram 2. Miter box top corners

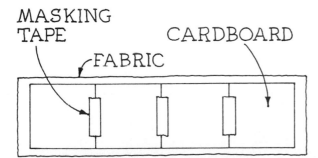

Diagram 1. Tape short edges of box sides and place on wrong side of fabric, padding down

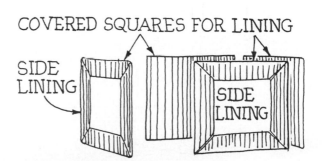

Diagram 3. Glue box side lining pieces to inside of box sides

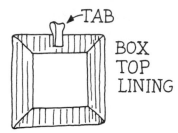

Diagram 4. Glue box top pieces together with tab between

Diagram 5. Blindstitch sides of box together

Diagram 6. Blindstitch box top to box side

6. Glue box bottom lining, right side up, to box bottom leaving ¹/₈-inch around all sides. Before gluing box top and lining together, fold a 1¹/₂-inch strip of ribbon in half and center on inside edge of box top to make lift tab **(Diagram 4)**. Glue box top lining, right side up, to inside box top, leaving ¹/₈ inch around all sides with the tab between as shown.

7. Fold box side piece to form a square and blindstitch short ends together, hiding beginning and ending knots within the fabric **(Diagram 5)**.

8. Blindstitch box bottom to all four lower edges of box sides.

9. Blindstitch edge opposite tab on box top to upper edge of one side to make a hinge for box top **(Diagram 6)**.

Large Box

Follow instructions for assembling small box, substituting larger box cardboard pieces and pieced Log Cabin sides as appropriate.

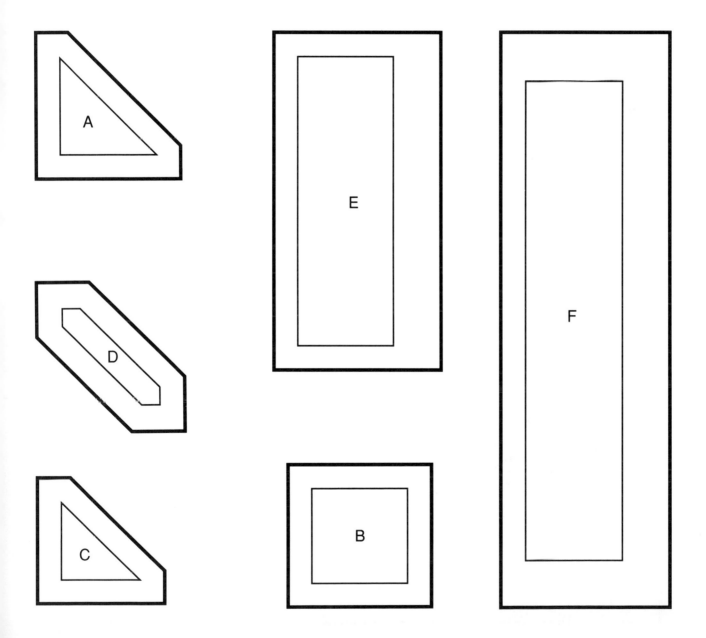

Churn Dash Box

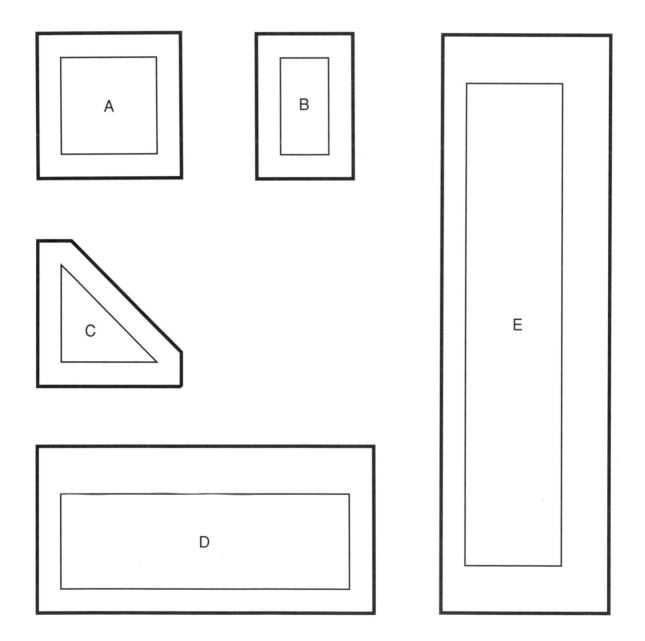

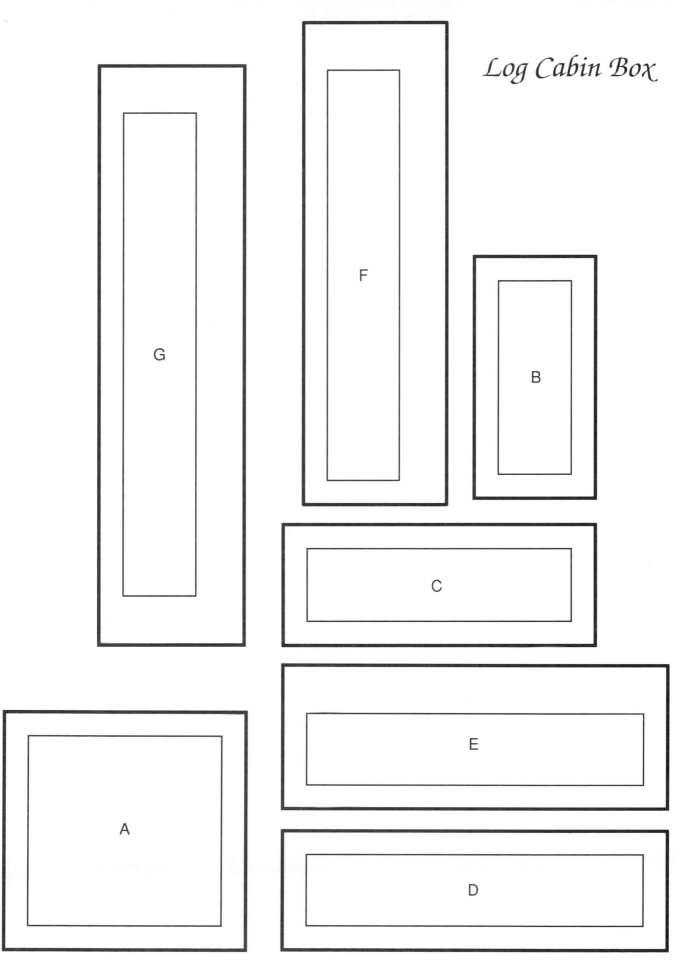

Log Cabin Box

SHADOW QUILTED COIN PURSE

By Sheri Kawahara-Fisher

Shadow quilting is a simple form of appliqué. The sheer overlay softens the colors of the fabric, creating a subtle effect that's perfect for wedding or baby gifts or for a romantic accent on accessories in the bedroom. Start with this easy coin purse; once you see how shadow quilting works, you'll find all sorts of applications.

SIZE

Purse measures 4 inches deep by 4 ¾ inches wide

MATERIALS

- 5¼ x 12¼-inch piece white cotton fabric
- 5¼ x 12¼-inch piece white organdy (sheer fabric)
- 5¼ x 12¼-inch piece coordinating lining fabric
- 5¼ x 12¼-inch piece polyester fleece
- Scraps of red, pink, and green fabric for appliqué
- One ¼-inch snap
- Water-soluble gluestick or fusible webbing

CUTTING

Pattern Piece	Number of Pieces
A	1 pink
B	1 red
C	2 green

On cotton, organdy, lining, and fleece, curve two corners as shown in **Diagram 1**.

ASSEMBLY

1. Using patterns, cut out flower or heart appliqué pieces, without seam allowances, and lightly tack or fuse in place on white cotton. Use photos as guides for placement.

2. Layer materials in the following order: polyester fleece, white cotton (with flower appliqué right side up), sheer fabric, then lining fabric with right side down.

3. Sew ¼-inch seam allowance around all edges, leaving a 2-inch opening for turning **(Diagram 1)**.

Coin Purse

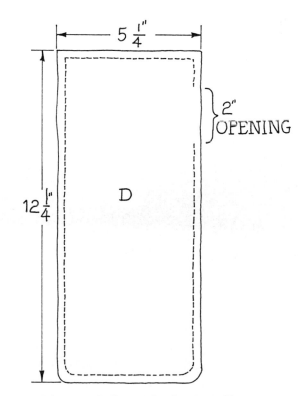

Diagram 1. Sew ¼-inch seam allowance around the edges, leaving opening

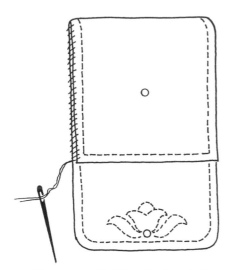

Diagram 2. Fold and slipstitch sides closed by hand. Add snaps

4. Clip corners, and trim seams if necessary. Turn purse right side out so that sheer fabric lies over the flower appliqué. Press purse lightly and slip stitch opening closed.

5. Hand stitch around all flower parts and heart in contrasting thread, being sure to stitch through all layers. Topstitch around coin purse, ¼ inch from outer edge.

6. Fold bottom up 4 inches to form purse and slip stitch both sides closed. Hand sew snap to purse (**Diagram 2**).

Heart Appliqué Pattern

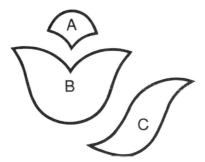

Flower Appliqué Pattern

CAROLINA BASKETS

By Karen Felicity Berkenfeld

This quilt was commissioned by Carolina, a restaurant in New York City, and hangs there now. The gray background is unusual and especially lovely combined with pink, but the pattern will work well with any contrasting colors.

SIZE

Block is 8⅛ inches square
Finished quilt is 68 x 80 inches

MATERIALS

- 2 yards light fabric
- 10 yards dark fabric (includes fabric for back of quilt and binding)
- 6 yards 1½-inch-wide light bias for ½-inch binding for 20 basket handles (F)
- Twin-size batting
- Templates for
  G: 8 ⅝ inches square
  H: 9 x 9 x 12 ¾-inch right triangle
  I: 6½ x 6½ x 9½-inch right triangle
  (all include seam allowance)

CUTTING

Block

Pattern Piece	Number of Pieces
A	220 light 100 dark
B	20 dark
C	40 dark
D	20 dark
E	20 dark
F	20 light
G	20 dark
H	14 dark
I	4 dark

Borders

Two strips 2½ x 58 inches, light
Two strips 2½ x 50½ inches, light
Two strips 9½ x 62 inches, dark
Two strips 9½ x 68½ inches, dark

PIECING

Basket Blocks

1. Sew one light A to one dark A along the diagonal to make a square (**Diagram 1**). Press seam open. Repeat for a total of 100 squares.

2. Sew together two A squares (**Diagram 2**). Press seams open. Repeat for a total of forty units.

Piecing Diagram

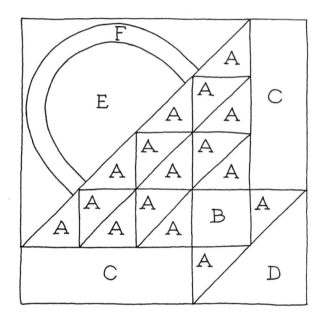

Diagram 1. Sew one light A to one dark A to make a square

Diagram 2. Sew together two A squares

3. Assemble A squares in rows as shown in **Diagram 3**. Sew one light A to the top of each row and one dark B to the bottom of last row. Press seams open.

4. Matching seams at intersections, sew together rows in order shown in **Diagram 3**. Sew one light A triangle to left side of first row. Press seams open. Repeat for a total of twenty units.

5. Sew one light A to the right of each C (**Diagram 4**), twenty with the diagonal facing in one direction, twenty with the diagonal facing the opposite direction.

6. Matching seams at the intersections, sew A-C units to adjacent sides of the pieced basket. Press seams open. Sew one dark D triangle to base of basket (**Diagram 5**). Press seam open. Repeat for a total of twenty baskets.

7. To make basket handle, appliqué bias binding (F) to large dark triangle E (**Diagram 6**). Press appliqué. Repeat for a total of twenty appliquéd handle pieces.

8. Sew handle sections to basket bases to complete blocks. Press seams open.

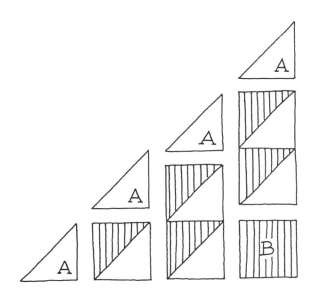

Diagram 3. Sew together A squares in rows with light A triangles at top of each row and one B at bottom of last row. Sew rows together

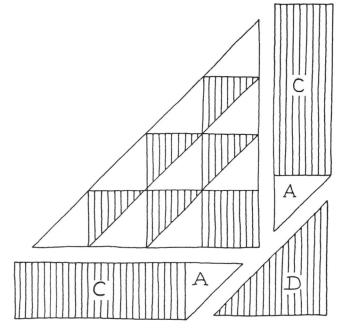

Diagram 5. Sew A/C unit to adjacent sides of the basket. Sew D to basket base

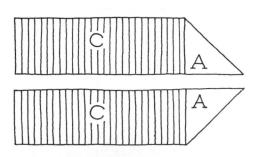

Diagram 4. Sew one light A to the right of each C, twenty with the diagonal in one direction, twenty with the diagonal in the other as shown

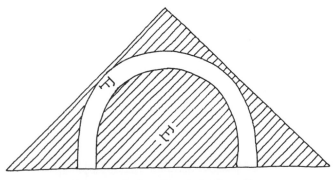

Diagram 6. Appliqué the handle (F) to E. Sew E to basket base

Quilt Assembly Diagram

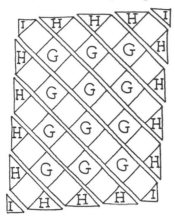

Diagram 7. Sew together the basket blocks alternately with G pieces to make eight rows as shown. Sew H's at the ends of each row and I's at corners as shown

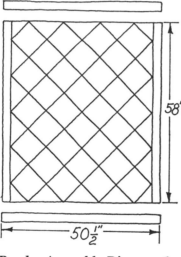

Border Assembly Diagram 1

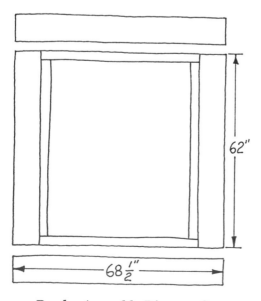

Border Assembly Diagram 2

9. Sew together basket blocks alternating with G (large dark squares) into eight rows as shown in **Diagram 7**. Arrange on the diagonal as shown. Sew H pieces to ends of each row and I pieces to corners. Press seams open.

10. Sew rows together, matching seams at intersections. Press seams open.

ASSEMBLY

11. Sew 58-inch borders to the right and left sides of the quilt top (**Border Assembly Diagram 1**). Press seams open. Sew 50½-inch borders to the top and bottom. Press seams open.

12. Sew 62-inch borders to the right and left sides of the quilt top (**Border Assembly Diagram 2**). Press seams open. Sew 68½-inch borders to the top and bottom. Press seams open.

13. The quilt was bound by folding the back to the front, turning under the raw edges, and blind stitching to the quilt top. An alternate method would be to bind the quilt with bias binding, following instructions on page xxiii.

QUILTING

14. Quilt as desired. The designer quilted feathered wreaths in the plain blocks and a feathered scroll along the borders.

234

Carolina Baskets

AN EXTRA BATCH OF BISCUIT PROJECTS

By Doris J. Carmack

Using the biscuit block technique described in Kitchen Biscuits, page 144, make a delightful puff quilt and pillow for your bedroom or den, a cushion for your favorite rocker, and a country basket lining.

AFGHAN QUILT

SIZE

Block is 3 inches square
Finished quilt is 39 x 57 inches

MATERIALS

- 3¼ yards fabric for A and 39½ x 57½ inch back
- ⅜ yard fabric B, C, and D
- 1¼ yards fabric E
- 2¼ yards muslin
- 5½ yards 2½-inch-wide ruffled lace
- 5½ yards ⅛-inch-wide satin ribbon
- Polyester filling

CUTTING

Pattern Piece	Number of Pieces
4-inch squares	61 fabric A 20 fabric B 28 fabric C 36 fabric D 102 fabric E
3½-inch squares	247 muslin

PIECING & ASSEMBLY

1. Make 247 biscuit blocks according to directions for Basic Biscuit Block, page 145. Sew together in rows following order in **Piecing Diagram**.

2. Stitch gathered edge of lace around entire outer edge of quilt.

3. With right sides together, sew quilt back to quilt top, leaving a 6-inch opening for turning. Trim corners to eliminate bulk, and turn right side out.

4. To make ribbon ties, sew a bar tack (narrow zigzag stitch and 0 stitch length with feed dog lowered so fabric will not move) over the center of a 3-inch piece of ribbon at each place marked with an "O" on the **Piecing Diagram**. Tie a knot with each piece of ribbon.

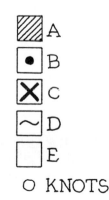

A
B
X C
D
E
O KNOTS

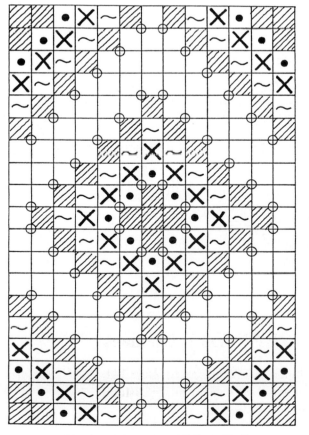

Piecing Diagram: Afghan Quilt

BRICK PILLOW

SIZE

Block is 3 x 1½-inch rectangle
Finished pillow is 12 inches square

MATERIALS

- 1 yard light print fabric
- ¼ yard dark print fabric
- ½ yard muslin
- Polyester filling
- 12-inch-square pillow form

CUTTING

Pattern Piece	Number of Pieces
4 x 2½-inch rectangles	10 light print 22 dark print
3½ x 2-inch rectangles	32 muslin
12½-inch square	1 light print for back
5-inch-wide strips for ruffle	light print (enough for length of 96–120 inches)

PIECING & ASSEMBLY

1. Make 32 biscuit blocks according to directions for Basic Biscuit Block, page 145. Sew together in rows following **Piecing Diagram**.

2. Make a ruffle, and assemble the pillow according to instructions in Pillow Primer, page xxviii.

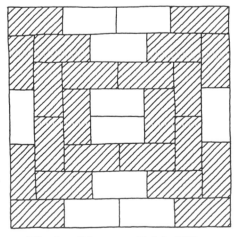

Piecing Diagram: Brick Pillow

ROCKER CUSHIONS

Biscuit cushions can be made for any size chair or rocker. You will have to measure chair back and seat to determine the finished block size. For example, the cushion pictured is seven blocks across. If the finished blocks are 2-inch squares, the width of the cushion will be 14 inches.

MATERIALS

- Fabric for biscuit blocks and cushion back (drapery remnants, corduroy, denim, or other sturdy fabric)
- Muslin for block backs
- Polyester filling
- Cording and bias binding or purchased piping
- ¼-inch ribbon for ties

PIECING & ASSEMBLY

1. Cut the required number of squares for blocks and backs for the desired cushion size. Make blocks and sew together in rows according to directions for Basic Biscuit Block, page 145.

2. To make piping, cut and sew bias binding according to instructions in Quilting Basics, page xxiii. Fold binding over cording (**Diagram 1**) and, using a zipper foot, sew close to cording as shown.

3. With raw edges on the outside, sew piping around cushion (**Diagram 2**).

4. Fold and pin ribbon ties to corners (**Diagram 3**).

5. Measure and cut backing for each cushion. Sew backing to front, right sides together, leaving an opening for turning. Turn and slipstitch opening closed.

Diagram 1. Make piping

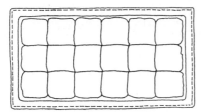

Diagram 2. Sew piping to chair cushion

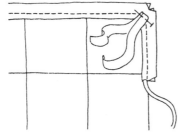

Diagram 3. Fold and pin ties to corners.

BASKET LINING

SIZE

Each basket is different and must be fitted as you go. The basket pictured required 250 biscuits 1½ inches square.

MATERIALS

- Scrap fabric in assorted prints and colors
- Muslin
- ½-inch bias tape, enough to cover outside rim of basket plus 1 inch
- 2½-inch-wide gathered lace, enough to cover rim of basket plus 2 inches
- Ribbon and silk flowers
- Polyester filling

CUTTING

For the basket pictured

Pattern Piece	Number of Pieces
2½-inch squares	30 each of 6 assorted fabrics 65 main color fabric
2-inch squares	250 muslin

PIECING & ASSEMBLY

Because the lining is fitted as you go, it is best to use fabrics randomly rather than working a pattern. This is a good scrap fabric project.

1. Following directions for Basic Biscuit Block, page 145, make enough blocks and sew into rows to form large rectangle to fit across bottom and up two sides of basket to within ½ inch below rim (**Diagram 1**).

2. Make enough blocks and sew into rows to form two smaller rectangles to cover remaining two sides of basket to within ½ inch below rim.

3. Before sewing side pieces on, fit all pieces into basket. Because most baskets are wider at the top, the lining will fit the basket bottom but be too small at the top edge. Add additional

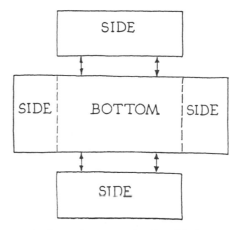

Piecing Diagram: Basket Lining

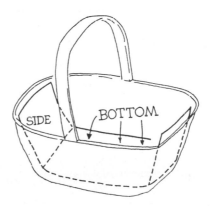

Diagram 1. Fit large rectangle of biscuits to bottom and sides of basket

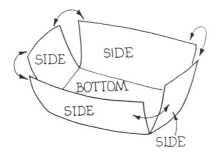

Diagram 2. Fold up the sides of bottom rectangle to meet side rectangles

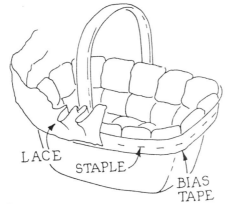

Diagram 3. Staple bias tape to outside rim of basket. Hand stitch lace on top of bias tape

biscuits to the sides of the large rectangle if necessary to fit. When satisfied with lining fit, sew together the sides of the rectangles, matching corners to form a box **(Diagram 2)**.

4. Count the number of biscuits around the top of the lining, make a circle of biscuits, and sew them to the top edge of basket lining.

5. Sew one edge of the bias tape on top of the raw edge of the top row of biscuits.

6. Fit the lining into the basket, fold over the bias tape to the outside rim, and staple it to the basket. (Note: to clear the handles, clip the bias tape on each side of the handles and fold it to the inside.) Hand stitch gathered edge of lace to bias tape around entire edge of basket. Lace will fall over bias tape to form the ruffle **(Diagram 3)**.

7. Decorate handle with bows, ribbons, and silk flowers as desired.

Rodale Press, Inc., publishes AMERICAN WOODWORKER™, the magazine for the serious woodworking hobbyist. For information on how to order your subscription, write to AMERICAN WOODWORKER™, Emmaus, PA 18098.